Praise for *The Perfect House*

"Rybczynski learned firsthand what made Palladio's houses so attractive, so imitated, so perfect—and so could you."

—*The Boston Globe*

"Insightful, deft . . . an easy-to-follow tour of Palladio's greatest legacy."

—*The Seattle Times*

"[A] wonderfully informative and evocative guide to both the elegant rooms of Palladio's villas and the fascinating history of how a humble stonemason from Padua became one of the most influential architects of all time."

—Ross King, author of *Brunelleschi's Dome*

"[A] deeply able and aptly enchanted guide."

—*Publishers Weekly*

"[Rybczynski] is one of our most original, accessible, and stimulating writers on architecture. . . . [*The Perfect House*] is a small but lasting gift to the reader."

—*Library Journal*

"Rybczynski leads us through Palladio's beautiful villas, illuminating each room for its own sake and in the process helping us understand what Palladio thought 'the perfect house' was, and where so many of our own ideas on that subject have come from. He puts his great historical and architectural knowledge to work to explain private houses—the small, the intimate, the domestic. The result is a delightful and enlightening book, full of warmth and intelligence."

—Cheryl Mendelson, author of *Home Comforts*

ALSO BY WITOLD RYBCZYNSKI

ANDREA PALLADIO BY GIOVANNI BATTISTA MAGANZA
(Centro Internazionale di Studi di Architettura)

The Perfect House

A Journey with the Renaissance Master
Andrea Palladio

WITOLD RYBCZYNSKI

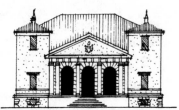

SCRIBNER

NEW YORK   LONDON   TORONTO   SYDNEY   SINGAPORE

SCRIBNER

1230 Avenue of the Americas
New York, NY 10020

Copyright © 2002 by Witold Rybczynski

First Scribner trade paperback edition 2003

SCRIBNER and design are trademarks of Macmillan Library Reference USA, Inc.,
used under license by Simon & Schuster, the publisher of this work.

For information about special discounts for bulk purchases,
please contact Simon & Schuster Special Sales:
1-800-456-6798 or business@simonandschuster.com

DESIGNED BY ERICH HOBBING

Set in Bembo

Manufactured in the United States of America

1   3   5   7   9   10   8   6   4   2

The Library of Congress has cataloged the Scribner edition as follows:
Rybczynski, Witold.
The perfect house : a journey with the Renaissance master Andrea Palladio /
Witold Rybczynski.
p. cm.
1. Palladio, Andrea, 1508–1580. 2. Architecture, Renaissance—Italy.
3. Architects—Italy—Biography. I. Title.
NA123.P2 R93 2002
720'.92-dc21   2002066838

ISBN 0-7432-0586-3
0-7432-0587-1 (Pbk)

Illustration Credits
Centro Internazionale di Studi di Architettura "Andrea Palladio,"
Vicenza: frontispiece; *I quattro libri dell'architettura* by Andrea Palladio,
published in Venice, 1570, facsimile edition published by Ulrico Hoepli Editore Libraio,
Milan, 1980: 53, 76, 82, 110, 128, 170, 188, 228; The British Architectural Library,
The Royal Institute of British Architects, London: 46, 47, 50, 51, 154;
Witold Rybczynski: 2, 6, 8, 14, 24, 26, 33, 34, 58, 62, 66, 67, 70, 78, 86, 97, 98, 102, 105, 112,
120, 123, 124, 132, 146, 150, 158, 174, 176, 180, 190, 193, 194, 202, 204, 208, 210, 212, 226,
235, 242, 248, 256, 260.

To Shirley, once more

CONTENTS

For one could not describe as perfect a building which was useful, but only briefly, or one which was inconvenient for a long time, or, being both durable and useful, was not beautiful.

—ANDREA PALLADIO

FOREWORD

he Villa Barbaro in Maser, north of Venice, was my first Palladio villa. It faced south at the top of a gentle slope, overlooking cultivated fields and vineyards. The gable end of the central portion was a delicately modeled temple front consisting of four giant half-columns supporting a pediment filled with sculptural figures. Two long arcades terminating in pavilions adorned with fulsome scrolls created an animated silhouette against a dark tangle of trees. The golden yellow plastered walls glowed in the afternoon sun. Photographs had not prepared me for the real thing; Palladio's design had the immediacy and fresh-ness of something built the day before yesterday. "You have to see these buildings with your own eyes to realize how good they are," wrote Goethe, who came upon this architecture when it was already more than two hundred years old. "No reproductions of Palladio's designs give an adequate idea of the harmony of their dimensions; they must be seen in their actual perspective."[1]

I, too, was smitten. That was in 1985. I wrote a short essay on Palladio, and two years later made some tentative notes for a book.[2] The notes were tentative because I was interested in the man as well as his buildings, and although he wrote a famous architectural book, the details of his personal life are sketchy. My editor was supportive but I was not sure exactly how to proceed, and the idea languished. I filed the Palladio notes away under "Ideas for Books" and forgot about them.

Years later, rummaging through the Ideas file, I came across the Palladio material. It read in part:

> The nineteenth-century discipline of art history applies the techniques of studying painting and sculpture to buildings, that is, it treats them primarily as works of art. But a building, even if it is designed with artistry, is also a product of clients' demands and economic constraints, of a way of life, of building technology, and of its surroundings. When a Venetian patrician hired Palladio to design a villa, he did so because he wanted a home, and if Palladio's career flourished, it was because he was specially skilled at fulfilling this requirement.
>
> It seems to me that it would be possible to learn a great deal about Palladio by looking at his buildings, not with the eye of an art historian but with the eye of an architect, and not only as works of the imagination, but as products of a particular time and place. Such a study would necessarily be impressionistic and personal; it is not intended to turn up new historical evidence (although it would rely on recent scholarly work), but rather to give the reader new insights, a new way of looking at Palladio's work.

My interest was rekindled. As it happened, I had just finished a book on architectural style, and style features in Palladio's work. Also, having recently written a biography, I was more confident about dealing with his life. I was on sabbatical from the university, with a book completed and time on my hands. It was spring and the airlines were offering bargain fares to Europe. It was not a difficult decision; I would take Goethe's advice, go back to Italy, and see the buildings with my own eyes.

I had already visited Palladio's churches in Venice, as well as his palazzos and public buildings in Vicenza—this time I would concentrate on the villas. They dot the flat Veneto plain north of Venice, chiefly clustered around the city of Vicenza. The houses stand at country crossroads, beside rivers and canals, and at the ends of tree-lined drives. Many were built as the seats of country estates, and are still surrounded by farm buildings and agricultural equipment, albeit tractors rather than horse-drawn wagons. In some cases, the rural settings have been transformed into prosaic backdrops of apartment blocks, garages, and suburban gardens. Even in such inhospitable surroundings, the villas maintain their noble presence, their unremitting sense of order, and their beauty. Most are occupied and lovingly maintained, the wear and tear of centuries erased or, at least, concealed. Others, no less captivating, show evidence of careless upkeep: cracked and peeling plaster, broken steps, sagging shutters. A few are in advanced stages of disrepair with crumbling brickwork and gaping windows. Of the roughly thirty villas attributed to Palladio, seventeen have survived largely intact.*

To British and American visitors, Palladio's villas are familiar objects in this foreign terrain. They recall country seats in Kent and Tidewater plantation houses in Virginia. Traces of Palladio are found in famous buildings such as Inigo Jones's Queen's House at Greenwich and Thomas Jefferson's Monticello, and in national symbols such as Buckingham Palace and the Mauritshuis in The Hague. The great portico of the White House in Washington, D.C., also owes a debt to Palladio's villas, as do many American small-town banks and courthouses. That

---

*Seven of the villas were either destroyed or drastically altered, four were not finished and exist only as fragments, one was never built, and the fate of one is unknown, as its location has never been determined.

a handful of houses in an obscure corner of the Venetian Republic should have made their presence felt hundreds of years later and halfway across the globe is extraordinary. It makes Palladio the most influential architect in history.

The villas of Palladio also mark an important moment in the history of the home: the beginning of domestic architecture—that is, the beginning of architects' interest in the private house. An architectural language previously reserved for temples and palaces was introduced to residential buildings. Much of the potent architectural symbolism associated with the home, whether it is the grand porch of a stockbroker's mansion in Connecticut or the modest pediment over the front door of an American Colonial bungalow, is derived from these sixteenth-century structures. It all starts with Palladio.

As the architectural historian James S. Ackerman pointed out, there are really two Palladios.[3] One was the author of *I quattro libri dell'architettura* (The four books on architecture). Published in 1570, this renowned architectural treatise influenced architects as different as Inigo Jones and Thomas Jefferson. While it included much information about the architecture of ancient Rome, and was written in a spare, dry prose, Palladio's treatise was not academic. "In all these books I shall avoid being long-winded and will simply provide the advice that seems essential to me," he cautioned the reader.[4] His practical suggestions take the form of straightforward recipes, such as "Rooms are built with either a vault or a ceiling; if with a ceiling, the height from the pavement to the joists will be the same as the breadth and the rooms above will be a sixth less in height than those below. If they are vaulted . . . the heights of the vaults in square rooms will be a third greater than their breadth."[5] In other words, in a room eighteen feet square, a flat ceiling would be eighteen feet high, and a vaulted ceiling twenty-four feet.

The accompanying woodcuts are simple line drawings. Dimensions abound, which gives the impression of a rationalist who believes that architecture is the result of predetermined recipes and mathematical formulas. This methodical approach to design accounts for his wide influence, particularly on gentleman amateurs.

The other Palladio was a builder, not a theorist. He might bend his own rules and make eighteen-foot-wide rooms with ceilings that were seventeen feet high, or twenty. An accomplished practitioner who sized up the situation—and the client—and sought inspiration from his surroundings, he sensitively balanced his humanist concerns with the practical requirements of each project. "He gave the most intense pleasure to the Gentlemen and Lords with whom he dealt," wrote a contemporary.[6] A consummate student of ancient Rome, he was at one and the same time an inventive designer and a conservative professional. This is the Palladio I hope to find.

THE PERFECT HOUSE

I

Godi

orty miles northwest of Venice, the flat plain that starts on the shore of the Adriatic runs abruptly into the base of the Dolomitic Alps. The foothills village of Lugo Vicentino overlooks the Astico River, whose broad valley must have been pretty once but is now an unsettled quilt of cultivated fields and large manufacturing sheds. The mixture of agriculture and industry is apparent in the La Casara restaurant, where I'm surrounded by a noisy crowd of farmers and factory workers enjoying their lunch hour.

After an excessive meal, which raises again the puzzle of how Italians get anything done in the afternoon, I take a stroll. The restaurant is on the outskirts of the village. The houses here are too new to be picturesque, but the neat buildings and well-kept gardens attest to the prosperity of the region. The suburban landscape is dotted with agricultural remnants: a renovated farmhouse, a stone barn, a fenced piece of pasture. At the edge of the built-up area the ground rises steeply and I can see the bare branches of an orchard. Farther up the hill, behind a forsythia hedge that is already blooming, a large rectangular building with a red-tile roof commands the scene. This is what I've come to see—Palladio's Villa Godi. Although Renaissance country houses are commonly referred to as villas, this use of the term is modern. In the sixteenth century, *la villa*

referred to the entire estate; the house itself was *la casa padronale* (the master's house), or more simply *la casa di villa.*

I drive my rented car up the winding road. "Placed on a hill with a wonderful view and beside a river" is how Palladio described the house, and despite its industrial excrescence the Astico valley still presents a spectacular vista.[1] The house sits on a man-made podium circumscribed by an imposing stone retaining wall. The curving, battered wall resembles a medieval bastion; the sturdy building, with its compact mass and severe symmetry, likewise has a military bearing. At first glance it could be an armory or a garrison post. As one gets closer, two features soften its severity: the plastered walls, which are painted a faded but cheerful buttery yellow and resemble old parchment, and an arcaded loggia, which is recessed into the center of the building and creates a shaded and welcoming entrance.

The caretaker lets me in through a large wrought-iron gate and I follow a path across the podium. The gravel crunches agreeably underfoot. The lawn is planted with conifers clipped into spheres and pyramids. A fountain, whose centerpiece is a statue of a nymph surrounded by cavorting cherubs, sprays water

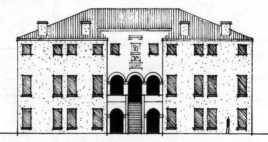

VILLA GODI

into a pool. I give her a sideward glance and hurry through the garden to the house.

The villa, which did not look large from a distance, turns out to be immense, almost as tall as a modern five-story building. The plain plastered walls are relieved by a regular pattern of windows with stone frames and slightly different details: a heavy bracketed sill for the lowest floor; a delicately modeled sill for the main level; and a plain surround for the attic. Square windows are pushed up against an elegant cornice just under the shallow eaves. The cornice is supported by a row of little repetitive blocks, a detail adapted from ancient Roman temple eaves decorations called modillions. These are the only classical references in this otherwise undecorated and austere façade.

"The master's rooms, which have floors thirteen feet above ground, are provided with ceilings," Palladio wrote, "above these are the granaries, and in the thirteen-foot-high basement are placed the cellars, the places for making wine, the kitchen, and other similar rooms."[2] This pragmatic stacking of warehouse and domestic uses originated in Venice, where land was scarce.[3] The tall Godi "basement" is entirely aboveground, so a long straight stair leads to the loggia. This spacious outdoor room faces west, which must give splendid views of sunsets over the peaks of the *altipiano* but leaves the main façade of the house exposed to the hot afternoon sun. It is unclear why Palladio turned the building this way—the preferred orientation was southern, and that view was equally fine. It may have had to do with how one originally arrived at the villa, since old maps show a long, straight approach road climbing the hill from the west. Or it may be explained by the fact that the villa is believed to incorporate parts of a medieval house that already existed on the site.[4] The citizens of the Venetian Republic had a reputation for penny-pinching, if not outright parsimony, and new houses were frequently built on top of old ones in order to save money by reusing foundations and walls.

The *intonaco,* or plastered stucco, of the walls shows marks where it was once incised to simulate the joints of stone construction. The entry in my old edition of the *Encyclopaedia Britannica* claims that Palladio's buildings were originally "designed to be executed in stone."[5] In fact, none of Palladio's country houses are built of stone; all are brick covered in plaster, which was the standard method of construction for rural buildings. The jointing pattern, which is faint today but was prominent when the house was built, was not meant to deceive. Like the wooden faux-stonework of George Washington's Mount Vernon, it produces a sense of scale as well as a pleasing decorative texture.

Not all the masonry is simulated. The most distinctive feature of the house is the three-arch loggia whose square piers, arches, and imposts from which the arches spring are all faced with stone. Two carved stone emblems adorn the wall above the loggia: an armorial shield with imperial eagles, symbols of the owner's nobility, and a rampant lion, the *stemma,* or coat of arms, of the Godi family. An inscription on the tablet below reads HIERONYMUS GODUS HENRICI ANTONII FILIUS FECIT ANNO MDXLII (Built by Girolamo Godi, son of Enrico Antonio, in the year 1542). The Godis, one of the most powerful and wealthy patrician families of Vicenza, owned large estates in the Vicentino. When the patriarch Enrico Antonio died in 1536, he bequeathed the lands in common to his three sons (the fourth was a priest). Girolamo took charge of the Lugo holdings, more than five hundred acres, which included the hilltop of Lonedo, where he started to build a villa the following year.

Small doors lead directly from the loggia to rooms on either side, but the large door in the center is obviously the main entrance. PROCUL ESTE PROFANI is carved into the stone frame. "Keep the unholy far away" may have been intended tongue in cheek, since the Godis were known to have had heretical tendencies. ET LIBERA NOS A MALO—"And deliver us from evil"— completes the sentiment on the inside. I read the interior inscription later, for when I open the door my attention is immediately arrested by the grand space—as Palladio, no doubt, intended. The cavernous room rises up to the roof— about twenty-five feet—and extends all the way to the rear of the house. This is the *sala,* or hall. The *sala,* which originated in medieval times, was a common feature of Venetian country houses. Always the largest room in the house, it was neither an entrance vestibule nor a living room, but a formal social space, "designed for parties, banquets, as the sets for acting out comedies, weddings, and similar entertainments," Palladio wrote.[6] The *sala* in the Villa Godi is lit by a large window, a triple opening with a semicircular arch in the center called a *serliana.** This end of the *sala* extends slightly beyond the rest of the house, and the additional narrow windows on the two sides give the effect of a large bay window, which not only illuminates the room but also affords views of the garden below.

The *sala* is flanked by eight large rooms—four on each side. Six of the rooms are identical, two are slightly smaller to make room for the staircases; the large rooms are each about eighteen by twenty-eight feet. This seems like a lot of space, but the bachelor Girolamo shared the villa with his brothers and their families. There are no corridors; instead, each room opens directly into the next. The doors and windows are exactly

---

*The *serliana* originated in antiquity and was revived by Bramante. It is named after the architect Sebastiano Serlio, who popularized it in a widely read treatise.

lined up so that standing in one of the rooms with my back to a window, I can look through four sets of open doors and see the corresponding window on the opposite side of the house. The stair, the loggia arcade, the front door, the *sala,* and the *serliana* are likewise carefully aligned. These precise geometrical relationships give the interior a sense of calm and repose. Everything appears in its place.

I walk around the house, or rather slide since I am obliged to wear felt slippers to reduce wear on the floors. These are *battuto,* an early version of terrazzo, made by slathering a mixture of lime, sand, and powdered brick across the floor, pressing milled stone chips into the hardening mixture with heavy rollers, then grinding smooth and oiling the surface. There are no other visitors, and the caretaker has left me alone. I swish from room to room. The doorways are low and the unpretentious doors of simple plank construction have wrought-iron strap hinges. The identical windows incorporate a charming feature: facing stone seats that transform them into little conversation nooks. The flat ceilings are supported by closely spaced wooden beams with ornamental carvings on the underside. The only room

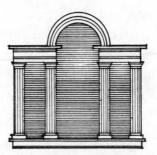

SERLIANA, OR PALLADIAN WINDOW

with a plaster ceiling is in the southeast corner of the house, a privileged position that gets the morning sun, summer and winter, and probably belonged to Girolamo.

The Godi house, which was begun about 1537, has the distinction of being Palladio's first villa; indeed, as far as we know, it was his first independent commission. The novice had moments of clumsiness, particularly in the front façade. The recessed entrance bay, for example, while welcoming, has a large section of blank wall over the loggia, which the heraldic coats of arms do not quite fill. The external staircase rises to a complicated landing in front of the loggia that distracts from the overall composition. The asymmetrical placement of the windows on the façade is disturbing. Instead of being equally spaced they are bunched together in pairs (to leave space for the fireplaces and chimneys, which are located on the exterior walls). Thirty years later, when Palladio was writing his architectural treatise, he included drawings of the Villa Godi but took the opportunity to smooth out these defects. Leaving the plan largely unaltered, he simplified the stair, reduced the number of windows and spaced them equally, and capped the central section of the house with a pediment.

The design of the villa is very successful in one key respect. Earlier Venetian villas often look like town houses transposed to the country, elegant but slightly ill at ease. Palladio manages to make the Godi both a polished work of architecture and a sturdy farmhouse. Like a country gentleman in a tailored hacking coat and muddy rubber boots, the villa fits into its surroundings, even as it holds itself above them. This quality would permeate all of Palladio's villas, which are both sophisticated and rustic, genteel and rude, cosmopolitan and vernacular.

The Villa Godi hasn't always been appreciated. Sir Charles Barry, the leading British architect of the early 1800s, thought

THE RAISED LOGGIA, WITH ITS THREE ROMAN ARCHES,
MARKS THE ENTRANCE TO THE VILLA GODI.

it "an unarchitectural pile."[7] Banister Fletcher, the nineteenth-century author of a long-lived architectural history, a bulky copy of which I owned as a student, considered the Godi's main façade "a very poor example of our master's genius."[8] The modern art historian Rudolf Wittkower criticized the Villa Godi as "retrogressive."[9] Indeed, as Wittkower pointed out, the design bears a resemblance to the Villa Tiretta, a country house built about forty years earlier near the village of Arcade, only thirty miles away.[10] In fact, the proportions of Godi are more robust than Tiretta, and the massing is much more accomplished. But the resemblance is a reminder that Palladio, at this early stage of his career, was not straying far from established local traditions. His conservatism is understandable. Most architects today begin their careers designing kitchen additions or weekend cottages. The Godi is a palatial residence on a dramatic site, for the richest family in town. A mistake here could stop one's career in its tracks; it is prudent to be cautious.

An architect's early work is often consigned to a back drawer. Some masters, such as Le Corbusier and Ludwig Mies van der Rohe, even suppressed their youthful efforts. Yet when the elderly Palladio was being interviewed by the painter and architect Giorgio Vasari, who was collecting material for *Lives of the Most Eminent Painters, Sculptors and Architects,* he specifically mentioned the Villa Godi.[11] And he included a description of the villa in his great treatise, *I quattro libri dell'architettura* (The four books on architecture), which he published near the end of his life. He may have made some mistakes and not broken new ground at the Villa Godi, but he was obviously proud of his first building. It couldn't have been an easy commission: a no-doubt demanding client used to getting his own way; an exceptionally large house; a dramatic site with a splendid view, but also perched on a slope and restricted in area; and existing buildings that had to be integrated into the design. Yet the novice pulled it all together and produced a handsome work of great gravitas and, yes, nobility. It is an exceptional accomplishment for a beginner.

A beginner in architecture but no stripling, for when Palladio was first mentioned as working on the Godi house he was already thirty-two years old. Renaissance architectural careers started late: Filippo Brunelleschi was forty-one when he entered the competition to design the dome of the cathedral in Florence; the great Donato Bramante was thirty-seven when he was called to rebuild St. Peter's in Rome; Vasari was forty when he designed his first building; and Michelangelo was forty-six before he applied his prodigious talent to architecture. Since there were no architects' guilds or associations in the sixteenth century, there was no period of formal training or apprenticeship. In that sense, to be an architect did not mean to be a professional; it meant, rather, to hold a position. Renaissance architects were generally mature men who had already distinguished themselves in some branch of the fine arts. Brunelleschi was a renowned goldsmith and clockmaker; Bramante and Vasari were accomplished painters; Michelangelo was a celebrated sculptor as well as a painter. Palladio stands out in this company, for when he entered architecture he was not famous nor did he have a background in the arts—he was a stonemason.

He was born in Padua in 1508, sixteen years after Columbus discovered America. It was November 30, St. Andrew's Day— or so legend has it—and the child was named Andrea. His father was either a miller or a maker of millstones, but in any case someone who delivered his products by boat, for he was called Pietro dalla Gondola; his mother was Marta, of whom little is known except that she was lame. Since the family lacked a hereditary surname, the son was called Andrea di Pietro dalla Gondola, or simply Andrea di Pietro. There is no record of any siblings, nor is anything known about his ancestors. Yet there is a telling detail associated with his birth: his godfather was a stonemason.

The city of Padua belonged to the Venetian Republic. The year after Andrea was born, war broke out between the Republic and the so-called League of Cambrai, the combined forces of the Holy Roman Empire, France, and Aragon, several city-states, and the papacy. Early in the war, the Venetians lost a decisive battle, and Padua was occupied by the enemy, changing hands several times as the war dragged on. Although the Republic ultimately regained most of its mainland possessions, including Padua, life did not return to normal for seven years. It was sometime during this turbulent period that Andrea lost his mother.

At thirteen, as was customary, the boy was apprenticed to learn a trade. He was placed with a local master mason, Bartolomeo Cavazza. Apprenticeship normally lasted five to seven years, but after only three years Andrea quit and moved with his father to Vicenza, about twenty miles away. Cavazza brought suit, as was his right, and the boy was returned to Padua, but a year later Andrea was back in Vicenza, this time for good. These events remain unexplained. Cavazza was no journeyman mason but a well-known *taipiera,* or stone carver, who fashioned architectural ornament for churches and convents as well as stately houses.[12] Would Andrea really break off such an advantageous relationship? More likely Pietro left Padua for his own reasons and took his only son with him. Moreover, the boy capriciously quitting his apprenticeship is out of character—the adult Palladio is always described as genial and steadfast, and there is evidence that Andrea remained on good terms with Cavazza.[13] In any case, he did not abandon his trade. At the age of sixteen, the *fante*, or apprentice, Andrea di Pietro was formally admitted to the Vicentine guild of plasterers, bricklayers, and masons.

Vicenza, with a population of about 20,000, was one of the smallest cities of the Venetian Republic, smaller than Padua and much smaller than Venice, whose 150,000 inhabitants made it one of the largest cities in Europe. Nevertheless, Vicenza was prosperous, surrounded by rich farmland that belonged to its many noble families. The city was well situated at the confluence of two rivers and beside an attractive hill, Monte Bèrico. Like all Venetian towns, it was surrounded by a protective wall, much damaged in the recent war. At the foot of the wall, on the Contrà Pedemuro, was located the so-called Pedemuro workshop, considered the leading stone-carving yard in Vicenza. It was here that Andrea continued his training. How did he land this plum position? Perhaps thanks to his godfather, who was a native of Vicenza. Or maybe his experience with a well-known Paduan master impressed Giovanni da Porlezza, co-owner of the workshop, who sponsored the boy at the guild and paid his initiation fee.

Andrea lived and worked on the Contrà Pedemuro for more than twelve years. There is little documentation about this formative period of his life, yet it should not be glossed over. The workshop, though specializing in carved stone, was also a construction company. Andrea learned not only how to carve a variety of building elements—door frames, portals, column capitals—he was also exposed to all practical aspects of building. This experience served him well. By the time he became an architect, he knew, and could precisely describe, not only *what* he wanted done but also *how* he wanted it done. If need be, he could pick up a stone chisel and give a convincing demonstration. This firsthand knowledge was unusual among Renaissance architects whose artistic background generally did not prepare them for dealing with construction issues.

Porlezza became Andrea's mentor (and probably a father figure, since Pietro dalla Gondola died before Andrea was twenty). Porlezza was often called upon to function as *capomaestro,* or master builder, since Vicenza had no architects, and from him Andrea learned about the design of buildings, including the rudiments of geometry and drawing. "Guided by a natural inclination, I dedicated myself to the study of architecture in my youth," Palladio wrote in *Quattro libri,* "and since I always held the opinion that the ancient Romans, as in many other things, had also greatly surpassed all those who came after them in building well, I elected as my master and guide Vitruvius, who is the only ancient writer on this art."[14] Vitruvius was a Roman architect whose *Ten Books of Architecture* was the sole architectural treatise that had survived from ancient times—the Renaissance builders' Rosetta stone. A medieval copy of the Vitruvian manuscript had come to light in 1415, and had long been studied by scholars in hand-copied form, but it was not until 1521 that an Italian translation—with added illustrations—became widely available as a printed book. Palladio was born only about fifty years after the invention of the printing press, and he was fortunate to live near Venice, one of the great European centers of the new printing industry. (The first Italian translation of Leon Battista Alberti's important architectural treatise *Of Built Things,* which had been written in Latin, would be published in Venice in 1546.) Porlezza probably had a copy of Vitruvius in his shop, and one can imagine Andrea poring over it in his spare time. Yet any ambitions he had in that direction were severely limited. Architects lived in Venice and Florence, and worked for

AT THE BUILDING SITE OF THE VILLA AT CRICOLI,
COUNT TRISSINO, A PATRON, ENCOUNTERED THE YOUNG
STONEMASON ANDREA DI PIETRO, SOON TO BE PALLADIO.

the grand *signori*; he was a mere stonemason. As a *popolano,* or commoner, he occupied a lowly social position. In Vicenza, as in most cities of the Venetian Republic, anyone engaged in the so-called mechanical arts was precluded from formal citizenship, as were newcomers; in Venice, fifteen years' residency was required for even partial citizenship.

When he was twenty-six, Andrea took a wife. This was somewhat unusual, for men generally married in their thirties or forties, when they were financially independent, and we do not know the circumstances of the marriage. We do know that his bride was named Allegradonna, and that she was the daughter of a carpenter. The record shows that she was in service as a maid, and that it was her mistress who provided the dowry: a bed, a pair of sheets, three new shirts, three used shirts, handkerchiefs, assorted clothing, and lengths of cloth.[15] The dowry was valued at about twenty-eight ducats (a far cry from the five to ten thousand ducats that accompanied a nobleman's daughter). The couple shared Andrea's room in the workshop after they were married, and it was another year or two before they could afford to set up their own household.

In 1537, the Pedemuro workshop received a commission to remodel part of a large house on an estate in Cricoli, just outside the northern city gate. The client was Count Giangiorgio Trissino, scion of one of the oldest families in Vicenza. The fifty-nine-year-old nobleman was more or less in retirement. He had spent most of his life as a diplomat and papal ambassador in Rome and elsewhere, and had only recently returned to Vicenza. Now, after a failed second marriage, he was ready to settle down. His new house at Cricoli was not to be merely a suburban retreat—he already owned a country villa as well as a residence in the city—but the seat of a new academy where he planned to introduce the progressive culture of Rome to the young men of his native Vicenza. Trissino was a formidable personage: a familiar of cardinals and popes, confidant of emperors, an intimate friend of that cultivated aristocrat Isabella d'Este and her infamous sister-in-law Lucrezia Borgia. His portrait hangs in the Louvre: large handsome features, a sensual mouth, and heavy-lidded eyes with a shrewd, penetrating gaze. He holds a beautifully bound book in his delicate hands, a symbol of his literary accomplishments. Trissino was a scholar and poet, the author of a celebrated tragedy, and a linguist. Well known throughout the Italian states, he was Vicenza's leading Renaissance humanist.

He was also an amateur architect. The Cricoli house that he was remodeling had been bought by his father. It was a *castello,* a type common throughout the mainland, or *terraferma,* of the Venetian Republic. Patterned on medieval fortified houses, *castelli* typically had four corner towers, often picturesquely crenellated, and a main façade with a central balcony or loggia. They were adorned with the delicate Gothic tracery that was popular during the Venetian quattrocento. Trissino was modernizing his house, removing the Gothic elements and completely rebuilding the loggia in the so-called *all'antica* style, based on the classical architecture of ancient Rome. His design was a literal copy of a garden loggia by the famous architect Raphael, whom he had known in Rome: a three-arched opening surmounted by pedimented windows, with Ionic pilasters below and Corinthian above.

It is not recorded exactly how Trissino encountered Andrea, but popular legend has them meeting on the Cricoli building site. While the story has been dismissed as apocryphal by some scholars, it seems a plausible explanation; after all, where else would a count meet a stonemason? We do not know exactly what it was that caught Trissino's eye, for surely it was he who initiated the encounter. Maybe he saw one of Andrea's sketches and recognized his innate ability. Or maybe he was talent spotting, for Trissino intended the membership of his future academy to include young men of different social backgrounds, not only the sons of his aristocratic friends. In any event, as Paolo Gualdo, a canon of the Cathedral of Padua who knew Palladio well, described it, the pair "developed a very close relationship."[16] This must have happened in 1537 or 1538, for by 1539, Andrea is mentioned as being a guest in the Trissino home.

"Finding Palladio to be a young man of very spirited character and with a great aptitude for science and mathematics," Gualdo recounts, "Trissino encouraged his natural abilities by training him in the precepts of Vitruvius."[17] *Training* may not be exactly the right word. Trissino was a man of taste but his architectural abilities were limited. His surviving sketches, for example, are clumsy and amateurish. I went one afternoon to see the loggia at Cricoli, which still exists. It's a handsome enough building that demonstrates his academic knowledge, but it gives the impression of a textbook exercise, stylistically correct yet curiously flat—a literary man's idea of architecture. Nor is it likely that Andrea was ever a full-time student at the so-called Accademia Trissiniana, which opened in the late 1530s. For one thing, he had a growing family to support—by this time Allegradonna had borne him three sons. Moreover, whatever his natural aptitude, lacking early schooling or tutoring, he would have been ill-prepared to undertake a humanist education. More likely, Trissino lent him books and invited him to sit in on classes. Yet the nobleman's influence was considerable. Trissino had lived in Rome and knew the city's leading artists and architects, and he could speak with firsthand authority about the latest currents of architectural thought, including the *all'antica* style, which, though it originated in Florence and Rome in the previous century, was still a novelty in the Republic. In that regard, the loggia at Cricoli, whatever its shortcomings, was an invaluable model for Andrea. He had had years of practical training in architectural decoration from Porlezza and, we can assume, years of personal reading; contact with Trissino provided an intellectual frame of reference for this informally acquired knowledge.

The Count was a restless spirit, and he spent much of the next two years traveling, often accompanied by his protégé Andrea. There were extended stays in Padua, which was not only larger than Vicenza but also the seat of an ancient university and the intellectual center of the Venetian Republic (there was no university in Venice proper). Andrea, who had left Padua as a sixteen-year-old apprentice, now found himself moving in very different circles. One of Trissino's friends who had a lasting influence on Andrea was Alvise Cornaro, a successful businessman and dynamic patron of the arts. He was an unusual character who, after an intemperate youth, had adopted strict dietary rules and preached moderation (years later—he would live to ninety-one—he published his celebrated *Treatise on the Sober Life*). Like Trissino, Cornaro was an architectural dilettante, but with an original bent; he was not a nobleman, and his ideas about architecture were those of a bourgeois. Cornaro described architecture as "ministering to the good comfort of men in their lodging, and to their other necessities . . . and in addition to this, it is beautiful as well."[18] He stressed the importance of personally examining ancient Roman buildings rather than simply reading about them in Vitruvius. Yet his approach to the past was pragmatic. "A building may well be beautiful and comfortable, and be neither Doric nor of any such order," he instructed, "as are in this city [Venice] the church of S. Marco and in Padua the Chiesa del Santo."[19] Such down-to-earth

thinking provided Andrea a practical counterbalance to Trissino's more theoretical view of architecture.

Padua offered several architectural examples of the *all'antica*
style, most by the recently deceased Veronese painter and architect Giovanni Maria Falconetto. Falconetto had been a protégé
of Cornaro, and a decade earlier had built two structures in his
patron's garden: a loggia used for theatrical presentations—some
of the earliest *comedia dell'arte* was performed here—and the so-
called Odeo, a pavilion used for musical performances. Both
buildings were skillfully designed and contained the first examples of architectural frescoes in the Veneto. Cornaro taught that
frescoed décor, which the ancient Romans also used, was both
attractive and economical. Falconetto's designs obviously served
as an inspiration for the Cricoli loggia, and his drawings,
including his measured drawings of Roman antiquities, were
available to Andrea for copying. Unlike Vicenza, Padua also
offered significant examples of actual Roman ruins, including
an impressive amphitheater, an open-air theater, and a ceremonial gateway. At Cornaro's house, Andrea was introduced to
several Venetians who were studying at the University of
Padua: the young noblemen Vettor Pisani, his cousin Daniele
Barbaro, and Giorgio Cornaro (no relation to Alvise), as well as
Pietro Godi, his future client's older brother.

Andrea also met two architects. One was Sebastiano Serlio,
an elderly man and a friend of Giangiorgio Trissino; he is
believed to have helped the Count with the design of the
Cricoli villa. Serlio was a Bolognese who had been trained as a
painter by his father and had then gone to Rome, where, at the
age of thirty-nine, he decided to become an architect. His life
was turned upside down in 1527 when the besieged city fell to
the army of the Holy Roman Emperor, whose Lutheran mer-
cenaries went on a weeklong rampage pillaging and destroying

hundreds of churches. The calamitous Sack of Rome, which a contemporary observer described as "rather the fall of a world than of a city," marked the end of an era.[20] It was also the end of papal patronage—at least for the moment—and many artists and architects left Rome in search of work. Serlio, now in his sixties, moved to Venice. His career did not flourish. He had a prickly disposition and was by inclination a scholar rather than a builder. He published several prints illustrating the classical orders, and in 1537 brought out the first volume of a treatise ambitiously titled *Tutte l'opere d'architettura, et perspectiva* (All the works of architecture and perspective), which would become an influential architectural handbook. In Serlio's book Andrea could study the ancient monuments of Rome. It is also likely that Serlio taught the young stonemason proper draftsmanship while he was in Padua, since Andrea's earliest surviving architectural drawings date from this period.[21]

The other architect was the Veronese Michele Sanmicheli, whom Palladio may already have known, since he was a distant relative of Porlezza. Sanmicheli was then about fifty, his career in full swing. Raised in Verona, as a youth he had gone to Rome, trained under the great Bramante, and, together with his friend Antonio da Sangallo, worked for the papacy. After the Sack, he, too, sought employment in the Venetian Republic. Sanmicheli's specialty was military architecture, and he was engaged by the Venetians to refit the battered fortifications of their *terraferma* towns and cities. At the time of Andrea's visit, Sanmicheli was rebuilding the walls of Verona. A skilled engineer, he was also a superb architect. Of Verona's Porta Nuova gate, Vasari would write that it was "done with so much judgment, cost, and magnificence, that no one thought that for the future there could be executed any work of greater grandeur or better design."[22] Sanmicheli had recently completed the mag-

nificent Palazzo del Tè in Mantua, which Palladio visited, and
he was building three more palazzos in Verona. His domestic
architecture exemplified the latest direction in Renaissance
classicism. Whereas an earlier generation of architects—Bramante and Raphael—had sought harmony and repose, Sanmicheli—like Michelangelo and Giulio Romano—stressed
drama and originality. He was interested in the past, but he freely
interpreted classical rules to great scenographic and emotional
effect.

Sanmicheli, an extremely successful practitioner, had an
unusual background: he was not a painter or sculptor; both his
father and his uncle were architects. He must have been a
compelling model for Andrea. There is every reason to suppose
that despite his humble origins, the Vicentine stonemason was
welcomed by these sophisticated and accomplished men.
Cornaro was no snob, and Serlio and Sanmicheli would have
been sympathetic sounding boards. The learned conversations,
the study of plans, the sketching of buildings, the drawing lessons, and the contact with men for whom architecture was a
subject of everyday vital concern, deepened Andrea's interest
and inevitably influenced his thoughts of the future.

Trissino had his own reasons for encouraging his protégé to
pursue an architectural career. The Count was a patriot. Not
that he was devoted to the Republic—quite the opposite, like
many Vicentine noblemen he considered Venice an oppressive
power (and had sided with Venice's enemies during the War of
the League of Cambrai, which later caused him problems). His
allegiance was to his native city. He had great hopes that his
academy would promote the dissemination of humanist culture, including architecture, and raise the level of intellectual life
in Vicenza. Postwar prosperity had arrived, and new construction would follow: palazzos in the city, houses on country

estates. But Vicentines lacked their own architect; there was no Sanmicheli waiting to come home. They could import an outsider, as the Venetians had done in commissioning the celebrated Florentine architect Jacopo Sansovino. But Trissino understood that greater honor would come to his city if it nurtured a homegrown talent, and in his estimation, Andrea di Pietro could be that person.

Of course, there's more than a little Professor Higgins and Eliza Doolittle here.* Andrea, whatever his abilities, was a diamond in the rough when Trissino met him. The nobleman had the wit to recognize Andrea's amiable nature and innate talent, and the foresight to perceive that his experience as a stonemason could be an invaluable asset. But the Count, a diplomat and courtier, wanted more. Renaissance architects and painters were generally uncouth, rough individuals who belonged to the artisan class.[23] He resolved to teach his protégé genteel manners—how to behave, speak, and dress. The stonemason might be a commoner, but he would be a man of refinement and taste to better command the confidence of noble clients. Andrea must have learned these lessons well, for later firsthand accounts invariably mention his gentle and well-bred disposition; according to Gualdo, he was a "most extraordinarily able and attractive conversationalist."[24]

The final step of the makeover involved finding a more impressive name than Andrea di Pietro. Renaissance architects regularly adopted professional names. Jacopo Sansovino was born Tatti; Giulio Pippi de' Giannuzzi, a Roman expatriate practicing in the Venetian Republic, called himself Giulio Romano, or simply Giulio. The mellifluously named Michele Sanmicheli had adopted the name of his birthplace, San Micheli,

*Not in any sexual sense—Trissino had a reputation as a ladies' man.

a village near Verona. Andrea di Pietro might have become Andrea Padovano, or Andrea Vicentino. Instead he took a far grander name: Andrea Palladio. It is generally assumed that Trissino proposed the name since he later used it in an epic poem. The Latin *palladius* means pertaining to sagacity, knowledge, or study, and is derived from Pallas Athena, the goddess of wisdom. It is a name to live up to.

An architect, however impressive his name, needs clients, and in Vicenza that meant the *nobili,* or patrician class. Trissino's judgment in such matters was widely respected. If he considered Andrea Palladio an architect, that would have been good enough for his wide circle of friends. In 1540, before the villa at Lonedo was finished, Pietro Godi recorded several separate payments to "Master Andrea, Architect." This is the oldest surviving record in which Andrea di Pietro, now known as Andrea Palladio, is called an architect. The transition from craftsman to architect was hardly instantaneous, however, for a year later legal documents still referred to Palladio as a "stonemason."[25]

One might have expected that to please Trissino and show off what he had learned, Palladio would incorporate classical elements into the design of the Godi house. He did no such thing. Although the three-arch loggia echoed a similar arrangement at Cricoli, it only served to underline the differences between the two designs. Trissino's delicate façade, with its carefully copied classical ornament, appears brittle compared to Palladio's sturdy proportions, his heavy massing and simplified details. Taking Cornaro's teaching to heart, Palladio made the Godi house "comfortable and beautiful" without incorporating classical orders. This may simply have been the guarded prudence of a novice, but it was also a clear signal that while he may have owed his new name to another, he intended to be his own man.

*   *   *

I return the next day to the Lonedo hilltop where the Villa Godi is perched. The house is officially closed, but the caretaker recognizes me from my previous visit and lets me in. I want to take a more leisurely look at the interior. The walls of the rooms are a cavalcade of Greek and Roman gods, legendary heroes, and cherubs, as well as landscapes, battle trophies, cornucopias, garlands, and swags. They cover every square inch. These figures, motifs, and patterns are applied in what was called *buon fresco,* a demanding technique that involved painting with water-based pigments on fresh, moist plaster. There was no room for error; the application of the pigment had to be swift and accurate, as the plaster stayed wet only one day. The themes at Godi are distinctly classical. In one room, a heavy painted beam runs around the room, as if supporting the ceiling, and is held aloft by monumental female statues. Between the statues are glimpses of a naturally rendered countryside peopled by reclining poets and watchful muses. On the walls of another room are the ruins of

THE MOUNTAINTOP OF LONEDO

a Roman temple, with Olympian gods populating the sky above the crumbling columns. The sole plaster ceiling is frescoed with a monumental oval depicting a beautiful woman (Virtue) standing over a hideous man in chains (Vice). The walls and the vaulted ceiling of the loggia are likewise painted with allegorical themes. The grandest decoration is naturally reserved for the *sala,* which is done up like an art gallery, with grand paintings in gilt frames—the *Rape of Europa,* the *Labors of Hercules*—all frescoed.

All the rooms are defined by a trompe l'oeil framework of architectural elements: columns, architraves, friezes, cornices, dadoes, and decorative moldings. This fictive architecture—and it is definitely architecture—is rendered in shadowed, three-dimensional perspective. The textures of faux marble and stone are so convincing that I find myself touching a door surround to check whether it is a facsimile or the real thing. Real windows and doors have imaginary counterparts on the opposite side of the room. The artist doesn't stop there. While some of the painted figures in the niches are white marble statues, others are rendered in lifelike colors and give the spooky impression that they are about to step off their pedestals. Realistic putti cavort just below the ceiling, their pink buttocks hanging saucily over the edge of the architrave. The frescoes not only depict allegorical classical themes and an architectural framework but also represent a whimsical illusion of reality. In one of the painted doors, a life-size man lifts the curtain for his companion and beckons him into the room. Elsewhere, a mischievous little boy sits on a ledge. In the hall, where painted windows complete with window seats echo the real thing, a relaxed gentleman in doublet and hose occupies one of the seats. Although the décor refers to ancient Rome, the ghostlike personages that look out at me from the walls are dressed in con-

THE FRESCOES AT THE VILLA GODI DEPICT HUMAN FIGURES
AS WELL AS TROMPE L'OEIL ARCHITECTURAL DETAILS.

temporary—that is, sixteenth-century—clothes. They both decorate and inhabit the space.

Many of Palladio's villas are frescoed. It is impossible not to be struck by the extreme contrast between the vivid style of the interiors and the simplicity of the exteriors, particularly in the case of the austere Godi house. In the past this led some historians to conclude that the frescoes were an afterthought. Lacking evidence to the contrary, it was also assumed that Palladio had nothing to do with the design of the frescoes, which were therefore regarded as distinct from his architectural vision. This attitude was summed up by Banister Fletcher, who observed that "interior decoration seems to have been somewhat neglected by our master, owing no doubt to a shortage of funds."[26] According to others, the rich décor actually undermined Palladio's design intentions.

The Godi frescoes were not begun until about 1552—that is, a decade after the villa was completed. The painter Gualtiero Padovano completed the loggia and the rooms in the south wing, and then unexpectedly—he was in his fifties—died. His replacement was a talented young painter named Giambattista Zelotti, who finished the work (except for one room that was painted by Battista del Moro). Before the painting began, Palladio was called back to Lonedo for additional work. He was asked to design a new main window for the *sala*. The original window was a thermal or Diocletian window—that is, a high, arched opening modeled on the windows found in Diocletian's Roman baths, or *thermae*. Palladio replaced this with the *serliana* that is there today. It is unclear exactly why this expensive alteration was made. Maybe Pietro Godi, who supervised this phase of the work, had his own ideas of what was fashionable. Some historians believe the window was altered to make more space for the frescoes.[27] In any case, an entry in Pietro Godi's account book reads: "Palladio. Gave him today, 4th July [1550] for the drawing of the Hall, one Hungarian crown [worth] 7 lire 14 soldi."*[28]

The drawing in question has recently come to light.[29] It is of paramount importance, writes Douglas Lewis, a curator at the National Gallery of Art in Washington, D.C., who unearthed it, "because its subject represents an aspect of Palladio's artistic creativity that has been unsuspected."[30] The drawing is what architects call an interior elevation, a view of one of the walls of the *sala,* the west wall opposite the *serliana.* It shows the frescoed architectural elements—pediment, pilasters, niches, dado. The entrance door and a ventilating grille are skillfully integrated into the composition (the east wall has a frescoed version of the same grille). The area for the figurative painting (Zelotti's *Rape of Europa*) is blank, and the statues in the niches are likewise left to the painter's discretion, but detailed notes specify the character of the surrounding decorative elements: "military trophies," "festoons," "gold frames," "cornice similar to the other [wall]." This drawing, in Palladio's hand, is conclusive evidence that the trompe l'oeil architectural framework frescoed on the walls of the Villa Godi is, in fact, his design. Since there is a record of eight comparable payments, it appears likely that he made similar drawings—since lost—for the other rooms. The frescoes, far from being extraneous, are an integral part of the architectural conception.

Palladio, who must have been inspired by Alvise Cornaro's endorsement of frescoes as a practical alternative to tapestries and wall hangings, probably recommended Padovano, who was part of Cornaro's Paduan circle. Nor is there any doubt that

*A modest payment since a pair of men's trousers cost about three lire.

Palladio was pleased with the results. "This gentleman [Godi], who has the most exquisite taste, has entirely ignored the expense and chosen the most gifted and remarkable painters of our time," he wrote. *Per redurla a quella eccellenza & perfettione, che sia possibile:* "In order to make it as outstanding and perfect as possible."[31] And so it is.

Che Bella Casa

must have driven by the house without realizing it. I know that I'm in the right hamlet—Bagnolo di Lonigo—but there is no sign of a Palladio villa. The building is supposed to be next to a river, but there's no water either; the highway is lined with small houses on one side and a massive grassy embankment on the other. A marker announces the next town, confirming that I've gone too far, so I turn the car around and head back. Rounding a curve, I glimpse a small arrow indicating "Villa Pisani." I miss the turnoff and again make a U-turn, not easy with trucks barreling up and down the road. A narrow track ramps up to the top of the embankment, which turns out to be a dyke enclosing the narrow Guà River. On the other side, a large roof sticking out of the trees must be the villa.

The road crosses a small bridge, and a short, tree-lined gravel drive leads down to a closed gate. There are two cars parked haphazardly among the trees, and I pull up beside them, get out, and ring the buzzer. A young woman dressed in jeans and a white shirt appears.

"Is it possible to visit the house?" I ask hopefully, knowing that some villa owners restrict access to visitors.

She smiles. "Come in. You can go wherever you like."

The gate is at the edge of a compound whose centerpiece is

a large square lawn. Palladio referred to this space as a *cortile,* or courtyard. It was originally bounded on three sides by columned porticoes, which were destroyed in the Second World War. Today the house encloses one side of the courtyard, and a long, two-story stone barn the other.

I take a turn around the *cortile.* Reaching the far side, I look back at the house. The white stucco is freshly painted and sparkles in the sun. The grand building is almost as wide as the Villa Godi, with a similar red-clay-tile roof, but the resemblance ends there. The design is both simpler and more complicated. Simpler, because from this side the house resembles a shoe box with a hipped roof that slopes on four sides. The fenestration reflects the same tripartite organization as the Godi—a basement, the main floor, and an attic—although there are fewer windows and they are equally spaced, which gives the façade a calmer, more considered appearance. A broad stair leads to a central door. The complexity arises from several subtle refinements. The basement is partially buried, lowering the main floor and reducing the height of the house. Rugged stonework frames the small basement windows as well as the corners of the house. At the level of the main floor, about six feet above the ground, is a horizontal stone molding called a water table since its function is to throw water away from the foundations. It is echoed by a second stone molding at the level of the windowsills. The two horizontal bands, which girdle the house, give it the appearance of sitting on a base. They also accentuate the horizontal proportions of the façade, whose most distinctive feature is a large arched window directly above the door. The arched window, a semicircle divided vertically into three unequal parts, is a thermal window similar to the one that was originally in the Villa Godi.

I walk around to the side of the house facing the river. Pal-

PALLADIO'S SIGNATURE THERMAL WINDOW DOMINATES THE REAR
OF THE STARKLY BEAUTIFUL VILLA PISANI.

THE RUSTICATED TEMPLE FRONT OF THE LOGGIA IS SURMOUNTED
BY THE PISANI FAMILY COAT OF ARMS.

ladio considered riverside locations to be advantageous for villas, "because the produce can be carried cheaply by boat to the city at any time, and it will satisfy the needs of the household and the animals; this will also make it very cool in the summer and will be a lovely sight, and is both useful and pleasing in that one can irrigate the grounds, the gardens, and the orchards, which are the soul and delight of the estate."[1] Unfortunately, the lovely sight is long gone. The view of the river is obstructed by a tall brick wall—a counterpart to the grassy embankment—built to contain spring floods. The Guà is one of many rivers that flows across the Veneto plain, fed by the melting snows of the Alps. In the process of controlling the level of water in their lagoon, the Venetians became master hydrologists whose canal and river system was the principal means of communication in the *terraferma*. The cinquecento owners of the villa traveled to their estate by boat—across the Venetian lagoon, up the Adige River, finally reaching the Guà. So, just as in many American plantation houses in Virginia, a Veneto villa's front door faced the river.

The centerpiece of the front façade is a three-arch loggia made of heavily rusticated stone. Rustication refers to stonework that is rudely chiseled, and laid with deep V-shaped joints, to create a rough and coarse texture. This loggia is as massive and imposing as one of Sanmicheli's monumental city gates, an effect that is accentuated by the flanking towers that resemble a medieval *castello*. Although the Villa Pisani, like the Villa Godi, was built on top of an older house, these towers were not a holdover from the past but were designed by Palladio.*[2]

I go up a flight of semicircular steps and enter the loggia. No

---

*Years later, Palladio used similar twin towers in the Villa Valmarana at Lisiera, and the Villa Thiene at Cicogna.

frescoes this time, but the long narrow space is vaulted, and at each end there is a large apse, or curved niche. It is a curious solution and not, to my eye, an altogether successful one. The two curved ends emphasize the length of the loggia, drawing attention away from what should be the main focus: the front doors. The tall doors lead directly into the *sala*. And what a *sala!* The splendid room rises more than thirty feet, and extends all the way through the house, a distance of about thirty-five feet. This is a much more complex space than the *sala* of the Villa Godi. The ceiling is not flat but vaulted, and the plan is not rectangular but cruciform, the four barrel vaults of the unequal arms intersecting in a great groin vault in the middle. Light streams in through the thermal window on the far wall; the two arms of the cruciform likewise have thermal windows, which are indirectly lit by skylights in the roof; the fourth thermal window, on the loggia side, is blank.

When Palladio wrote *Quattro libri,* he devoted two chapters to villas, distinguishing the country houses of "noble Venetians" from those of "gentlemen of the *terraferma*" such as Girolamo Godi. The Venetian chapter opened with the Bagnolo house, home of "the magnificent Counts Vettor, Marco, and Daniele, the Pisani brothers."[3] The Pisanis, Palladio's first Venetian clients, belonged to one of the city's leading families. Merchants and landowners, they had been an important presence since the twelfth century, and had long been members of the Gran Consiglio, the governing body of the Republic. The branch of the family that commissioned Palladio was known as the Pisani del Banco, since its members specialized in banking. The brothers were newcomers to Bagnolo. Their father had bought the estate, which had been confiscated from a turncoat Vicentine nobleman, after the war. The house had been badly damaged during the fighting, and in 1542, on the occasion of

Vettor's betrothal, they decided to replace it with a grander structure.

The Pisanis' status on the five-hundred-acre estate (soon to be expanded to fourteen hundred acres, chiefly devoted to growing rice) was that of feudal lords, with all the accompanying privileges. Their exalted position was reflected in Palladio's design. The *sala* was not only a social area, it was where the Counts received their tenant farmers (who owed their lords one day of labor a week), where they listened to petitions and grievances, dispensed justice, and presided over public ceremonies. Hence the imposing vaulted space that resembles a Roman basilica. It is likely that the frankly monumental entrance loggia and the twin *castello* towers—age-old symbols of the feudal aristocracy—were also chosen because Palladio considered them suitable for the residence of such "magnificent" clients.

Vettor Pisani was the oldest brother and head of the family. He was only twenty-one when he commissioned Palladio, whom he had met three years earlier in Padua while a student at the university.[4] Vettor was an unusual young man, who had not yet reached his majority (which in Venice was twenty-five years) but clearly knew his own mind. While he was presumably acquainted with Sanmicheli and Serlio, he chose an unknown and relatively inexperienced architect. For Palladio, a novice from the *terraferma* hinterland, the Pisani commission represented a remarkable opportunity.

Palladio was lucky. Although he missed the golden age of the Venetian Republic by more than a century, in some ways he could hardly have lived in better times for an architect. For hundreds of years Venice had been a maritime powerhouse, the commercial intermediary between western and central Europe, and the Middle East and the Orient. During the fifteenth century, the island city emerged as one of the important land powers of the Italian peninsula, holding sway over an area that stretched as far west as Bergamo, northeast into Friuli, and south to the Po Valley. The chief reason to conquer these territories was to control the overland trade routes from Venice to northern Europe, but starting in the 1540s, exactly the time that Palladio embarked on his architectural career, the role of the *terraferma* changed. Wealthy Venetians began to invest heavily in mainland agriculture—land reclamation, irrigation canals, and drainage schemes. Historians do not agree about the exact reason for this newfound interest, but it was probably a combination of factors. Thanks to the growth of the Turkish empire, the discovery of alternative trade routes, and the growing naval power of the Baltic states, England, and the Low Countries, Venice was no longer dominant in international trade, and wealthy Venetians needed new vehicles for their investments. As Venice grew, the demand for food increased and so did its price, and the flat, rich lands of the *terraferma*—drained and irrigated—were ideally suited to agriculture.[5] Land also provided a good hedge against inflation. Finally, there is no doubt that the merchant elite of Venice were attracted by the image of spending part of each year on country estates in suitably grand villas.

Palladio began the Villa Pisani only five years after the Villa Godi, yet its design is far more ambitious and accomplished than his first commission—and much more original. The most important experience a beginning architect can have is to build, for it is on the building site that he sees his ideas realized, gains self-confidence, and learns from his mistakes. The prominence of the Villa Godi, and the continuing patronage of Count Trissino, quickly led to other Vicentine commissions. The first was a large town house for the Civena family. The

Palazzo Civena, today a nursing home, is a handsome two-story structure, facing the Retrone River, with a covered arcade at street level for pedestrians.* The following year, the Da Monte family likewise commissioned a residence in town, a small building with a rusticated base and a second floor with a central *serliana*. These two commissions were followed by a pair of villas on the outskirts of Vicenza, one for Giuseppe and Antonio Valmarana, cousins who had inherited an estate at Vigardolo outside Vicenza, the other for Tadeo Gazoto, a merchant who owned land in the nearby village of Bertesina. Neither house was as big or as prominent as the Villa Godi, but both would offer Palladio an opportunity to take his architecture in a new direction. The catalyst for this development was, again, Giangiorgio Trissino.

In the summer of 1541, Palladio accompanied the Count on a two-month visit to Rome. Rome was the site of the greatest concentration of antiquities in Italy: the crumbling remains of the Roman Forum, triumphal arches and temples, the hulking remains of several Imperial baths, the Colosseum, and the best preserved of the ancient monuments, the Pantheon, an enormous circular temple capped by a great dome. The importance to Palladio of experiencing these sites firsthand was immense. Later, it was common for budding architects to visit Rome, but in the sixteenth century this was not the case, particularly for Venetians. Although Palladio had studied Vitruvius and other secondary sources, and visited antiquities in Padua and Verona, the architecture of Rome was a revelation. "I set myself the task of investigating the remains of the ancient buildings that have survived despite the ravages of time and the cruelty of the bar-

---

*Although today grandly referred to as palazzos, in Palladio's time the large town houses of the nobility were called simply *case della città*.

barians," he recollected, "and finding them much worthier of
study than I had first thought, I began to measure all their parts
minutely and with the greatest care."[6] His admiration for
Roman architecture was unbounded: "It will be obvious to
anyone not entirely devoid of common sense that the methods
by which the ancients built were excellent because the ruins of
so many magnificent buildings survive in and outside Italy
after such a vast amount of time and so many changes and falls
of empires; because of this we have absolute proof of the
extraordinary virtue of the Romans which otherwise, perhaps, nobody would believe in."[7]

Palladio was following in the footsteps of quattrocento
architects such as Filippo Brunelleschi, who was responsible for
what is generally considered the first classical building of the
Renaissance—the Ospedale degli Innocenti in Florence. Turning away from what he judged the rude disorder of Gothic,
Brunelleschi went to Rome to study the monuments and
adopted an elegant and spare architectural style loosely based
on ancient precedents. The classical connection was later elu-
cidated and given a theoretical underpinning by Brunelleschi's
friend Leon Battista Alberti, whose *Of Built Things* was a
reworking—and updating—of Vitruvius. By the time Palladio
visited Rome, Bramante and Raphael had produced bodies of
work that were explicitly inspired by the ancient monuments of
Rome. Or what was left of them. With notable exceptions, such
as the Pantheon, most of the temples and bath buildings existed
only in fragmentary form. Although several popes had begun
excavating the ancient ruins during the preceding century,
the remains were still largely covered by a thousand years of
accumulated debris.

Palladio made his own detailed archaeological surveys using
a measuring tape, a plumb line, and a circumferentor, a primi-

tive surveying instrument that consisted of a compass with a sighting device. He demonstrated a scholarly bent and ultimately acquired such an intimate knowledge of the ancient city that in 1554 he would publish two guidebooks, one on churches and the other on antiquities—*L'Antichità di Roma*— a standard reference that would go into more than thirty editions over the next two centuries.[8] "Every great architect finds his own antiquity," James Ackerman wisely observed.[9] Palladio found his version climbing over ruins and poring over his field sketches, trying to decipher and comprehend this distant past. For the Renaissance, ancient Rome was chiefly an imagined re-creation, yet it was a potent fiction that encouraged architects to dream on a big scale. Palladio made ingenious, and sometimes fanciful, reconstructions. In the case of the Baths of Agrippa, for example, which were almost completely destroyed, he portrayed the building in frontal view and cross section. Although these drawings were a serious attempt to portray "what might have been," the powerful, vigorous images are as much a reflection of Palladio's architectural interests as they are of ancient Rome.

He made precise drawings of capitals, friezes, and entablatures, meticulously dimensioning each torus and fillet. He copied details. He sketched moldings, either drawing them by eye or modeling their outlines with a thin strip of lead that he used as a drawing template. The purpose of this activity was twofold. Drawing, which involves long periods of intense scrutiny, internalizes the subject (in a way photography does not begin to approximate); Palladio was schooling his eye and trying to better understand what he was seeing. He was also compiling a visual lexicon to which he could refer when he was working. Classical buildings of the type that Palladio designed depended on numerous details, especially moldings—around doors and windows, surrounding fireplaces, at dados and cornices. His field sketches provided an invaluable catalog of models.

As an archaeologist, Palladio was concerned with accuracy, but as a designer he was looking for beauty. Describing the octagonal Baptistery of Constantine at St. John Lateran, an early Christian building in Rome, he wrote: "In my opinion this temple is modern and made from the spoils of ancient buildings, but, because it is beautifully designed and has ornaments that are exquisitely carved in a great variety of patterns that the architect could make use of on many occasions, I thought it essential to include it with the ancient buildings, particularly because everybody supposes that it is ancient."[10] The entrance loggia to the Baptistery was a long space with an apse at each end, which probably provided the model for the loggia at the Villa Pisani. Another reconstructed plan, also drawn during the 1541 visit, shows the Baths of Titus and includes a vaulted cruciform hall that reappears, in reduced form, as the Pisani *sala*. The point is not that Palladio was copying ancient precedents, but rather that in the process of documenting and re-creating the past he was discovering solutions for the present.

Rome also provided Palladio with the opportunity, no less important, to see the work of his contemporaries. These included Sanmicheli, Giulio, and da Sangallo, as well as their predecessors, Bramante and Raphael. Bramante had died in 1514 and Raphael in 1520, so their designs were, in a sense, somewhat old-fashioned. Yet Palladio was drawn to their architecture. He was definitely a provincial—a hayseed in the big city—but he was not swept up by the latest trends. Bramante's bold rustication impressed him; so did his unusual exterior stair in the Cortile del Belvedere, whose semicircular (concave) steps rise to a circular landing, whence a second set of (convex) semicircular stair continue into the building. This and the succeeding Roman visits were a crucial part of Palladio's architectural training; Raphael had worked under Bramante, and Giulio under Raphael, but Palladio had no master to emulate. Like Michelangelo, he made his own way.

Trissino, who continued to take a lively interest in Palladio's architectural education, introduced him to the most ambitious—if unfinished—private building project in Rome, a villa designed by Raphael for Cardinal Giulio de'Medici, later Pope Clement VII. The palatial retreat, today known as the Villa Madama, was Raphael's idealized vision of an ancient Roman villa, and his design included garden loggias, terraces, water features, and an open-air theater. The centerpiece was to be a circular entrance court more than one hundred feet in diameter. Work started in 1518, and when Raphael died two years later, the vast complex was only half-finished. It was damaged during the Sack of Rome, repaired, but never completed. When Palladio saw it, the building had been standing unoccupied for two decades, the walls of the incomplete court forming a great semicircle, the immense apses and unfinished colonnades as forsaken and overgrown as their ancient models.

The Villa Madama made a strong impression on Palladio, who drew a measured plan of what had been built. He also must have copied details, for Raphael's rusticated basement windows reappeared in the basement of the Villa Pisani. In a more general way, the Villa Madama showed Palladio how a modern building could be based on the study and creative interpretation of ancient precedents. Raphael, whose client was one of the most powerful men in Rome, was inspired by the luxurious pleasure-villas of the late Roman Republic. These sprawling complexes survived in ruins such as those of Hadrian's villa at Tivoli, or in ancient texts, notably Pliny the Younger's detailed description of his seaside villa at Laurentum. Such pleasure-villas were characterized by a variety of partially enclosed outdoor spaces: atria, courtyards, porticoes, loggias, airy colonnades, sunny terraces, walled gardens with pools. The Villa Madama, even in its unfinished state, includes not only the semicircular forecourt but also garden walls and a garden terrace built above giant semicircular recesses that overlook a fishpond. These structures are not part of the house proper, but amplify its architectural impact, extending the villa into the landscape.

The idea of enlarging the architectural presence of a house by means of walls, garden structures, and outbuildings must have appealed to Palladio, who was familiar with Pliny's writing. But the Roman imperial villas and the Villa Madama were much larger than anything Palladio was asked to build—Raphael's circular courtyard alone could accommodate the entire Villa Pisani with room to spare. So Palladio turned to a passage of Vitruvius that described the typical Roman country house with "an atrium surrounded by a paved portico." At the Villa Pisani, Palladio enlarged the atrium into a courtyard. His design for the porticoes was wonderfully simple: a continuous shed roof resting on a back wall and supported by columns. The structures were not completed until the 1560s, and it is unclear whether they followed the simple design that Palladio sketched in an early plan, the more elaborate design illustrated in *Quattro libri,* or some modified version. They were, in any case, impressive— Vasari singled them out as "most beautiful."[11]

The porticoes enclosed a formal, ceremonial space. Despite Palladio's claim that the courtyard was for "farm use," it was hardly a barnyard with piles of manure, rooting pigs, and clucking chickens. A 1569 plan of the Pisani estate that hangs in the villa shows a second courtyard that is across the road from the villa and is obviously intended for agricultural use.[12] The stables and storage rooms around the formal *cortile* were for the convenience of the immediate household. The surface of the *cortile* was probably gravel, and it would have resembled a piazza, while the porticoes provided a protected space around the edge, just like the arcades of many Vicentine towns. The introduction of such urban features into a country estate is another aspect of Palladio's delicate balance of sophistication and rusticity, of bringing city people—and city life—into the country.

When Palladio designed features like the *cortile,* he did so entirely on paper; Renaissance architects sometimes built wooden models of their designs, but only for large buildings such as churches. Palladio was a particularly able draftsman—neat, skillful, precise.* Drawings were always made in ink since pencils were unknown, and graphite and graphite holders were not invented until 1565.[13] Sometimes he started with a light underdrawing using a crayon or a piece of metallic lead. His chief drawing instruments were wooden rulers, set squares, metal dividers, and compasses. He sketched and drew with a quill pen, using purplish black iron gall ink made from oak apples; today, as the iron has oxidized, the ink has turned various shades of sepia and brown.[14]

There was no such thing as tracing paper. Palladio drew on heavy, hand-laid, watermarked paper that came in octavo sizes—about sixteen by twenty inches. Paper was not particularly rare or expensive, but he was frugal in its use and most of his drawings are small, no larger than a modern sheet of typing paper. The sheets tend to be crammed with drawings. He once covered a small sheet with no fewer than twenty plan variations for a palazzo.[15] The freehand ink sketches are only postage stamp–size but include details such as staircases. In one variation

---

*As far as is known, Palladio generally did his own drawing and rarely relied on assistants.

the stair is oval; in another, circular; in the third, rectangular; and the *sala* changes from a square to a rectangle to a cross. Slightly larger-scale plans include scribbled dimensions and details such as fireplaces. Palladio often made such preliminary sketches on the backs of his old drawings; the palazzo plans are on the back of a sheet containing a façade and cross section of a Roman temple.

Four surviving drawings by Palladio of the Villa Pisani offer an extraordinary glimpse into his working method. He recorded his first idea on the back of a sheet containing a pre-liminary version of the Villa Valmarana.[16] The lightly drawn, freehand Pisani sketch is a floor plan, and shows the thicknesses

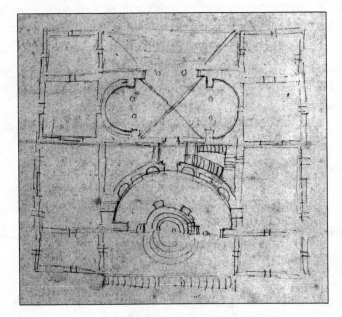

PALLADIO'S FIRST SKETCH OF THE VILLA PISANI, 1541
(RIBA, XVII/2 *verso*)

of the walls as well as the location of doors, windows, and fireplaces. There are four rooms on each side of a rectangular *sala*
with apsidal ends; an *X* marks the cross-vaults of the ceiling.
The most striking feature of the plan is a colonnaded semicircular loggia cut into the front of the house. Historians believe
that this unusual device, called a hemicycle, was inspired by
either the Villa Madama's truncated circular courtyard or by
Bramante's Cortile del Belvedere, which Palladio had also seen
in Rome. His version differs significantly from Raphael's in its
smaller size, its function (as the entrance to a house), and in
being roofed.

Palladio's sketch is striking for its symmetry—that is, one side

PALLADIO'S DRAFTED PLAN, 1541
(RIBA, XVII/18 *verso*)

of the plan is a mirror image of the other. "Rooms must be distributed at either side of the entrance and the hall," he wrote, "and one must ensure that those on the right correspond and are equal to those on the left."[17] He went on to glibly explain that this was desirable for structural reasons, which is not actually true. In fact, like all Renaissance architects, Palladio favored symmetry for aesthetic reasons (and not only in plans, façades were symmetrical, too). "Look at Nature's own works," Alberti had pointed out, "if someone had one huge foot, or one hand vast and the other tiny, he would look deformed."[18] Palladio also often made analogies between buildings and the human body, once pointing out that "just as our blessed God has arranged our own members so that the most beautiful are in positions most exposed to view and the more unpleasant are hidden, we too when building should place the most important and prestigious parts in full view and the less beautiful in locations concealed as far from our eyes as possible."[19] Thus, in the Pisani plan, the "less beautiful" stairs are hidden in a leftover space behind the hemicycle.

Palladio obviously made this hurriedly scrawled sketch for his own use, but the next surviving plan was probably intended for his client, since it is carefully drafted.[20] Drafted drawings required two steps. A contemporary of Palladio described the process: "For the fair copy of buildings we draw the line with an ivory nib, and then with a pen."[21] The ivory or ebony nib was used to score invisible guidelines into the paper. There are signs that Palladio frequently modified these ghostly preliminary drawings before the final inking. The ink lines were drawn using a ruler; decorative elements on façades such as wreaths, statues, or rustication were drawn freehand. Palladio often applied a diluted ink wash to accentuate the thickness of the walls in plans, to pick out loggias and windows in elevations, or to add shadows.

The results are drawings of great clarity—and striking severity. Rooms are rarely labeled and furniture is never shown, though key room dimensions are included; there are never titles and rarely notes; there are no decorative borders. Occasionally, Palladio added a scale bar.* These do not appear to be construction drawings in the modern sense. They may have been shown to the foreman to establish the main dimensions of the foundations, but it is likely that illiterate artisans depended on verbal instructions and sketchy overall directions. In any case, such drawings were too precious—and fragile—to leave on the building site.

The design of the Villa Pisani was considerably simplified in the drafted plan. Palladio changed the apsidal ends of the *sala* to small niches and reduced the number of rooms from eight to six. At the same time, he added a square vaulted space, a sort of large vestibule, between the loggia and the *sala*. The sequence of small, medium, and large rooms, each with a different proportion (a small rectangle, a square, a large rectangle), was an exact copy of the arrangement in Trissino's villa at Cricoli.

The third surviving plan, likewise drafted in ink, is drawn at a smaller scale and includes not only the house but the entire *cortile*, with columned porticoes on two sides and a wall across the end.[22] Palladio drew the river with fanciful curlicues (and redundantly labeled it *fiume*). The house plan is further refined. In the previous versions, the rooms on each side of the *sala* are simply placed one behind the other; now the largest rooms are ingeniously turned ninety degrees so that their long side faces the courtyard. Presumably at Pisani's request, the

---

*Modern architectural drawings are made to a small number of standard scales. In Palladio's time, scales were a matter of personal choice and convenience.

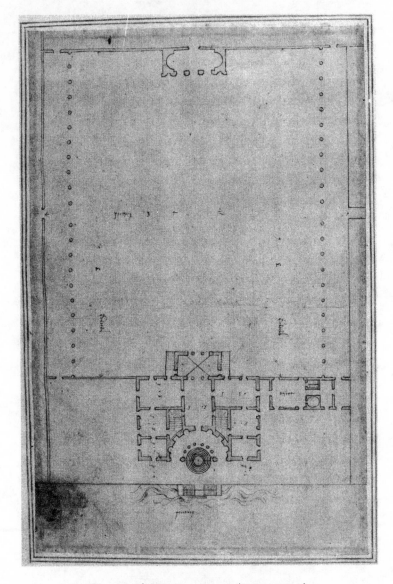

Palladio's site plan, 1541 (RIBA, XVI/7)

PALLADIO'S FOURTH PLAN WITH A FRONT VIEW, 1542
(RIBA, XVII/17)

public rooms have been drastically simplified: the *sala* has lost its apses, and the square vaulted vestibule has been entirely eliminated. On the other hand, the hemicycle is now more elaborate, with a semicircle of columns defining the Bramantesque stair.

Palladio is not finished yet. Pisani must have demanded larger rooms, judging from the fourth surviving plan.[23] Palladio adds complicated corner niches in the smallest rooms, making them hexagonal in plan. In the process of modifying the room sizes, he reconfigures the layout of the *sala,* making it T-shaped with a cross-vault in the center. He must believe the planning process is at an end, for now—and only now—he turns his attention to the exterior of the house. This sheet combines the floor plan with a drawing of the entrance façade—façade above, plan below. Two *castello* towers frame the hemicycle, which is overlooked by a large thermal window that brings light into the *sala.*

This drawing corresponds exactly to what was built in all respects but one: Palladio took out the hemicycle and replaced it with a rectangular, three-arch loggia. We do not know exactly when this change occurred. Since no drawing of the plan with the redesigned loggia has come to light, some historians conjecture that the change was made after construction had begun (the area beneath the loggia and the hall has no basement, so it is impossible to verify if the foundations were altered).[24] The shape of the roof on this side of the house is complicated, as if it were the result of a last-minute alteration. What prompted such a drastic revision? It has been suggested that the late change was demanded by the client, and may even have been made without Palladio's authorization.[25] But why would Vettor Pisani, who had approved the hemicycle in several preliminary versions, suddenly change his mind? Surely not to save money, for he was fabulously wealthy, and the final loggia with its complicated apsidal ends and real stone facing—not a plaster facsimile—was hardly inexpensive. In any case, it is unlikely that the young nobleman second-guessed his architect on aesthetic matters.

It is not unusual for a novice designer to fall in love with an idea, only to suddenly discover—often late in the day—that he has made a mistake. Palladio's design process for the Villa Pisani, as shown by the four surviving drawings, was one of both progressive refinement and trial and error. He may have come to the conclusion that while Raphael's hemicycle looked impressive in a palatial structure overlooking the Tiber, it was ill-

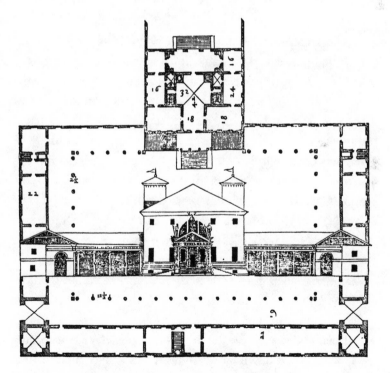

THE FINAL PLAN AND COURTYARD FAÇADE FROM *QUATTRO LIBRI*

suited to a relatively small country house on the tiny Guà. I think he was right. His fussy little hemicycle, with its niches and columns, risked not only looking pretentious but also detracting from the *sala,* which had become the focus of his design. The hemicycle had to go. (And it never returned; while Palladio sometimes incorporated a hemicycle as a garden feature, he never again used it in a villa.)

Palladio replaced the hemicycle with a more conventional rectangular loggia, but couldn't resist adding apsidal ends recycled from his first sketch-plan. Since the shallow loggia required less depth than the hemicycle, he enlarged the *sala,* adding a short arm and turning the T-shaped room into a cruciform. On the exterior, he returned to a theme that he had begun to explore in two earlier villas. The Villa Valmarana, which still stands, is a solid little building covered by a simple gable roof. Palladio transformed the gable into a schematic pediment—the shallow triangular gable of an ancient temple—by outlining the eave with a molding that became a short, interrupted entablature cornice, similar to one he had seen in Rome on an ancient temple.[26] (Or at least that was the way he drew the façade—the builders of the villa left out the cornice, just as they did not follow his complicated design for the window surrounds.) In the Villa Gazoto the pediment motif is more pronounced. The façade, modeled on a palazzo by Bramante, is divided into seven bays separated by flattened columns, or pilasters. The three central bays have arches opening into a loggia, above which is a large triangular dormer. It is perched rather tenuously on top of the simplified frieze that extends the full length of the house, but it is unmistakably a pediment.

Palladio designed the pilasters of the Villa Gazoto according to the rules laid down by Vitruvius. The so-called architectural orders, whose origin is Greek, are the foundation of classical architecture. The main elements of an order are the entablature, or beam, and the supporting columns. The entablature has three parts: the architrave, or lowest section; the frieze in the middle; and the cornice immediately under the eaves. The column consists of a base (often defined by moldings), a shaft (which can be plain or fluted), and a capital, or headpiece. Vitruvius described three orders—Doric, Ionic, and Corinthian—whose chief distinguishing feature was their capital: Doric capitals had simple moldings; Ionic capitals had volutes, or spirals, like the horns of a mountain ram; Corinthian capitals incorporated stylized acanthus leaves. Alberti identified an additional ancient Roman order that came to be known as Composite since it combined Ionic volutes and Corinthian leaves, while Serlio added the Tuscan order (a sort of simplified Doric), which Vitruvius had mentioned but did not describe. The five orders were often given human attributes: Doric was considered manly, Ionic womanly, and Corinthian maidenly. The undecorated Tuscan order was often used for utilitarian buildings, elegant Ionic in houses, rich Corinthian in ceremonial buildings, and Composite when an extra degree of luxury was called for. Palladio favored Ionic in the porticoes of his villas and rarely used Composite columns, but that is what he gave Gazoto, who had become wealthy speculating in salt in Treviso and probably wanted a showy house.

Palladio believed that in using a temple pediment on a house, he was following a Roman custom. "The ancients also employed [pediments] in their buildings, as one can see from the remains of temples and other public buildings," he wrote, "it is very likely that they took this invention and its forms from private buildings, that is, from houses."[27] He was careful to write "likely," since, in fact, there was no hard evidence for his supposition. Characteristically, he also saw practical advantages to pediments. "In all the buildings for farms and also for some of those in the city I have built a tympanum [the triangular panel inside the pediment] on the front façade where the principal doors are," he explained, "because tympanums accentuate the entrance of the house and contribute greatly to the grandeur and magnificence of the building, thus making the front part more imposing than the others; furthermore, they are perfectly suited to the insignia or arms of the patrons, which are usually placed in the middle of façades."[28] Gazoto, being a commoner, had no armorial crest.

Palladio took the Villa Gazoto's three-arch loggia and pediment as his model for the Villa Pisani, but instead of the Composite order, he used the plainer Doric, and added heavy rustication to the piers. He had already tried this motif, which he adapted from Sanmicheli's Verona city gates, in the portal of the Palazzo Civena. He placed the Pisani coat of arms in the center of the tympanum. At first glance the loggia appears unexceptional; however, Palladio was not merely repeating an earlier solution. He replaced the schematic frieze with a full Doric entablature, including an architrave, a frieze with triglyphs and metopes, and a cornice. The result is a complete representation of a Roman temple: columns, entablature, pediment. Or rather the ghostly shadow of a temple front, since the flattened pilasters and stylized capitals almost disappear into the heavy rustication. It is as if Palladio was not quite sure that he was doing the right thing. Yet this tentative design marks a historic moment, not only in his architectural development but in the history of Western architecture. It already holds the promise of numerous English country houses and Georgian plantation houses. All colonnaded entrance porticoes and pedimented house fronts share an architectural DNA that can be traced to the Villa Pisani.

The three villas—Valmarana, Gazoto, and Pisani—Palladio built after his heady Roman summer show a definite evolution, from interrupted pediment, to pediment, to full temple front. The next logical step would have been that most characteristic of Palladian features: the columned portico. However, architecture is not biology; ideas in design do not develop according to simple determinism. Palladio did explore the temple theme further—a few years after starting the Villa Pisani, he designed the Villa Thiene, a country house that incorporated a flattened temple front with giant pilasters rising the full height of the house. But in other villas he continued to use pediments without pilasters. A country house of this period that Palladio designed for Biagio Saraceno has a three-arch loggia as plain as the Villa Godi.

The symbolic use of a temple pediment on the front of a house was not, strictly speaking, Palladio's invention. It had been suggested a century earlier by Alberti, who, while cautioning that "the pediment to a private house should not emulate the majesty of a temple in any way," allowed that "the vestibule itself may be ennobled by having its façade heightened slightly, or by being given a dignified pediment."[29] Alberti's suggestion was taken up by the Florentine architect Giuliano da Sangallo (the uncle of Antonio da Sangallo, who had worked with Sanmicheli), who included a complete *all'antica* temple porch with freestanding Ionic columns on the front façade of Lorenzo de'Medici's villa in Poggio a Caiano. Completed by 1492, this is the first temple-fronted villa of the Renaissance. The porch, however, is awkwardly related to the house—it appears stuck onto the façade—and it did not inspire other architects. During the 1530s, just before Palladio started his architectural career, three prominent villas were built in the Venetian Republic. Sanmicheli, who knew da Sangallo well, built the Villa La Soranza

VILLA VALMARANA

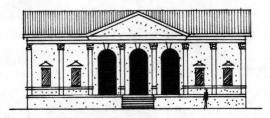

VILLA GAZOTO

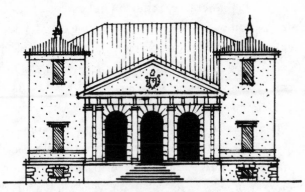

VILLA PISANI

Praise for Jennifer Solow's dazzling debut novel *The Booster*

"Solow has neatly dropped her literary beach towel next to the spot of sand occupied by Kate White and Sophie Kinsella."

—*The Boston Globe*

"A deliciously guilty pleasure."

—Farrah Weinstein, *New York Post*

"*The Booster* is taut and also fraught with the real value of luxury goods."

—*New York Daily News*

"Jennifer Solow's writing talent is clearly evident. . . . A solid, well-written first effort."

—*The Tampa Tribune*

"A thoughtful and sometimes piercing character study."

—Bookreporter.com

"Solow brings something new to this genre."

—Janet Maslin, *People*

"Jennifer Solow is an inspired and refreshing addition to the world of women's literature."

—Jane Green, author of *The Other Woman* and *Jemima J*

This title is also available as an eBook.

"[*The Booster*] will keep you guessing (and laughing and gasping) until the very end."

—Zink magazine

"Loved it! Jennifer Solow is a clever funny writer, but a bad, bad, wicked, evil girl."

—Simon Doonan, author of Nasty: My Family and
Other Glamorous Varmints

". . . filled with New York City observations so exact and unflinching, you feel like Solow packs a hidden camera—a truly fun read with dark humor, big heart, and plenty of chutzpah."

—Jill Kargman, coauthor of The Right Address and
Wolves in Chic Clothing

"A brilliant, scary, and very funny first novel."

—Allison Lurie, Pulitzer Prize–winning author of Foreign Affairs

"*The Booster* is a roller-coaster ride through the high times and the tribulations of fabulous city life. It shows that real New Yorkers don't go down without a fight!"

—Cynthia Rowley, designer

"A sharp novel."

—Harper's Bazaar (Hot Pick for March 2006)

"Jennifer is taking over where *Sex and the City* left off."

—David Evangelista, CBS Early Show

"This debut author has buckets of talent and her first release is sure to win her many admirers."

—Romantic Times

in Castelfranco, not far from Vicenza. The simple structure (which no longer exists) had a central arcaded loggia but no pediment. Falconetto, perhaps with Cornaro's collaboration, built a villa for the bishop of Padua inspired by the Villa Madama, but did not include a pediment either. Nor did Jacopo Sansovino, who built only one villa in the Veneto, also near Padua, an impressive, palazzolike structure surrounding an inner courtyard. So when Palladio added a temple front to the Villa Pisani, he was neither following a current fashion nor copying something he had seen elsewhere.

Of all the applied arts, architecture is the least progressive—that is, while engineering and technology evolve, architecture itself, its forms and spaces, is constant. A Renaissance fireplace is not as efficient as a modern gas furnace, but a Renaissance building, judged purely architecturally, can be as good as, or even better than, a modern one. Architecture, especially great architecture, does not become obsolete. That is why Palladio looked at Bramante, and I am looking at Palladio.

When Palladio visited Rome, he experienced the antiquities both as archaeology and architecture. The Villa Pisani is a relic of a distant time, yet it is also a house in which I could imagine living. This impression is no doubt heightened by the fact that the villa is somebody's home. In 1976, the Countess Cornelia Ferri de Lazara, a Pisani descendant, began an ambitious project to restore the architectural integrity of the house. Not only was the building in a dilapidated state, during the eighteenth century it had suffered multiple indignities such as the infilling of the arches of the loggia, which was subdivided into small rooms, the addition of a catwalk across the *sala* linking the two sides of the attic, and the crude infilling of ground-floor windows to minimize a Napoleonic fenestration tax. These changes were undone. When the basement, which had flooded and was full of silt, was excavated, it was discovered that over the years, perhaps in an attempt to control the flooding, the ground around the exterior of the building had been raised more than two feet. With the original levels reestablished, the house regained its base, and the façades their original proportions.

Palladio's architectural intentions have been restored, yet the house does not feel like a museum. The furnishings are, for the most part, contemporary—tasteful but unpretentious sofas and easy chairs, coffee tables, sisal mats, a Heitzmann grand piano. The rooms, while commodious, are not overwhelming. After the uniform room sizes of the Villa Godi, Palladio developed an arrangement that he would follow for the rest of his career. "There should be large, medium-sized, and small rooms," he recommended, "one side by side with the next, so that they can be mutually useful. The small ones should be divided up to create even smaller rooms where studies or libraries could be located, as well as riding equipment and other tackle which we need every day and which would be awkward to put in rooms where one sleeps, eats, or receives guests."[30] In the Villa Pisani there is a small-medium-large suite of rooms on each side of the *sala*. The large rooms face the courtyard and are entered directly from the *sala*. One is furnished as a living room, the other as a kitchen (the kitchen was relocated here in the eighteenth century when the basement flooded). The medium-sized rooms are next, the one adjacent to the kitchen furnished with a dining table and chairs, the other used as an informal sitting room—a collection of old maps hangs on the walls. The small rooms are within the corner towers, and because they are entered directly from the loggia, probably served as antechambers or reception rooms. Unlike the other rooms, they have domed ceilings.

Several features add to the domestic atmosphere. The rooms
are bathed in light. The large amounts of glass are not unusual
by modern standards, but they were exceptional in sixteenth-
century European houses whose "glazing" was generally oiled
paper or canvas. It was only in the Venetian Republic, which led
Europe in glassmaking, that glass was plentiful and relatively
inexpensive.[31] Palladio took full advantage of this material, and
provided many large leaded-glass windows, which accounts for
his uniformly bright interiors. The walls of the Villa Pisani are
white. With the exception of a single decorated vaulted ceiling,
there are no frescoes in the rooms. As in the Villa Godi, the window niches are fitted with two little seats composed of stone
slabs supported on delicate columns. The medium and large
rooms have fireplaces, the small square rooms have none, suggesting that they were not used for sleeping, at least not in winter. The fireplaces are important decorative elements, with
elaborate stone mantels, differently carved in each room. The
interiors have a simple charm and are not so very different from
those of a modern house, although the sixteen-foot ceilings of
dark stained wooden beams are much taller.

Combining rooms of different sizes within a rigidly rectangular plan requires skill, all the more so when the plan also has
to accommodate extraneous elements such as stairs. In the
Villa Pisani, two stairs, one on each side of the *sala,* are hidden
within the fabric of the walls. Palladio went to some lengths to
explain why he had not bothered to provide these stairs with
natural light, since they "serve only the rooms at the bottom and
at the top of the house, which are used for either granaries or
mezzanines."[32] Mezzanines, or *amezati,* were distinct from the
attic spaces, and despite their name were not balconies but
second-floor rooms with lower ceilings, usually used as servants'
quarters. In the Villa Pisani, *amezati* were located in the two

THE SALA OF THE VILLA PISANI IS A GRAND RECEPTION ROOM
WITH A THIRTY-FOOT CEILING THAT RISES THE FULL HEIGHT
OF THE HOUSE.

castello towers. Today, these rooms, like the attic spaces, have been converted into bedrooms.

After visiting the villa I sit down on a wooden bench in the *sala* and write in my notebook. The house is absolutely still. This is a remarkable room. The overhead vaults are fully frescoed, possibly by Bernardino India, a Veronese who worked regularly with Sanmicheli, or by Francesco Torbido, a pupil of Giulio—the attribution is unclear. The walls, on the other hand, are painted white. The architectural décor consists of giant Doric pilasters with carved stone capitals and bases and a stone frieze supporting the vaults. The presence of actual, rather than frescoed, interior architecture, as well as the complicated vaulting, attests to Vettor Pisani's magnanimous building budget. The *sala* is largely unfurnished, as it was in Palladio's day. Nor are there any fireplaces—the cavernous space would have been impractical to heat. The absence of such domestic features, as well as the tall vaulted ceilings and the bright light, make me feel that I am outdoors. It is almost as if Palladio were underlining the difference between the domestic rooms and the grand *sala*.

The doorways leading to the rooms beside the *sala* have elaborate stone surrounds and architraves that make them resemble exterior doors. It is known that the Pedemuro workshop was involved in the construction of the villa, and it is likely that Palladio himself did some of this carving. Despite Trissino's support, and an encouraging string of commissions, he was not yet a full-fledged architect; the fees for designing two town houses and three villas over five years would hardly have supported his family. Like most Renaissance architects, Palladio needed official patronage—a secure position with an annual salary—and that seemed far in the future. For the moment, he prudently kept his day job.

*   *   *

The afternoon is coming to a close and it's time to go. Reluctantly, I make my way to the gate, which is locked. There is a car parked next to mine, so there must be somebody still here. The small room that functions as an office is empty. I call out, but no one answers. Going around the corner, I knock on a small door, but no luck. Partway down the length of the barn, arched openings lead into an arcaded loggia. The dark space beyond is empty except for a parked minivan. Continuing along the building, I approach a second arcade. Hearing a buzzing noise from somewhere inside, I go into the dark interior. The noise is louder here, the familiar high-pitched whine of an electric table saw, an anomalous modern sound in these old surroundings. There is a light at the far end of the cavernous space. Behind a partition is a carpentry shop, or rather a musical instrument maker's shop; a man and the young woman who earlier let me in are leaning intently over a burnished piano case. They are wearing ear-protectors and are obviously engrossed in their work. Sheepishly I ask if someone could unlock the gate.

Luigi and Paola Borgato, whose workshop this is, build pianos to order. Every year they produce three or four nine-foot grands. The Borgato piano is highly regarded—I later learn that the London-based concert pianist Radu Lupu owns one.

"Grazie mille," I say to Paola Borgato as I leave.

I want to tell her how much I've enjoyed my visit, and how much I appreciate the care with which the villa has been restored and maintained, and what a magical place this is. But all I can manage in my rudimentary Italian is *"Che bella casa."*

III

The Arched Device

oiana Maggiore is a hamlet about twenty miles south of Vicenza. It sits in the flat, low-land plain that was the Venetian Republic's agricultural mainstay and is still farming country. It is a brisk morning, and the sun is shining brightly. The surrounding fields are freshly turned, ready for spring planting. The Villa Poiana is on the outskirts of the hamlet, plainly visible behind a long brick wall next to the road. I park the little rented Opel on the grass verge beside the wall and walk back to the gate.

The gate opens to a walled forecourt. The entire area seems to have been recently graded, and in many places the scrubby grass has been scraped away to reveal patches of raw earth. The building is hardly an obvious successor to the Villa Pisani—no triple arches, no rustication, no pilasters, no temple front. Instead, the most distinctive feature of the façade is a tall arched opening that leads to what I assume is an entrance loggia. The broad surround of the archway is punctuated by five round holes or *oculi*—literally, eyes. The arc of platter-sized *oculi* is like a cartoon of a juggler's act. Yet there is nothing whimsical about this sturdy building. The horizontal moldings of the façade, the square piers that support the loggia, the three arches, even the elaborate bracketed architraves over the windows, are plastered brick—only the windowsills are stone. Since everything

AT THE ENTRANCE OF THE VILLA POIANA IS A STATUE
OF THE ROMAN GOD NEPTUNE; ABOVE IT IS AN ARC
OF CIRCULAR OPENINGS, OR OCULI.

is freshly painted white, the massive building appears to be carved out of a single block of chalk. No doubt the absence of even rudimentary landscaping exaggerates the effect, but the house has a no-nonsense soldierly presence that the five circles only underscore. Just let me catch you smiling, it dares.

The client was Bonifacio Poiana, a *cavaliere,* or knight, of a long-established Vicentine family. The Poianas—the word means "buzzard" and the bird appears on their coat of arms—had a long history of military service, providing cavalry to the Venetian Republic. They also had a long history at Poiana Maggiore—their fifteenth-century fortified villa complex, including a medieval tower, stands across the road from the villa. Bonifacio Poiana bought the land for his new house in 1547, and soon after engaged Palladio. Palladio was still a stonemason when he first met the *cavaliere;* it was for his wife, Lady Angela, that Allegradonna had worked as a maid.

Seen close up, the façade is not what it appears to be. The *oculi* are not holes but deep recesses, nor are the plaster walls plain, they are incised with a masonry pattern. The entrance arch, whose simplified square piers seem to be a part of the wall, is actually the center of a highly stylized *serliana.* And

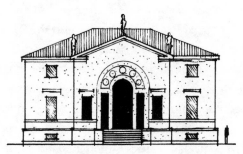

VILLA POIANA, THE FRONT

what look like two more windows on each side of the entrance, with identical pediments and surrounds, are really apertures opening into the loggia. The loggia is reached by a wide stair, a short climb since the basement is partially buried. Lowering the house is Palladio's accommodation to the surrounding flat landscape site. The horizontal impression is accentuated by the water table, which neatly turns into a parapet at the stair abutments, and by a second flat molding that surrounds the building at the level of the windowsills. The panels below the windows protrude slightly, creating additional shadow lines.

The large hipped roof has a gable over the loggia. Instead of a full triangular pediment, however, Palladio interrupts the horizontal entablature and merely hints at a temple front—the same device that he designed for the Villa Valmarana. At Poiana he accentuates the effect of a frontispiece by pushing the whole central section of the façade slightly forward (the reverse of what he did at the Villa Valmarana, where the central section is slightly recessed); it's only a few inches, but the resulting shadow line makes a subtle but unmistakable separation. The Villa Poiana reprises a number of motifs from Palladio's earlier houses: it has the Spartan plainness and massiveness of the Villa Godi; the *serliana* of the Villa Valmarana is here, although in highly abstracted form; the central pediment of Gazoto is repeated in the gable over the loggia; and the moldings recall similar devices at the Villa Pisani. Yet this is not a collage. Palladio combines the different parts seamlessly—the house is all of a piece.

The pediment of the Villa Poiana is accented by three life-size statues. The female figures represent drama, sculpture, and music. Two additional statues—Hercules and Neptune—stand on the stair abutments, guarding the entrance. These statues were installed late, in 1658, but they followed the illustration in *Quattro libri*. Palladio generally embellished the exterior of his buildings with sculpted likenesses of human figures, although he was not the first Renaissance architect to do so; Sanmicheli placed sculptures on the roof parapet of the Palazzo Canossa in Verona in 1537. Like Sanmicheli, Palladio took his cue from the ancient Romans. Vitruvius mentions that the pediments of certain temples are "adorned in the Tuscan fashion with statues of terra-cotta or gilt bronze."[1] By the time Palladio saw the ancient ruins, the statues had long since disappeared—looted or simply fallen—but he surmised their presence from the empty niches and bare pedestals, and included statues in all his drawings of historical reconstructions. "Nobody should be surprised that I have put such a plethora of statues in these buildings," he explained, "because one reads that there were so many in Rome that they looked like another population."[2] *Another population* is exactly what I think of as I look up at the figures on the roof of the Villa Poiana. The statues are not only allusions to antiquity, allegorical symbols, and attractive ornaments silhouetted against the sky, but also protective icons. Le Corbusier defined architecture as "the masterly, correct and magnificent play of masses brought together in light." The Villa Poiana is all that, but the statues are a reminder that the masses are, literally, subordinate to the human presence.

I go around to the back. The design of the sides, which in the earlier houses is haphazard, is perfectly symmetrical. The rear façade is almost a mirror image of the front, although without a loggia. Between the piers of the *serliana* is a large set of solid doors, reached by an exterior semicircular stair similar to that of the Villa Pisani. The doors are surmounted by a miniature thermal window and an arc of five *oculi*, although here the circles are real windows. According to some historians, the *oculi* motif may have been copied by Palladio from Bramante (who in turn copied it from early Christian churches); or it may have been inspired by the *oculi* and stylized *serliana* of Sansovino's Loggetta in the Piazza San Marco, begun the previous decade.[3] The rear façade of the Villa Poiana represented an important stylistic development for Palladio. The earliest Renaissance architecture was urban, and walled towns and cities were extremely dense so that buildings, churches as well as residences, generally had but a single façade, facing the street. On the other hand, country houses were freestanding. Palladio's first houses dealt awkwardly with this new freedom; I have the impression that he was not quite sure what to do. The backs of the Villa Gazoto and the Villa Valmarana, for example, were utilitarian and unresolved architecturally; the Janus-like Villa Pisani had handsome front and back façades, but they could have belonged to two different buildings. In the Villa Poiana, Palladio skillfully used variations on the *serliana* motif to create an interesting visual relationship between the front and the rear of the house while, at the same time, giving predominance to the former. Domestic architects have repeated this simple but original theme for centuries.

As often happens in architecture, the breakthrough design of

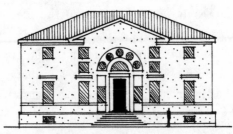

VILLA POIANA, THE BACK

the Villa Poiana was actually the result of hasty improvisation. A few years earlier, around 1544, Palladio had been commissioned by a Vicentine nobleman named Bartolomeo Pagliarino to build a small villa. A rough draft of the plan has survived, showing the house surrounded on three sides by expansive walled courtyards.[4] The small house has a T-shaped *sala* flanked by two rooms and two *camerini*—small rooms—and fronted by a projecting loggia with a *serliana*. Before construction could begin Pagliarino unexpectedly died, and the project was shelved. When Palladio received the Poiana commission, he dusted off the Pagliarino drawings.[5] (This is not unusual; Frank Lloyd Wright frequently adapted unbuilt house designs; Mies van der Rohe's National Gallery in Berlin started life as an office building in Cuba.) Palladio redrew the plan of the house using the same overall dimensions and the same cross-vaulted, T-shaped *sala,* although he simplified the projecting loggia and changed the configurations of the walled courtyards to fit the new site in Poiana Maggiore.[6]

This drawing is neatly drafted and dimensioned, suggesting that it was intended as the final version. However, on the back of this sheet are two rough sketches.[7] One is a slightly revised plan of the house. Palladio tried moving the interior wall so that the loggia was deeper and the T-shaped *sala* was rectangular. The other is a sketch of the front of the house, showing the *serliana* opening. After finishing this sketch, Palladio must have turned the sheet around to show the drawings to someone—perhaps Poiana?—who was sitting across the table from him. While explaining the design, Palladio idly jotted dimensions on the upside-down floor plan. I once had a teacher who insisted that we rotate the plans on our drafting tables from time to time to see them afresh. Palladio always drew his plans so that the entrance faced the bottom of the page; looking at the Poiana plan upside-down, he must have realized that if he made the *sala* the loggia, and vice versa, the house would be greatly improved. The new loggia would have more light, and the *sala* would align with the front and back doors.

The change was approved, and that is how the house was built. It appears that this correction may have occurred after construction started, for there are superfluous structural walls in the basement that correspond to the earlier plan.[8] For the exterior, Palladio simply duplicated the *serliana* on the front façade, and since the loggia was now wider, he turned what had been *sala* windows into windowlike openings (he never repeated this makeshift solution). There was one final modification. Bonifacio Poiana apparently decided that he wanted to expand his small house in the future, for the plan in *Quattro libri* showed four additional rooms in projecting wings on the east and west sides of the house.*

The surviving drawings of the Villa Poiana suggest a different Palladio from the conservative novice of the Villa Godi and the careful designer who evolved the plan of the Villa Pisani. Like all architects, he had learned to think on his feet and respond quickly to a client's demands. Unlike a novelist or a painter, an architect cannot squirrel himself away in his studio; he often makes important design decisions in the field, sketching and thinking on the fly. This does not imply sloppiness. For example, the final Poiana loggia is definitely superior to the earlier versions; the two wings are not a tacked-on afterthought but enclose intimate gardens. Directly in front of the entrance, Palladio designed a large walled *cortile*. "On one side are the courtyard and other places essential for farm life,

---

*Poiana never enlarged the house, although in 1606 a descendant completed the east wing.

on the other a garden which mirrors that courtyard, and in the area at the back the orchard and a fishpond," he wrote.[9] This functional separation of formal entrance, farmyard, and pleasure garden represents a sophisticated evolution in Palladio's thinking. The farmyard had porticoes along two sides, in the manner of the Villa Pisani; the garden was simply walled. These walls and porticoes were destroyed in the nineteenth century, and today the surroundings of this splendid house are barren: no gardens, no trees, no fishpond, a cornfield where the orchard once stood.

The Villa Poiana was begun after 1547 and finished six or seven years later. The 1540s were a busy decade for Palladio. His next clients after Vettor Pisani had been the Counts Marc'antonio and Adriano Thiene. The brothers, who belonged to what was reputedly the wealthiest family in Vicenza, had originally commissioned Giulio Romano to design a palatial town house, but after Giulio's death in 1546, Palladio took over. The enormous structure occupied an entire city block on the Corso, Vicenza's main street. Not to be outdone, the Thienes' newly married brother-in-law, Iseppo da Porto, commissioned Palladio to design another house, farther down the street. The beautiful façade of the Palazzo da Porto marks the first time Palladio designed statues for the attic story of a building; erected years later, they are likenesses of Iseppo and his son. Meanwhile, the country house commissions kept coming. In addition to the relatively modest villa for Biagio Saraceno, Palladio started a large country house for the Thiene brothers, who had become enthusiastic patrons and, in the case of Marc'antonio, a friend. The Thienes owned an estate beside the Tessino River at Quinto, on the outskirts of Vicenza, where Palladio devised an unusual twin-house, with elaborate suites of rooms for each

brother on two sides of a common entrance loggia and *sala*.*
The design included a large courtyard surrounded by colonnades, which was an interpretation of the ancient villas
described by Vitruvius.

Palladio was making his mark among the Vicentine *nobili,* but
the commission that represented his breakthrough was yet to
come. It concerned the Palazzo della Ragione, or Palace of Justice, which stood on the Piazza dei Signori, Vicenza's beautiful
main square, the site of a twelfth-century tower and of the
omnipresent emblem of the Republic, a column topped by the
winged lion of St. Mark. The old palazzo, an imposing Italian
Gothic building erected in the 1450s, had been Vicenza's
answer to the Doge's Palace in Venice. Built on medieval foundations, it incorporated shops on the ground floor and above,
under a wooden keel-like roof, a cavernous meeting room for
the city's governing Great Council. The rectangular building,
whose enormous copper roof resembles an upturned washtub,
was surrounded by a delicate two-story loggia added in 1496.
Only eighteen months after the loggia was completed, a large
section collapsed. The war postponed repairs and succeeding
generations of city fathers took no action. Wealthy Vicentines
built grand houses for themselves, but they were generally
niggardly when it came to paying for public works (unlike
Padua and Verona, Vicenza never modernized its city wall
after the war). When the remaining loggia of the Palazzo della
Ragione started showing further signs of weakness, it was
merely shored up with temporary props.

Finally, a committee was appointed to deal with what had

---

*Adriano Thiene died in 1550 and Marc'antonio a decade later.
Marc'antonio's son continued construction, but neither the villa nor
the palazzo were completed.

become a civic embarrassment, though only after Venice agreed to subsidize part of the cost of repairs. Between 1538 and 1542, Vicenza sought the advice of a series of eminent architects. Jacopo Sansovino, who was state architect of Venice, was consulted first; he was followed by Sebastiano Serlio. A few years later, Michele Sanmicheli was brought from Verona, and lastly the celebrated Giulio Romano was invited from Mantua. Still, the committee vacillated. The causes were a lack of political will and fiscal prudence—this was a major expenditure of public funds for the small city. In addition, there was dissatisfaction with the visiting experts. Sansovino seemed uninterested in the project; Serlio was vague—he was probably thinking of his impending departure for France (where he would remain for the rest of his life); for some reason, Sanmicheli made a poor impression on the committee; only Giulio's ambitious proposal to reconfigure the surrounding piazza in addition to restoring the loggia had some support.

In 1546, Giulio, though only in his early fifties, died. Sensing an opportunity, Palladio, who had not been consulted, threw his hat into the ring. He had been sketching solutions of his own as early as 1540, and as a member of the Pedemuro workshop had worked on repairs to the palazzo. Joining forces with his old master Porlezza, he submitted a proposal to the committee, which was sufficiently impressed to forward the design to the Great Council.

Palladio had the support of such influential members of the council as Godi, Thiene, and da Porto, yet even his most partisan admirers could not argue that he was in the same league as the famous visiting experts. The Great Council, cagily withholding judgment, authorized the construction of a large wooden mock-up of one bay of Palladio's proposal on the piazza as a trial. This was done, but still no decision was taken.

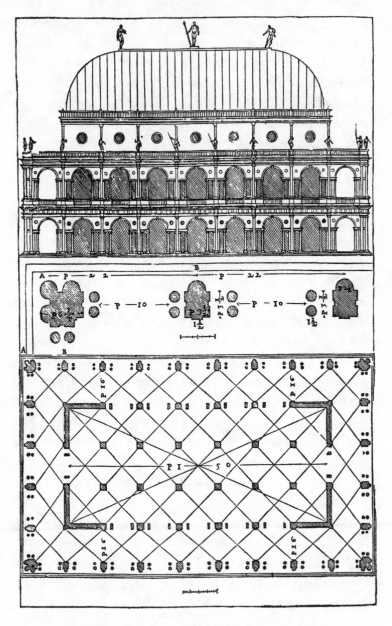

THE BASILICA, FROM *QUATTRO LIBRI*

Eighteen months later, Palladio (by then Porlezza had dropped out of the picture) was commissioned to make additional drawings and models. It was another three and a half years before matters came to a head. The Great Council considered three alternatives: rebuilding the original design, Giulio's proposal, and Palladio's scheme. On April 11, 1549, by an overwhelming vote of ninety-nine to seventeen, the council chose Palladio's design and appointed him superintendent of the project.[10]

It was a moment of triumph for the forty-year-old Andrea. He was now, in effect, the city architect of Vicenza. For this position he was paid a monthly salary of five gold scudi, about three hundred modern dollars.[11] The conversion is misleading since it is impossible to accurately compare the cost of living in cinquecento Italy with today, but it was not a huge sum— Giulio had received fifty scudi for just two weeks' consultation. Five scudi a month was about what Palladio would have earned as a stone carver.* Nevertheless, since the building promised to take decades to complete, this stipend would at least guarantee his family a modest living, leaving him free to augment his income with private commissions.

Palladio's proposal for rebuilding the arcades of the palazzo was remarkable, as practical as it was original. He kept the same number and size of bays as the existing loggia, and rather than demolishing the old structure, he encased the remaining columns in new material to create heavier, stronger piers. He also preserved some of the existing gallery vaulting, thus avoiding the risk of further endangering the stability of the building. Sixteenth-century builders could not take structural solidity for granted. A large section of Bramante's Cortile del Belvedere

---

*The fact that Palladio could not command a large salary no doubt influenced the Great Council's deliberations.

PALLADIO'S FIRST PUBLIC PROJECT, UNDERTAKEN WHEN HE WAS
FORTY-ONE, WAS THE BASILICA—VICENZA'S CITY HALL.

had collapsed during its construction, and a vault of Sansovino's library in Venice had failed only a few years earlier (causing the architect to be briefly jailed). But it was not enough merely to enlarge the supports; Palladio's challenge was to reinforce the structure without creating unpleasantly dark interiors. His ingenious solution, arrived at only after exploring several alternatives, was to make each bay not a simple arch but a *serliana.* The arched device had a number of practical advantages: it effectively lightened the piers—both visually and physically—allowing plenty of sunlight into the interior of the loggias; it reduced the span of the arches by almost fifty percent, which lessened the chance of collapse; it also addressed a peculiar problem of the medieval building, which had an odd trapezoidal plan and irregular bays. By using *serlianas,* Palladio was able to use identical arches, while adjusting the dimensions of the side beams to fit the varying dimensions of the bays. No doubt the experience of adjusting the design of new villas to fit existing foundations, as he had done with Godi and Pisani, served him well.

What probably appealed most to the Great Council was the style of Palladio's architecture. Although he carefully accommodated his design to fit the Gothic building, his loggias were boldly and uncompromisingly modern in appearance. Old buildings were frequently rebuilt in old styles, as the Doge's Palace would be after it burned down some years later, but Palladio well understood that the Vicentines wanted something new. Using *serlianas* in an arcade had been done before, notably by Sansovino in the upper floor of St. Mark's Library, which Palladio had seen under construction during his first visit to Venice. He greatly admired Sansovino, but the similarity with the Venetian project is superficial. Like most cinquecento architects, Sansovino stressed the horizontality of his long building by making each floor different; Palladio's novel solution was to repeat the *serliana* motif on both floors, emphasizing the gridlike character of the façade. The result was simultaneously more modern and more suggestive of antiquity.

Palladio's design is nothing more than a screen wrapped around an existing building. But what a screen! It is entirely built of hard, white Piovene limestone, and it is *thick*. To further strengthen the arcade, and to resist the lateral thrust of the fifteenth-century building, Palladio uses paired columns to support the *serliana* arches, so the screen wall is actually about five feet deep. And it is a very complicated screen, combining half-columns, full columns, pilasters, arches, and entablatures. The large half-columns, which correspond to the piers, rise a full floor to support an architrave. The lower columns are Doric, the upper Ionic. Like all Renaissance architects, Palladio believed that in multistory buildings the orders should be used in strictly hierarchical fashion. "Doric will always be placed under the Ionic, the Ionic under the Corinthian, and the Corinthian under the Composite," he wrote.*[12] The Doric entablature is decorated with traditional garlanded bucrania, or depictions of ox skulls, a reference to the sacrificial function of ancient Roman temples. The *serlianas,* supported on paired columns, are inserted within the almost square bays. In the triangular spaces between the arch and the entablature Palladio pierces *oculi* that subtly mimic the round windows of the great hall above. The other nod to the existing building is the vaults that support the galleries, which are not classical frescoed barrel vaults but

---

*Palladio was influenced by Sebastiano Serlio, whose treatise suggested a hierarchy among the five orders. Serlio seems to have invented this "rule"—Vitruvius has nothing to say on the matter—based on the façade of the Colosseum.

Gothic-style brick cross-vaults. Thanks to such subtle stylistic accommodations, Palladio accomplished the improbable feat of wedding an *all'antica* loggia to the immense Gothic box.

According to Vasari, who saw the lower level of the loggia almost complete, the Basilica, as Palladio called his building, was "much renowned."[13] This single work would assure its maker a prominent place in the architectural pantheon—and Palladio knew it. "I have no doubt at all that this building can be compared to antique structures and included amongst the greatest and most beautiful buildings built since antiquity," he observed.[14] The Basilica represents Palladio's peculiar position with respect to the architectural currents of his time; for despite his awareness of the latest fashion, his provincial status kept him out of the mainstream. Thus, while the Basilica was not in the style of Sanmicheli and Giulio, it did manipulate classical elements in an emotive, mannered fashion. For example, the entablature of the *serliana* created the illusion that it was interrupted by the half-columns, just as the half-columns created the illusion that they, and not the piers behind them, supported the arcade. "How hard he worked at that," marveled Goethe on his visit to Vicenza in 1786, "how the tangible presence of his creations makes us forget that we are being hypnotized!"[15]

Every evening I walk across the Piazza dei Signori, from the trattoria where I regularly eat dinner to my hotel. The ivory-white Basilica shimmers in the moonlight. Goethe characterized architecture as frozen music, which well describes this extraordinary building. I don't know what kind of music Goethe heard when he looked at the Basilica, but I hear percussion—the great jazz drummer Philly Joe Jones, my boyhood idol. The tall half-columns are the steady rhythm beat of the bass drum, which Palladio accentuates by breaking the extremely deep cornice and projecting it forward over each capital. At the attic

A DETAIL OF THE LOGGIA, FROM *Quattro libri*

level, a statue above each column provides a high-pitched cymbal clash. The two levels of the arcade keep slightly different times, the lower Roman Doric, with its staccatolike frieze, is more articulated, while the upper Ionic is more delicate and smooth. At the end of the building, which is nine bays long, a cluster of three columns (topped by three statues) marks a pause—a drum roll—and the beat continues around the corner. The arches of the *serlianas* weave a sinuous backbeat, which is punctuated by the double tom-tom pulse of the *oculi,* and the rim-shots of the keystones, which are in the form of *mascheroni,* or grotesque masks.

Despite the masks and statues, the muscular loggias of the Basilica are relatively plain. The plainness emphasizes the Basilica's three-dimensional sculptural quality. In a typical vertical section of the loggia I count at least fifty distinct projecting and receding planes (compared to perhaps half a dozen in a modern façade). The vigorous modeling of cornices, moldings, and entablatures, the deep frieze, and the orchestrated play between solid and void create a chiaroscuro effect that represented a new interest for Palladio.

He owed his awareness of modeling to Giangiorgio Trissino. In September 1545, shortly before Palladio was to submit his first design for the Basilica, the Count took him on a five-month excursion to Rome—Palladio's second visit. The entourage included Marco Thiene, who was a cousin of Marc'antonio, and Giambattista Maganza, a painter who had been a pupil of Titian and became Palladio's close friend and sometime collaborator. Marco Thiene described the outing as a "travelling Academia Trissiniana." Some historians believe Trissino arranged the trip precisely at this critical juncture to offer Palladio a further opportunity to hone his architectural skills.[16] In that case, the architect Palladio could not have missed in Rome was

Michelangelo, who had just begun work on St. Peter's and on the Capitoline Hill complex. While there was nothing yet built, Palladio would have been able to study models and drawings, which would account for the vigorous and sculptural Michelangelesque quality of the Basilica loggias.

It would be another three years before the Great Council appointed Palladio architect of the Basilica. Trissino was still Palladio's strongest supporter, and he likely played a behind-the-scenes role in the early deliberations of the building committee, but he was not in Vicenza during the final debate. He had become embroiled in a bitter dispute with his son by a first marriage, whom the Count wanted to disinherit. It was an ugly feud. At one point, Trissino broke into his son's house looking for papers, and the son in turn had bailiffs eject his sickly, seventy-year-old father from his Cricoli home. The matter went before the magistrates, who not only found in the son's favor but cruelly stripped Trissino of all his possessions, including his precious villa. Unable to reverse the decision, the embittered—and now impoverished—Count left Vicenza and moved to Rome. He stayed in Marco Thiene's house, where, ill and suffering from gout, he heard of Palladio's Basilica appointment. Trissino may have had the good news from Palladio himself. According to Paolo Gualdo's contemporary account, Palladio was in Rome in December 1549, at the behest of Pope Paul III.*[17] It is heartening to think of mentor and protégé meeting one last time. Giangiorgio Trissino died the following year, a copy of his beloved Vitruvius by his bedside.

*   *   *

*The Pope, perhaps hearing of the Basilica project, wanted advice on the design of St. Peter's, but he died as Palladio was en route to Rome and nothing came of the request.

I am reminded of the Basilica as I walk up to the loggia of the Villa Poiana. Palladio designed the villa just as he was finalizing the plans for the Basilica, and obviously *serlianas* were uppermost on his mind. The tall arched opening leads into a long, barrel-vaulted space with white walls and a beautifully frescoed ceiling. A cross-vault in the center echoes the archway of the *serliana*. The semicircular fresco over the door depicts the Poiana coat of arms and an assortment of military trophies, anomalously edged by a border of gay wildflowers. On the projecting architrave of the door frame, a bust of the bearded *padrone*, Bonifacio Poiana, gazes sternly down on his callers. The large door is locked.

I go around to the side wing and what appears to be a service entrance. There's a small car parked next to the house. A temporary signboard announces that the commune of Poiana Maggiore is in the process of refurbishing the villa—that accounts for the raw, graded earth, the brand-new rainwater gutters around the roof, and the patches of fresh plaster on the walls. I tap on the window.

A woman opens the door. She's wearing rubber gloves and a kerchief around her head. I can see a mop and pail behind her. I ask if it's possible to visit the house, explaining that I've come from Philadelphia. She seems happy to be interrupted.

"Come in," she says. "I'll show you around."

The large room in which we are standing occupies the entire east wing. A door at the far end leads into the central block. We enter a square room with crescent-shaped quarter-vaults, or lunettes, in each corner. The space is bare—none of the rooms is furnished—but the interior has obviously been recently restored to its original state. (In the 1950s, the villa had been converted into a tenement, subdivided, and rented to six local families.[18]) We pass into a *camerino,* perhaps once used as an

THE ARCHED MOTIF OF THE SERLIANA IS ECHOED IN THE WINDOW
OVER THE DOOR AS WELL AS IN THE VAULTED CEILING.

intimate cabinet or study, with an elaborate cross-vaulted ceiling and frescoes. The subjects are *grottesche*—grotesques—fanciful figures of satyrs, cherubs, monkeys, and parrots. They are the work of Bernardino India, who may have done the ceiling frescoes at the Villa Pisani.

From here, we enter the *sala*. As usual it is the tallest room, with ceilings about thirty feet high, although less grand than the cruciform hall of the Villa Pisani. The walls, devoid of architectural ornament, are painted white. The ceiling, partially frescoed, is a simple barrel vault. Light enters the room through small arched windows at each end, and through windows on each side of the doors; the *oculi* in the rear wall project sunny circles onto the floor. The arc of *oculi* is repeated on both end walls of the *sala*—circular windows at one end, recesses at the other. The vault itself corresponds exactly to the semicircular archway of the façade. The effect is very beautiful. In each new villa Palladio is achieving a greater sense of unity, not only relating the back to the front but also the interior to the exterior.

Across the *sala* is a reverse sequence of rooms: a small study, a medium-size square room, and finally a larger room.

"La Sala degli Imperatori," my guide announces.

I am obviously supposed to be impressed. The room is the same size as the *sala* and the raised coved ceiling makes it almost as tall. Walls and ceiling are covered in frescoes. The flat panel on the ceiling depicts a Roman equestrian battle scene, fierce but curiously bloodless. The walls have painted niches filled with statues of Roman war heroes—the emperors. A painted window looks out on an Arcadian scene in which an old man extinguishes the torch of war on the altar of peace, probably a reference to the Peace of Bologna, which in 1529 officially ended the Cambrai war. These frescoes are the work

of Anselmo Carnera, who was also working with Palladio on
the Palazzo Thiene. The painted architectural framework of
Ionic columns and niches in the Sala degli Imperatori bears a
marked resemblance to the drawing of a "Corinthian hall" in
Quattro libri. "They [the Romans] made the vault either semicircular or coved, that is, its *frezza* [the radius of the cove] was
a third of the breadth of the hall," Palladio wrote, "and it had to
be decorated with compartments of stucco and paintings."[19]
The layout of the room in the Villa Poiana precisely follows
this recommendation, which makes it likely that the overall
design of the painted décor, as in the Villa Godi, was Palladio's
responsibility.

The woman beckons me to follow her back to the *sala*
where a door leads to a staircase. The brick treads are illuminated
by natural light, since Palladio thoughtfully provided a window
looking onto the loggia. The stair goes down to the basement. Here the construction is brick: heavy walls, vaulted ceilings. The extremely low vaults—I can almost touch the
ceiling—are reinforced by iron tie-bars; the floors are brick. It's
surprisingly bright, the whitewashed surfaces reflecting the
light that enters through the small windows. There is nothing
improvised about the design: the intersecting curves of the broad
vaults have the simple but affecting beauty that straightforward
engineering sometimes achieves. Although the basement is
empty, I imagine it as a bustling place, with large tables for food
preparation, cooking fires, ovens, and rows of copper and cast-
iron pots. Much of the cool space would have been used for
food storage: casks of wine, containers of olive oil and vinegar,
barrels of pickles and salted meats, hams and sausages hanging
from the ceiling. On rainy days there would have been racks of
clothes drying, for laundering was also done here.

We go back to the stairs and climb all the way to the attic.

Partway up is a low-ceilinged *amezato* built above the *camerino*, which has a lower ceiling than the larger rooms. There is a square window, almost at floor level. A few steps up is the attic's counterpart to the square room. Since the heavy, brick walls of the villa are load-bearing, the plan of the main floor repeats on every floor. There is no floor above the Sala degli Imperatori; instead, the rough back of the coved ceiling swells up like a huge balloon. Palladio built ceilings in different ways. Flat ceilings that supported a floor were made of closely spaced wooden beams (as in the Villa Godi and the Villa Pisani) or of brick, if they were vaulted. The vaulted ceiling of a room that was not required to carry a floor was lighter, made of plastered cane lath supported on a structure of wood. That is the case here.

My redoubtable guide leads me downstairs, crosses the *sala,* and takes me up the second stair. Palladio villas often have two staircases, which were needed when the upper portion of the *sala* divided by the attic in two, or when the space below the *sala* was unexcavated. Walking around the attic is like being in a large barn, since the roof is supported by an open framework of crisscrossing wooden trusses, the huge timbers, about a foot square in cross section, banded together with wrought-iron straps. The large timbers came from forests high up in the mountains and were more expensive than stone, which is why masonry arches were used whenever possible. The wooden trusses carried purlins, smaller beams to which clay tiles were attached; the underside of the tiles is plainly visible since there are no ceilings.

Palladio described the attic of the Villa Poiana as a *granaro,* or granary.[20] Agricultural productivity in the sixteenth century was low, less than ten bushels per acre of cultivated land. Since a part of the land was regularly left fallow—and land was also used for grazing, vineyards, and hay and vegetable production—a large

Vicentine estate of four hundred acres produced only four or five hundred bushels of wheat, rice, millet, and barley.[21] Such a valuable harvest had to be kept in a secure place, especially as the owner was not always in residence. When I later calculate the storage capacity of the Poiana attic, it turns out that filled to a height of four feet, it could easily accommodate six *thousand* bushels. Evidently, the attic wasn't only a granary. It was also used as a box-room, a seasonal store for clothes and furniture, and not the least, as living quarters for servants. This explains the many windows and why country houses without agricultural lands, as well as town houses, had similar attics.

The basement and the attic of a villa are like the backstage of a theater: the delicate architecture of the owner's rooms is supported on vaults as massive as catacombs, and covered by timberwork as hefty as a railroad trestle. The Villa Poiana is not just an achievement of Palladio the designer, it is also an accomplishment of Palladio the builder. "There are three things in every building that have to be considered," he writes in the opening lines of *Quattro libri,* paraphrasing Vitruvius, "these are usefulness or convenience, durability, and beauty."[22] Usefulness related to planning, beauty to aesthetics, and durability to construction. Palladio took construction seriously. In his treatise, he devoted the first eleven chapters to such mundane topics as where to find good building sand, how to make lime, and the best way to build foundations. Like Alberti, Palladio followed Vitruvius's lead in emphasizing technique, but unlike that patrician scholar, the ex-stonemason knew at firsthand what he was talking about. And he built well, as this 450-year-old house attests.

The tour over, I thank my guide profusely and bid her good-bye. There is time for one last stroll around the exterior of the house. The sun is higher than when I arrived, and the architrave and the moldings throw sharp shadows on the wall. The deeply shaded *oculi* and dark loggia interior contrast sharply with the dazzling white walls. The masterly chiaroscuro effects attest to the lessons that Palladio has learned while designing the Basilica, just as the *serliana* entrance and the pediment refine themes that he has explored in earlier houses. The impression is of a mature architect fully in control of his medium. But what sort of architect? Thanks to the influence of *Quattro libri,* and the systematic analyses of Palladio's villa plans, Palladianism has come to represent, at least in the public's eye, a sort of architectural recipe: a central hall, a pediment, a couple of columns. In 1992, one enterprising Yale art historian, in collaboration with a Microsoft software engineer, devised a computer program that was capable of generating innumerable "Palladian" villa plans and façades according to predetermined geometrical rules.[23] Despite the authors' numerous caveats, this mechanical approach leaves the distinct impression that designing a Palladio villa was simply a matter of rigidly adhering to a few simple rules. Palladio himself contributed to the perception that he was a disciplinarian. "And though variety and novelty must please everybody, one should not, however, do anything that is contrary to the laws of this art and contrary to what reason makes obvious," he wrote, "so we can see that the ancients also made variations, but that they never departed from certain universal and essential rules of this art, as we shall see in my books on antiquities."[24]

Yet what is striking about the Villa Poiana is not how Palladio follows rules, but rather how he invents. The Villa Poiana is full of novel ideas such as the projecting wings, the extremely low basement, the stair windows looking into the loggia. Some of these features will reoccur in later houses, others will not. The chunky abstracted *serliana* appears only once more, in the Villa

Forni, a small house probably built in the 1540s. The *oculi,* for example, appear in the *sala* of the Villa Caldogno, which has circular and elliptical windows, but they are concealed within the loggia. The wonderful arc motif of Poiana is unique. Although the demands of the client, and the character of the site, influenced the distinct personality of each villa, the chief reason for the variety was Palladio's restless imagination.

This restlessness makes Palladio curiously modern. He is not modern like Ludwig Mies van der Rohe, who really was disciplined and whose later work, typified by the Seagram Building in New York, consisted of a rigorously controlled number of architectural elements: I-beam mullions, plate glass, travertine slabs. Nor is Palladio like Louis I. Kahn, who laboriously developed his own architectural vocabulary of brick and precast concrete, which was sometimes brilliant but often cramped and confining. Rather, Palladio resembles the Swiss-French genius Le Corbusier. Le Corbusier, too, published his architectural ideas and formulated many architectural rules, but his fecund creativity periodically drove him in new architectural directions, bending and often breaking his earlier pronouncements.

It sounds farfetched to compare Palladio, who was constrained by traditional building methods and by his admiration for the past, with a modernist firebrand such as Le Corbusier, who embraced new technology and wanted to rewrite, if not destroy, history. But Palladio was part of an architectural revolution that was more profound—and of considerably longer duration—than its twentieth-century counterpart. It is true that he lived at the end of that revolution—Brunelleschi's seminal Ospedale degli Innocenti was already almost a hundred years old when Palladio was born. Yet Palladio occupied a unique position in the Renaissance. Working in Vicenza, far from the architectural centers of Florence and Rome, he had to discover the *all'antica* style for himself. He built on the achievements of his predecessors and shared some of the romantic outlook of his contemporaries, but his architecture was neither jaded nor mannered; it had the fresh first blush of discovery—of true Rinascimento—which is probably why it proved so influential.

IV

On the Brenta

any of Palladio's villas are in out-of-the-way places and my directions are sketchy. Getting back to Vicenza, where I am staying, is easy— I just follow the road signs. It's only once I arrive in the city that I run into trouble. My hotel is in the historic center, a medieval maze of narrow, winding streets further complicated by a frustrating profusion of one-way signs, so if it's dark by the time I get back, I usually get lost. The ride becomes increasingly nerve-racking as I juggle glancing at my map, peering at street names, and keeping abreast of the rush-hour traffic. Vicentine drivers are polite but relentless—and fast. Eventually I give up trying to navigate, and instead look for a familiar landmark near my hotel. Once I see the floodlit façade of the Museo Civico, I know I'm home.

The municipal museum is a converted Palladio building, originally a nobleman's residence. The impressive structure occupies a conspicuous site at the eastern edge of the historic center, where the Corso crosses the Bacchiglione River and joins the old Venice highway. In the sixteenth century, the open space between the palazzo and the river was called the Piazza dell'Isola and housed an outdoor cattle market. Adjacent to the market was the town wharf, where barges from Padua, Venice, and elsewhere unloaded their cargoes. People as well as goods traveled by water in the Republic, and in many ways, this was Vicenza's front door.

The Palazzo Chiericati was one of several commissions that came to Palladio following his appointment as architect of the Basilica. The client was Count Girolamo Chiericati, a leading citizen who, as a member of the Basilica building committee, had backed Palladio. In 1550, after inheriting three small houses facing the Isola, Chiericati commissioned Palladio to build a grand residence in their place. A cattle market might seem an unwelcome neighbor, but Chiericati guessed—correctly—that new construction would transform the area; it was up to Palladio to expedite the change. This was a challenge. The building plot was awkwardly shaped—more than a hundred feet wide facing the piazza but only about fifty feet deep. To overcome this constraint—and gain extra space on the upper floor—Palladio shrewdly suggested that Chiericati petition the city council to permit the building to encroach on the piazza in the form of a public arcade "for the comfort and ornament of the whole city."[1] Covered pedestrian arcades were a familiar feature of Veneto towns, and the proposal was accepted.

The shallow plot could not accommodate the deep, courtyard type of town house that Palladio had designed for Thiene and da Porto. Yet the site had other benefits. While these earlier palazzos were on narrow, cramped streets, hemmed in by their neighbors, Chiericati's house would be freestanding, its broad façade fronting a piazza and with a fine view to the lazy Bacchiglione River and water mills on the far bank. The prospect was almost countrylike. Perhaps that is why Palladio planned the town house like a villa, not introverted but outward-looking. He elevated the main floor by raising the basement partially aboveground. On each side of the entrance hall he placed suites of small, medium, and large rooms, as well as staircases. He repeated the plan on the upper floor, adding a large *sala* above the entrance hall; the third floor contained the attic. All these features were adapted from his villas, but on the exterior Palladio created something new: the entire hundred-foot façade overlooking the piazza was a commanding two-story loggia.

This loggia was not supported by arches and piers but by freestanding columns. In his early villas, Palladio had only *suggested* columns. Since a house consists chiefly of walls, if an architect wished to use the grammar of classical architecture—that is, columns—he could do so only by attaching flat pilasters or half-columns to the walls' surfaces. This was not a satisfactory solution, for, as Goethe shrewdly observed: "[Palladio's] major problem was that which confronts all modern architects, namely, how to make proper use of columns in domestic architecture, since a combination of columns and walls must always be a contradiction."[2] The Palazzo Chiericati neatly resolved the contradiction: Palladio simply separated the columns and the walls, juxtaposing the columned loggia with the house proper. Put

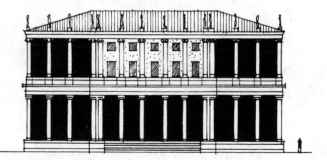

PALAZZO CHIERICATI

that way, it sounds simple enough, but it had taken him almost a decade to arrive at this fortuitous solution.

He made the discovery in a related project. The same inheritance that made Girolamo Chiericati owner of the Isola properties provided his brother, Giovanni, with an estate on the outskirts of the city. Giovanni, likewise an admirer of Palladio, commissioned a small villa.[3] The house still stands, surrounded by open fields, still part of a working farm, somewhat neglected, its architectural presence crudely compromised by an attached modern farmhouse and barn. The plan is unremarkable: a square *sala,* flanked by two suites of small, medium, and large rooms. However, instead of a recessed three-arch loggia, there is a splendid freestanding portico whose classical pediment is supported by four giant Ionic columns, rising the full height of the house.

When I go to look at the Villa Chiericati, the friendly farmer who lives next door asks me if I am German. Many Ger-

VILLA CHIERICATI

man architects come to look at the house, he explains. I can sense that he is puzzled why this rather decrepit structure attracts so much attention.

"There are porticoes descended from this one all over the world, even in the United States, where I live," I say. "This is a historic building."

I am not exaggerating. What started in 1485 as the mere suggestion of a temple pasted to the front of a Medici villa has grown into the real, three-dimensional thing. No Renaissance architect had ever done anything quite like this before; indeed, the Chiericati portico marks a great event in the development of Western architecture. For the next four hundred years, architects will design and build countless variations of the temple portico, adorning country houses, mansions, royal palaces, and presidents' homes, not to mention churches, museums, and banks. In the seventeenth century, Claude Perrault will make it the centerpiece of the Louvre; in the eighteenth century, it will front E. M. Barry's Royal Opera House in Covent Garden and Samuel Blodgett's First Bank of the United States in Philadelphia; in the early 1800s, the great German architect Karl Friedrich Schinkel will use it on the Berlin Theater; and more than a hundred years later it will reappear in John Russell Pope's imposing National Gallery of Art in Washington, D.C. It is likely that when twenty-first-century architects tire of titanium swirls and jagged metallic zigzags, they will return to find new inspiration in this ancient device.

Construction of the Villa Chiericati proceeded extremely slowly and only the basement and the bare outlines of the main floor were completed by 1558, when Giovanni's death put a stop to construction. The house remained in this unfinished state for the next two decades; Palladio must have despaired of ever seeing the villa finished, for he did not include it in *Quattro libri*. Yet he was obviously excited about the new portico since he immediately used it in another villa. That is my next destination: the Villa Foscari.

The house is better known as La Malcontenta, supposedly named after an unhappy—and allegedly unfaithful—wife who was locked up here by her suspicious husband. In fact, the hamlet was known as Malcontenta long before the villa was built, after the neighboring marshes that offered refuge for outlaws, or *malcontenti*.[4] I've been looking forward to visiting this villa ever since I first read the evocative name and saw lyrical photographs of its imposing portico, surrounded by weeping willows and reflected in the still waters of the Brenta.

I look out of the car window, which is streaked with rain. Instead of the Brenta and weeping willows, all I see is the grimy industrial outskirts of Mestre, the port of Venice: factories and warehouses, interspersed with dreary apartment buildings. Can this really be the place? A sign announces the Ristorante Palladio, so the villa can't be far away. I park the car in front of the restaurant and continue on foot. Around the bend, next to the road but separated by a low steel barrier, a narrow canal comes into view, its surface barely two feet lower than the pavement. The sluggish Brenta is exactly as John Ruskin described it 150 years ago, "a muddy volume of yellowish-gray water, that neither hastens nor slackens, but glides heavily between its monotonous banks."[5] Hardly a picturesque sight but it suits this ashen, overcast day.

The Brenta, which empties into the Venetian Lagoon a few miles away, was a key *terraferma* navigation route. The modern excursion boat that takes tourists for cruises up the canal covers the six miles from the city to Malcontenta in two hours. This is probably about the same length of time it took sixteenth-century Venetians to make the journey in a *burchiello,* or luxury barge, pulled by mules. The owners of the villa must have made this short trip many times, for theirs was a special kind of country house, not the administrative center of a farm but a city dweller's country getaway.

The concept of rural retreats was popularized by the fourteenth-century poet Petrarch, who had built a small house (which still exists) outside Padua, and spent the last five years of his life "surrounded by olive groves and a vineyard . . . far from alarms, noise and commotion."[6] A hundred years later, urban "noise and commotion"—not to mention the summer heat and pestilential atmosphere—had become intense and the countryside offered a popular alternative. By Alberti's time, it was necessary to distinguish between country houses that were associated with agriculture and those that were intended for pleasurable escape. "The fortunate will own a villa as a summer retreat," he wrote. "By this means they enjoy all the advantages to be found in the country, of light, breeze, open space, and views."[7] Many of Alberti's wealthy Florentine neighbors built such villas in the hills overlooking the city. Associating the *villa suburbana* with antiquity, he quoted an ancient Roman poet on the pleasures of villa life:

> How in the country do I pass the time?
> The answer to the question's brief:
> I lunch and drink, I sing and play,
> I wash and dine, I rest. Meanwhile
> I Phoebus quiz
> And Muses frisk.[8]

Venice was larger than Florence, and being built on the water was more crowded and unhealthy. To temporarily escape

Unusual stairs lead to the tall loggia of the Villa Foscari,
also known as La Malcontenta, which overlooks
the Brenta Canal.

such conditions, wealthy Venetians built summer houses on the island of Murano, next to the glass factories whose hot exhausts were curiously believed to be beneficial to one's health. The island of Giudecca was another favorite location.[9] Eventually, villa builders moved farther out, and the banks of canals such as the Brenta, which provided convenient access from the city, likewise filled up with summer retreats.

Phoebus, the god of the sun, is not much in evidence today as I walk beside the murky Brenta. The villa comes into view, or rather a corner of its portico, behind a stand of weeping willows; a giant Ionic column and a glimpse of pediment announce "Palladio villa" as unmistakably as a billboard. Alberti advised that a suburban villa "will be most attractive, if it presents a cheerful overall appearance to anyone leaving the city, as if to attract and expect visitors."[10] As I observe La Malcontenta, "cheerful" is not the word that comes to mind—this is the most dramatic portico I've ever seen, with giant columns rising the full height of the house. The monumental effect of the portico is magnified since the house itself, while not particularly large, is raised on a story-high podium and looms over the narrow Brenta across a short stretch of lawn. The flooding at the Villa Pisani had taught Palladio to build riverside basements above-ground, but he also seems to have acquired a taste for verticality, for he has made the basement—and the attic—exceptionally high, producing a house that is even taller than the two-story Palazzo Chiericati. And just as that building faced a piazza, Palladio pushed La Malcontenta toward the canal, ensuring that the visitor stepping out of his *burchiello* experienced the full dramatic impact of the monumental portico.

The main floor is reached by two exterior stairs, one on each side. The frieze of the broad entablature carries a Latin inscription commemorating the men who commissioned the

house: NICOLAUS ET ALOYSIUS FOSCARI FRATRES FEDERICI FILII
(The brothers Nicolò and Alvise Foscari, sons of Federico).
The Foscari brothers were wealthy Venetian nobles, descended
from a famous fifteenth-century doge. I can imagine them
examining a drawing of Palladio's latest design, the as yet
unbuilt Villa Chiericati, and instructing him, "We like this
plan, but make the portico larger. We want our friends and visitors to be impressed." Palladio turned up the architectural
volume; the Malcontenta portico is not only taller than the
portico of the Villa Chiericati, it is supported by eight columns
instead of four.

The column was the basic module of ancient Roman architecture, and its diameter was the dimensional module that
determined the sizes of the other parts of the building, including the space between the columns, or the intercolumniation.
Vitruvius described five types of intercolumniation, ranging
from 1½ to 3 diameters, but strongly recommended the so-
called eustyle "with the intervals apportioned just right."[11]
Eustyle, which required the space between the columns to be
equal to 2¼-column diameters, was Palladio's favorite, too.
Roman temple fronts always had an uneven number of bays—
typically three, five, or seven—and the central bay opposite the
entrance door was sometimes made slightly wider so that "a free
passage will be afforded to those who would approach the statues of the gods," according to Vitruvius.[12] Palladio usually followed this practice, and the five-bay portico of La Malcontenta
has a wider bay in the center. This serves no practical function,
since one enters the portico from the side, but the larger space
emphasizes the central axis of the house.

The tall house behind the portico is massive. The brick walls
are faced with a Venetian type of stucco called *marmorino,* a
mixture of powdered seashells and travertine marble dust mixed

with lime. This was plastered onto the walls, then pressed with a hot iron, which made an integrally colored, shiny surface that resembles soapstone. As in most of Palladio's villas, the stucco is incised with a masonry pattern, the joint lines here conspicuously highlighted with reddish paint. The effect is almost crude, but it strikes me as authentic. The roof is crowned by a wide dormer window whose gable creates a second, smaller pediment above the portico. On each side of the dormer are exceptionally tall chimneys with characteristically bulbous Venetian caps. In fact, despite its rural surroundings, the imposing house distinctly recalls a Venetian palazzo. This grand—almost grandiose—façade is the work of a Palladio who is less interested in chiaroscuro and history than in solemn monumentality. Like some of Michelangelo's works, the portico of La Malcontenta conveys a sense of *terribilità*—"sheer awe."[13]

To get to the villa I have to walk a short distance back along the canal's edge until I find a bridge. A track leads to a gate where a dour old woman dressed in black collects the entrance fee. "The villa is a private residence; inside it is forbidden to touch or use the furnishings, to take photographs

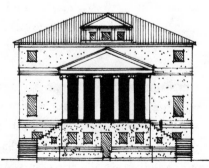

LA MALCONTENTA

and to smoke," reads a baleful warning in Italian, English, French, and Japanese. "During your visit, please be careful on the staircase outside since there is no handrail and on the waxed pavement inside."

A curving path leads to the front of the house. Close-up, the podium is even more impressive—it must be all of fifteen feet high. I have to crane my neck to see the tops of the Ionic columns. I climb the staircase carefully, for as the ticket warns, there are no handrails. Above the generous portico, heavy rustic beams support clay roof tiles whose underside is plainly visible, the rude construction emphasizing the heavy load that is carried by the burly columns. There are no railings between the columns, merely a stone parapet just the right height for sitting. Now the architectural reason for the podium is clear—it's the ideal vantage point from which to greet visitors arriving by boat. From up here, the Brenta looks almost picturesque.

The front entrance is immense—fourteen feet high, twice as tall as a conventional door. Above is a cartouche commemorating the 1574 visit of Henri de Valois, who stopped in Venice on the way to Paris to accede to the throne. The doors must have been opened wide for the future king, but I enter through a low aperture cut out of one of the panels. The spectacular *sala* is cruciform in plan, similar to the Villa Pisani but even taller, with a soaring, barrel-vaulted ceiling. The surfaces of the walls and ceilings are frescoed with allegorical and mythological subjects within a trompe l'oeil architectural frame of giant Ionic columns that mimic those of the portico. It is likely that Palladio designed the architectural décor, for the frescoes are painted by the same Giambattista Zelotti with whom he had recently decorated the Villa Godi. As at the Villa Godi, Zelotti replaced a painter who died on the job, Battista Franco. The dramatic vaults offered Zelotti greater scope for his talents, and above the orderly framework of columns, niches, and door frames, nymphs, gods, and goddesses run riot. The frescoes are faded and somewhat damaged, evidence of the hard treatment that La Malcontenta has received over the years. In 1848, the house was occupied by Austrian troops besieging Venice; during the First World War it was a field hospital; and in the years following it was used for storing grain and for the cultivation of silkworms. A subsequent restoration has not entirely erased the marks of a century of abuse. The frescoes are easy to see since the *sala* is exceptionally bright—the south-facing wall opposite the door is almost entirely windows, rectangular openings below and the large semicircle of a thermal window immediately beneath the vault. Palladio always provided plenty of fenestration but here he outdid himself.

La Malcontenta is currently owned by descendents of the Foscari brothers. Easy chairs and divans line the walls of the *sala,* but the effect is distinctly undomestic, more like the waiting room of a railway station than a salon; the great space would best have been left empty. The *sala* is flanked by suites composed of the usual small, medium, and large rooms. The rooms have varied décor and different types of domed and vaulted ceilings. The smallest rooms are decorated in the so-called Pompeiian style, walls and ceiling vaults frescoed with satyrs and winged cherubs. Zelotti painted one of the square rooms—today used as a bedroom—to resemble a vine-entwined arbor; the other room is beautifully decorated by Franco with ruined columns and giant, contorted Michelangelesque figures.

The floor plan of La Malcontenta is a virtual duplicate of an early version of the Villa Chiericati, which had a complicated vaulted cruciform *sala.*[14] Apparently, Giovanni Chiericati had balked at the expense and demanded something simpler. Palladio complied, but in his usual persistent way he did not give up on the idea, and when the Foscari brothers approached him, he must have shown them the earlier plan.

A young woman serves as a docent at La Malcontenta. It turns out that she is an architecture student for whom this is a part-time job. I ask her if I can see the attic, and she tells me that it's not open to the public but shows me a book about the villa that contains plans of all the floors. The attic appears to be an exact duplicate of the main floor, with two suites of rooms and a cruciform central space directly above the *sala*.[15] The upper *sala* is lit from each end by dormer windows.

Clearly, in a suburban villa there was no need for a granary. In fact, Palladio specifically referred to the upper rooms of La Malcontenta not as *granari* but as *camere,* or rooms. "The upper *camere* are like mezzanines," he wrote, "because of their lack of height, which is only eight feet."[16] The villa was originally designed for two bachelors, but Alvise Foscari became betrothed while the house was under construction, and it is likely that Palladio altered the upper rooms, adding the unusual dormer windows, in order to provide more space for the expanded household.[17] Thus Palladio subtly modified his design, solving a practical problem, adding a second floor disguised as an attic, and, as usual, creating beauty in the process.

Since I can't go upstairs I borrow the docent's book on the villa and leaf through its pages. The author is a Swedish professor who visited the Veneto almost forty years ago with a group of architecture students. They toured Palladio's villas, ending up at Malcontenta, where they spent several days taking precise measurements of the house, particularly the rooms. Their purpose was to compare the villa with the plan in *Quattro libri,* where the room dimensions are prominently noted. It is well known that Palladio favored certain room shapes. "There are seven types of room that are the most beautiful and well-proportioned and turn out better," he wrote, and listed them: round, square, and several rectangular shapes of predetermined proportions.[18] He was directly quoting Vitruvius, who devoted an entire chapter to the subject. In practice, Palladio did not use all seven shapes equally; he most often made rooms square, sometimes a square and a third, and sometimes a square and a half.* According to *Quattro libri,* these are the proportions of the small, medium, and large rooms that flank the *sala* of La Malcontenta.

Palladio did not explain why these room shapes "turn out better" (neither did Vitruvius). Rudolf Wittkower, in an influential book on the architectural principles of the Renaissance, published in 1949, speculated that Palladio based the proportions of his rooms on music.[19] He quoted a memorandum in which Palladio drew an analogy between architectural proportions and musical harmonies: "The proportions of the voices are harmonies for the ears; those of the measurements are harmonies for the eyes. Such harmonies usually please very much, without anyone knowing why, excepting the student of the causality of things."[20] According to Wittkower, Palladio's "measurements" were based on sixteenth-century musical theory that expressed notes as numerical ratios. This complicated explanation is difficult to summarize, but the gist of it is that the dimensions that Palladio used for rooms, *salas,* and porticoes form ratios that

---

*Twenty-one of the twenty-three villas in *Quattro libri* include room dimensions. Of the 211 rooms thus described, 56 are square, 27 are a square and a half, and 22 are a square and a third. The other recommended proportions appear less frequently: a square and two thirds, and two squares, account for only eight each; two rooms are round, and only one is a root-two rectangle (based on the diagonal of a square). In other words, Palladio followed Vitruvius's recommendations only about half the time.

were based on specific musical intervals such as fourths, fifths, major sixths, and so on. For example, according to Wittkower, at La Malcontenta the dimensions of the rooms (twelve by six-teen, sixteen by sixteen, and sixteen by twenty-four Venetian feet) and the width of the *sala* (thirty-two feet) form a series that represents the "keynote" musical theme, also present in the por-tico and the spacing of the columns.*[21]

Although Wittkower's theory is fascinating, it suffers two serious shortcomings. First, Palladio made no mention of har-monic proportions in *Quattro libri* whatsoever; surely if musical harmonies had played a role in his designs he would have included a discussion of the subject. Second, Palladio's use of

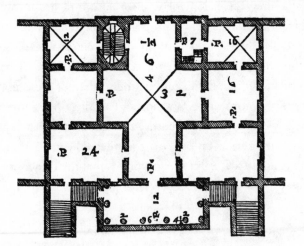

PLAN OF LA MALCONTENTA, FROM *QUATTRO LIBRI*

*Palladio used either Vicentine feet or Venetian feet, depending on the project's location. A Vicentine foot was about fourteen modern inches; a Venetian foot was slightly shorter.

dimensions that can be fitted into Wittkower's musical scheme is extremely inconsistent. Two Scottish scholars, Deborah Howard and Malcolm Longair, analyzed all forty-four of the measured plans of palazzos and villas in *Quattro libri* (whereas Wittkower had examined only eight villas) and found that although certain numbers reoccurred, Palladio frequently used odd dimensions, even in those instances when he could have easily adjusted the numbers.[22] They concluded that "[Palladio's] dependence on musical harmonic proportion was by no means as great as Wittkower implied . . . his preference for harmonic dimensions probably resulted either from his use of certain favorite room shapes, or from the practical advantages of using simple, easily divisible numbers."[23]

Howard and Longair wisely pointed out that an architect of Palladio's intelligence and experience would not have suggested that a beautiful building could only be designed by simply following a single proportional theory.[24] The world of building is messy; an architect learns to balance conflicting demands. Vitruvius himself allowed that "when there are other unavoidable obstructions, it will be permissible to make diminutions or additions in the symmetrical relations—with ingenuity and acuteness, however, so that the result may not be unlike the beauty which is due to true symmetry."[25] Palladio did this all the time. For example, concluding a chapter of *Quattro libri* devoted to room vaults, he wrote, "There are other heights for vaults which do not come under any rule, and the architect will make use of these *according to his judgment and practical circumstances* [emphasis added]."[26] At La Malcontenta, the Swedish professor and his students found a major inconsistency in the room dimensions: the attractive small rooms that were described as twelve Venetian feet wide in *Quattro libri* are actually ten feet wide, hence their proportions are not a square and a third.

THE REAR OF THE VILLA FOSCARI, WITH ITS DOMINANT
THERMAL WINDOW, IS QUITE DIFFERENT FROM THE FRONT.

Whether this was the result of practical circumstances or Palladio's judgment is not known.

The back of La Malcontenta faces a long lawn with double rows of trees on either side. The façade is dominated by a large thermal window and, like the Villa Pisani, the rear of the house bears little resemblance to the front. Or at least that is the first impression. In fact, just as he did at the Villa Poiana, Palladio created a subtle continuity between the front and the back. "The cornice goes all round the house and forms the tympanum above the loggia and on the opposite side of the house," he wrote. "Under the gutter there is another cornice that runs above the tympanums."[27] He replicated the tripartite organization of the river façade by pushing the central portion, corresponding to the portico, slightly forward. He repeated the pediment, though with an interrupted horizontal cornice, allowing the arched top of the thermal window to extend up into the tympanum. The window patterns of the basement and attic floor are identical, including the rooftop gable window with its miniature pediment.

There is no exterior stair in the back; the only way to get to the garden from the *sala* is to go down one of the internal staircases, through the basement, and out a central door. Why didn't Palladio repeat the portico on the garden side, or at least provide a recessed loggia and a stair on this, the south side of the house? It could not have been a question of cost—this was an expensive house. Perhaps he wanted to heighten the contrast between the private side facing the garden and the public side facing the Brenta. The flat rear façade also emphasizes the intense thrust of the projecting portico and gives this feature pride of place.

I take a last look at the front of the house. Seen up close, the

palatial façade is unusually animated. The water table at the base
of the building is unplastered brick, and brick reoccurs in a
heavy flat molding, called a fascia, that surrounds the house at
the main-floor level, and again in a narrower terra-cotta band,
corresponding to the entablature of the portico that defines the
attic story. The shafts of the columns are also bare brick. Palladio used similar brick columns in several projects. "Mine eye
hath never beheld any columns more stately of stone or marble,"
recorded Sir Henry Wotton, who was British ambassador to
Venice twenty years after Palladio's death, "for the bricks having been first formed in a circular mould, and then cut before
their burning into four quarters or more, the sides afterwards
join so closely, and the joints concentrate so exactly, that the pil-
lars appear one entire piece, shewing how in truth we want
rather *art* than *stuff* to satisfy our greatest fancy."[28]

The brick columns at La Malcontenta resemble elegant
smokestacks, but to a sixteenth-century observer brick columns
would appear merely robust. Their redness contrasts sharply
with the white *marmorino* walls. The sloping eaves of the pediment as well as the terra-cotta cornice of the roof are also red.
The two-tone color scheme is strikingly different from
Palladio's other villas and recalls the exuberant polychrome decoration of Venice's famous late Gothic buildings—the stone-
and-brick Campanile of San Marco, or the white-and-pink
marble of the Doge's Palace. Was he pandering to his Venetian
clients? "The architect is frequently obliged to accommodate
himself to the wishes of those who are paying rather than
attending to what he should," he once wrote, betraying an
uncharacteristic note of wry resignation.[29] On the whole, and
despite his rare complaint, Palladio, like so many Renaissance
artists, received exceptional support from his rich and powerful
patrons. He also used his considerable personal charm to influ-

ence his clients, and the relatively small number of stillborn projects attests to his powers of persuasion. But architects are always in a poor position to resist the demands of "those who are paying." This weakness is compounded when a wide social gulf separates them from their clients, as it did in the sixteenth century.

In Palladio's case, the gulf was particularly wide since he had risen from the ranks of the building trades, rather than from the—slightly—more prestigious fine arts. The only other important Renaissance architect to overcome the stigma of having been a manual worker was Antonio da Sangallo, who had started his career as a carpenter and ended by succeeding Bramante as architect of St. Peter's. "I may be called Master Antonio," da Sangallo once bragged, "but I would not exchange my life in Rome with anyone whatsoever."[30] This was no empty boast—though not achieving the status of *signor,* he became wealthy and lived on a grand scale. So did Giulio, who had been invited to compete for the Basilica. After coming to the Venetian Republic from Rome, he had built himself a splendid house in Mantua.*

James Ackerman has described the financial relations between Renaissance architects and their clients as a "mystery."[31] Painters had elaborate written contracts that specified not only payment schedules but also details such as the subject and the quality of the paints, the colors, and even what was to be painted by the master and what could be delegated to assistants.[32] Architects had emerged only in the previous century, replacing the medieval master builders, or *capomaestri.* On large public buildings archi-

---

*Giulio's financial success was also the result of his artistic production, including frescoes, paintings, and a notorious series of pornographic prints.

tects were usually paid a monthly retainer, but for private commissions, as far as we know, they did not have formal contracts.
They were paid for delivering individual drawings—and they
were not paid much. For example, Palladio received only four
gold scudi for the plan and façade drawings of the Palazzo
Chiericati. Such payments were sometimes augmented when
additional details (for moldings, capitals, brackets, fireplaces) were
required, and when supervisory visits to the building site were
made, but the actual amounts seem to have been at the discretion of the client. The record shows that over the two years that
the Palazzo Chiericati was under construction, its owner paid
Palladio a total of fourteen gold scudi and *"una soma de peri"*—
a load of pears.[33]

There is no complete record of Palladio's financial situation
at this time, but one thing is certain: the income from his private commissions was modest. His close friend the poet and
painter Giambattista Maganza once observed wryly, "Uncle
Andrea, what he earned he spent."[34] Since there is no indication
that Palladio was extravagant, this can only be taken to mean
that his income barely covered his expenses. He continued to
receive a monthly stipend for his work on the Basilica—more
than half of the lower arcade facing the Piazza dei Signori had
been completed—but this was not sufficient to support his large
family, which now included four sons, Leonida, Marc'antonio,
Orazio, and Silla, and one daughter, Zenobia. Until he was fifty
years old, Palladio earned so little that he did not even appear on
the city's tax rolls, and when his name was finally recorded, it
was in the lowest bracket.[35]

The solution to Palladio's financial problems was a salaried
position in Venice. His reputation in provincial Vicenza did not
count for much in the Most Serene Republic, but through his
villa commissions he now had several influential backers among

the Venetian nobility. Daniele Barbaro, whom he had met in Padua a decade earlier, introduced him to Jacopo Contarini, a powerful minister in the Republic, a dilettante, and a scientific scholar who was also an architecture enthusiast. Contarini invited Palladio to stay in his house whenever he visited the city.[36] Such contacts were important, yet the 1550s was hardly an auspicious time to establish a professional presence in Venice. Sansovino and Sanmicheli, the two Grand Old Men of architecture, were still on the scene. The brilliant Sansovino was firmly ensconced as *proto,* or construction manager, to the Procurators of St. Mark's, who were responsible for the buildings around the piazza, and in this capacity was in effect Venice's official architect. Hale in his seventies, he showed no sign of retiring. Sanmicheli, still the chief military architect of the Republic, was likewise active and currently designing the magnificent Palazzo Grimani on the Grand Canal. The latter promised to be the last major private project for some time, as the Venetian economy was entering a recession.

Starting in 1554, Palladio made several attempts to gain a Venetian foothold. He applied for the salaried position of *proto* of the salt magistracy, which managed the salt monopoly and was responsible for the majority of Venetian public works, but he did not get the job. A few years later, he entered an architectural competition to replace the old wooden Rialto bridge (Palladio had already built a large, hundred-foot bridge in timber for one of his villa clients). Although the competitors included Michelangelo as well as Sansovino, who was the clear favorite, the authorities temporized, and the expensive public project was set aside, not to be undertaken for another thirty years. Palladio also participated in a competition for a new main staircase (now called the Scala d'Oro) for the Doge's Palace. Sansovino and Sanmicheli submitted a joint entry and, not surprisingly, won. With Daniele Barbaro's help, Palladio finally did receive a commission—to design a new façade for the cathedral of Venice. Yet before construction could begin, the Patriarch died and his successor abandoned the project.*

Thus at the time that he was designing La Malcontenta, the forty-five-year-old Palladio, although growing in creative power, was blocked from large public commissions. What frustration he must have felt. So, as architects sometimes do, he used domestic commissions to demonstrate his architectural ideas. Le Corbusier did the same thing in the 1920s when he made white-walled suburban villas outside Paris manifestoes for his new modern architecture; Robert Venturi launched his career—and postmodernism—with a complicated little house designed for his mother in Philadelphia; and Frank Gehry signaled his startling new talent with an idiosyncratic remodeling of his own house, a bungalow in Santa Monica. La Malcontenta's great imperial portico, which would be seen by dozens of Venetians passing on the Brenta—or on the road, which was the main ground route to Padua—really was a billboard; not only for the Foscari brothers but also for Palladio's particular vision of Roman classicism.

---

*The façade of San Pietro, near the Arsenale, was finally realized forty years later, after Palladio's death. Although his design was not followed exactly, the church is still worth a visit.

V

Porticoes

he main street of Piombino Dese, a large village east of Vicenza, is Via Roma. The busy artery is lined with unremarkable apartment buildings and neon-fronted shops. It's Sunday morning and there's not much traffic. A parking lot near the church is temporarily occupied by a traveling amusement park whose single attraction resembles a huge lazy Susan. Children line up to get on, then scream as the ride begins to turn, slowly at first, then faster and faster, finally tilting and turning at the same time. The more daring boys leave their seats to crawl, crablike, across the angled floor. Strobe lights flash, and noisy calliope music is piped over loudspeakers.

Across the street, rising behind a brick wall, the stately portico of the Villa Cornaro overlooks the raucous spectacle. The juxtaposition of the fun fair and the villa makes me think of a scene in a Fellini film. The villa more than holds its own. It looms a full two stories high, its extremely tall portico, shaped like a temple front, silhouetted against the sky. Two stories doesn't sound impressive, but when each floor is thirty feet high and the house has a basement and attic, it is the equivalent of a six- or seven-story building.

This privately owned house is open to the public on selected days during the summer, but since it is off-season I've made arrangements for a special visit. I'm to meet the custo-

VILLA CORNARO

dian at eleven o'clock this morning at a nearby cafe called—what else?—the Caffè Palladio. He turns out to be a pleasant young man who tends the bar. After his replacement shows up, we cross the street to the villa, where he unlocks a heavy gate that lets us into the garden. He suggests that I walk around the grounds while he goes inside to open the window shutters.

The reason for the extreme height of the pediment is evident; it sits atop not one but two porticoes—a double-decker. The double portico—Corinthian over Ionic—projects forward like La Malcontenta, but has side walls in place of columns on the sides. These walls have arched openings that echo the arched windows whose prominent keystones are part of the masonry pattern scribed into the stucco walls. The central block of the house is flanked by two side wings. According to Palladio, one wing was used for the kitchen and housekeeping activities, and the other housed rooms for the servants. He did not explain the reason for not locating the kitchen in the basement—it may have had to do with reducing the distance to the upper floor, for he did the same thing in his other two-story houses.

On the rear, instead of a flat façade Palladio built *another* double portico. It is a twin of the first with six Corinthian columns above and six Ionic below, and the same triangular pediment, but instead of projecting out from the house it is recessed. This mirror image combination is an extraordinary architectural one-two punch.

Palladio's client was Giorgio Cornaro (no relation to Alvise Cornaro), another young Venetian nobleman. The Cornaros—Corner, in Venetian dialect—were a branch of the fabled Contarini, one of the original twelve families that founded the city in the seventh century. They were known as the Cornaro della Regina in recognition of Giorgio's great-aunt, Caterina

Cornaro, who had been Queen of Cyprus at the end of the fifteenth century. (After surrendering sovereignty of her island
realm to the Venetian Republic, she moved to the nearby village of Altivole.) The Piombino lands had belonged to the
Cornaro family for generations, and in 1551, when Senator
Girolamo Cornaro died, they were divided between his two
sons, Andrea and Giorgio. Andrea as firstborn received the
bulk of the holdings, which included an impressive house in the
village, designed some years earlier by Sanmicheli.[1] Giorgio, who
intended to marry, promptly set about building his own house.
He had inherited several hundred acres in scattered parcels, but
he chose a site next to his brother's villa. It is a measure of Palladio's growing reputation that he received the commission to
design a villa that was obviously meant to rival, if not outshine,
its illustrious neighbor.*

The cramped site made this difficult. It was a narrow rectangle of land extending back from the main street. Palladio was
obliged to accommodate a long barn and a working farm
court on half the site, which left only about an acre to build
on—the equivalent of a large American suburban lot. Except for
the Villa Godi, whose ramparted podium was relatively con-
stricted, most of Palladio's villas had large sites on which he
could lay out forecourts. Here he could not create an impression
of grandeur by spreading out, so he did the next best thing—he
went up.

Palladio responded to the particular demands of his clients—

---

*The Cornaro family were long-standing architecture buffs. Two
of Giorgio's uncles had built famous houses in Venice, the Palazzo Cor-
ner della Ca' Grande, designed by Sansovino, and the Palazzo Corner
Mocenigo on San Polo, designed by Sanmicheli; his Contarini ancestor
Marin had built (and largely designed) the famous Cà d'Oro on the
Grand Canal near the Rialto bridge.

THE TWO-STORY PORTICO OF THE VILLA CORNARO
WAS PALLADIO'S ANSWER TO A NARROW SITE.

The SOUTH-FACING LOGGIAS OF THE VILLA CORNARO
ARE A MIRROR IMAGE OF THE FAÇADE AND PROVIDE
A SHELTERED SITTING AREA.

that was part of his success as a residential architect—but he often developed ideas simultaneously in several projects. At the same time he was building the Villa Cornaro, he was working on two other houses. One was a villa for Francesco Pisani (a kinsman of Vettor), just outside the city gates of Montagnana, a walled town south of Vicenza; the other was a house for Signor Floriano Antonini on the outskirts of the city of Udine. Both were two-story houses in suburban locations with double porticoes. Altogether, there are eight double porticoes in *Quattro libri,* five villas and three town houses. The front double portico of the Villa Cornaro is unique, however, since it projects forward, making this one of Palladio's most impressive frontispieces.

With houses such as the Villa Chiericati, La Malcontenta, and the Villa Cornaro, Palladio at last created the architectural prototype that combined the temple architecture of antiquity with a modern house. The latter was simplicity itself: a plastered brick box with carefully proportioned openings, unifying moldings and fascias, and masonry patterns scribed on plastered walls. The box was adaptable—it could have wings, a lower or taller basement, one floor or two. The interior was conveniently subdivided vertically into service basement, family rooms and *amezati,* and a storage attic. As for the portico, it could front a recessed loggia or a projecting porch, be one level or two, and have more or fewer columns, to suit.

The rear garden of the Villa Cornaro, unlike the front, has room to breathe. The long spread of lawn looks out on farmland, a view that cannot have changed much since the sixteenth century. At the end of the lawn is a curious seven-arched bridge, said to be designed by Palladio, that leads over a fishpond to an imposing set of gates. I'm looking at the bridge when the custodian comes around the corner of the house. He tells me that a road once led over the bridge, through the gates, and straight across the fields to the edge of the property, about a quarter of a mile away. I'm not sure I agree with him when he says that this was the original front entrance (*Quattro libri* clearly indicates that the villa faced the street). Yet the house's two-sided character no doubt reflected two different approaches: one from the village street and the other along the country road flanked by orchards, which would have made a more attractive arrival for visitors coming from Venice, about twenty miles away.

Since the back entrance is obstructed by temporary scaffolding, we go around to the front. The outside stair, which extends the full width of the portico, is unusual. Palladio was always experimenting with entrance stairs—semicircular stairs at Piombino, a simple broad sweep at Poiana, double stairs at Malcontenta—in order to create a dignified way to bring people up to the portico. Here he designed a series of three steps interrupted by slightly inclined landings. The result is a sort of ramped stair. Instead of simply climbing, we glide up the stately ascent.

The front door opens into a shallow vaulted vestibule, with doors leading to rooms on either side. Straight ahead is the *sala,* a large squarish room.* Since there is a similar room immediately above, the ceiling is flat rather than vaulted, but drama is provided by four intersecting beams resting on four immense, freestanding Ionic columns, one in each corner of the room. Palladio designed several variations of the square *sala* in his two-

---

*The dimensions of the *sala* in *Quattro libri* are 32 feet by 27¼ feet, not one of Vitruvius's recommended shapes. The rooms at the Villa Cornaro are likewise oddly dimensioned—16 by 26½, 11 by 32, and 10 by 16—another example of Palladio exercising his "judgment."

story houses, all inspired by ancient examples. "[Roman halls] were called tetrastyle because they had four columns," he wrote. "They made these square and built columns there in order to make the breadth proportionate to the height and to make the structure above stable."[2] Like the *sala* of the Villa Pisani, this has the feeling of an outdoor space, an impression magnified by the giant columns. Unlike that room, however, this is a dynamic, three-dimensional space, the columns creating a central cube of space with a sort of aisle around the edges. Sunlight from a profusion of windows in the south-facing wall creates patterns across the clay-tile floor. The room is particularly bright since the walls are not frescoed but white.

Palladio further responded to Cornaro's demand for pomp and circumstance by including another feature from antiquity: niches for life-size statues. The stucco figures, added twenty years after Giorgio's death by his son, represent eminent Cornaro ancestors: the stern paterfamilias Marco, wearing his Doge's cap; his grandson, Zorzi the Elder, a famous military commander who acquired the Piombino lands; Zorzi's granddaughter, the beautiful Caterina, wearing a crown; her brother Zorzi, another soldier and Giorgio's grandfather; Giorgio's father, Girolamo, who fought for the Republic in Crete and Padua; and Giorgio himself, bearded and heavyset, who died in action commanding a Venetian galley in a war against the Ottoman Turks.

We pass through the other rooms, whose layout follows the same L-configuration as in La Malcontenta—small, medium, and large—each with a different type of ceiling vault. This plan is repeated on the upper floor (which is closed to visitors). My guide scrupulously describes each of the wall and ceiling frescoes. To my eye, the biblical paintings and the blowsy stucco reliefs are an alien presence and do not enhance Palladio's architecture. These rococo adornments were commissioned in the eighteenth century by Giorgio Cornaro's great-great-grandson; he would have done better to leave well enough alone.

The villa remained in the Cornaro family until the beginning of the nineteenth century, when it passed to a succession of private owners. During the 1950s and 1960s the house was a parochial kindergarten, then stood vacant, and was finally bought—by an American—and restored. The house changed hands again in 1989. I remember coming upon the improbable advertisement in the real estate pages of the *New York Times Magazine:* "Palladio Villa for Sale." The current owners, likewise Americans, have furnished the house attractively with period pieces. My guide refers to bedrooms, living room, and dining room; Palladio did not use such terms. He gave precise names

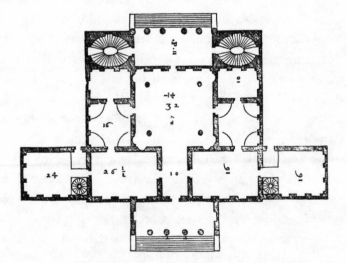

PLAN OF VILLA CORNARO, FROM *QUATTRO LIBRI*

only to utilitarian rooms: wine casks and foodstuffs were stored in the *cantina*; food was prepared in the *cucina* and served from the *dispensa* (pantry); the servants ate in the *tinello,* or servant's hall. But the important rooms on the main floor, other than the *sala,* were simply called *camere* or *stanze,* anterooms were *anti-camere,* and rooms located beyond the main room were *post-camere.* Palladio did not label such rooms according to their function because in cinquecento villas and palazzos rooms did not have predetermined uses; people slept and dined and social-ized all over the house. Although formal banquets were held in the *sala,* everyday meals were taken in one's room, which was furnished somewhat like a modern hotel room, with beds, wardrobes or chests, tables, chairs, and settees. Most rooms con-tained several beds, children sharing the room with their par-ents, guests with one another. Standards of privacy were, of course, different, for sixteenth-century residences did not have corridors—people simply passed through one room to get to the next. Only the master of the house warranted a private room—which Palladio called a *studiolo,* or study—where he kept money, papers, valuables, and books. Such small rooms were also called *stanze piccole*—little rooms—and were often created by subdividing a *stanze* after the house was built.

The Italian word for furniture is *mobilia,* and furniture was moved from room to room, which is why Palladio did not draw tables or chairs in his plans (nor, as far as we know, did he ever design any furniture). Rooms were often used seasonally, north-facing rooms in the summer, and south-facing in the winter. Room adornments—tapestries, easel paintings, can-dlesticks—were likewise portable. Much sixteenth-century furniture is foldable or demountable, for furniture was also moved from house to house. When Cornaro relocated his household from Venice to Piombino, to oversee the harvest, say, or to avoid an epidemic, he traveled with bedsteads, linens, and table silver.

The simple exterior of the Villa Cornaro masks six or seven different floor levels. Since this was a two-story house, Palladio provided two grand stone staircases, oval in plan and brightly lit by windows on three sides; smaller wooden spiral stairs in each wing were for the use of the servants. The Villa Cornaro has no fewer than twelve rooms and two *salas,* not including the service rooms in the two wings, and the *amezati* over the smallest rooms, which accommodated the large household staff. It is likely that the Cornaro family lived on the upper floor, whose high-ceilinged rooms caught the cooling summer breezes and were more private; the downstairs was probably reserved for occasions of state. The cavernous upper *sala,* which extends up into the roof space, does not have columns, which made it useful for dancing and dramatics. If it was occasionally crowded with people, that also explains the structural function of the four supporting Ionic columns below.[3]

The Villa Cornaro was hardly a "machine for living in," as Le Corbusier once described a modern house; it was an elegant stage on which Giorgio and his family could lead their privileged lives. There was finery, but comfort was rudimentary by modern standards. The small and large rooms had fireplaces, but the medium-sized rooms and the *salas* were unheated. The elegant oval stairs were only accessible from the loggia, which meant that to go upstairs, one had to go outside. There was no plumbing. Servants carried hot water for bathing up to the rooms from the kitchen. Palladio provided the villa with indoor privies, in alcoves behind the main stair. In the house that he was building at the same time in Montagnana, he also incorporated indoor privies—two-holers. He assured the reader of *Quattro libri* that the privies "do not smell much because they were put in a place away

from the sunlight and have some vents, leading from the bottom
of the pit through the thickness of the walls, that let out at the top
of the house."[4] The vents may not have worked as intended, for
these are the only indoor privies recorded in *Quattro libri*.

"You can stay in the garden as long as you like," my guide tells
me as he locks up the house. "Just shut the front gate when you
leave."

I take some photographs of the portico, then go to the back
garden, where I sit on the bridge parapet, writing up my notes.
The utter simplicity of the house is charming. The basement is
unplastered brick, with a stepped brick band separating it from
the plastered walls above. Whereas the front façade has arched
windows—rare in Palladio villas—the ones in the back are
square as well as arched, with arches in the scribed masonry
pattern. Such a transparently scenographic device only makes
the majestic porticoes more substantial.

It's after one o'clock and time to go. The carnival ride is
silent, the children have gone home for lunch. I cross the street
to the Caffè Palladio to get a bite to eat. The young man has
left and the place is empty. Ordering a ham and cheese sandwich and a glass of beer, I take a table by the window. The sandwich arrives—it is grilled, provolone and prosciutto—and I
munch contentedly, staring absentmindedly out of the window
at the villa, which is plainly visible across the street. Piombino
must have been only a hamlet when the house was built, yet
the surroundings already were less than pastoral. Perhaps that's
why the villa does not really look out of place; it is, as it was
always intended to be, the finest house in town.*

---

*The architectural competition between the two Cornaro villas was
settled in the 1770s when Sanmicheli's house was demolished.

From a distance the double portico looks very familiar, actually very American. There are similar two-story pedimented porches all across the United States, particularly in the South, where a columned porch in front of a mansion is synonymous with "plantation house." Drayton Hall is a famous plantation house outside Charleston with several Palladian features: a symmetrical plan, a regular window arrangement, pronounced moldings, blocky modillions supporting a cornice under the eaves, and prominent double porticoes. It was built almost two hundred years after the Villa Cornaro. A series of unusual individuals and fortuitous events leads from Piombino Dese in the hinterland of the Venetian Republic, to the backwoods of a remote British colony on the Atlantic seaboard of the New World.

The complicated story begins in Jacobean England with a remarkable architect, Inigo Jones. A portrait by Van Dyck shows Jones in his late sixties, a handsome bearded man with unruly hair flowing from under a silk skullcap, and a deceptively mild look considering a biographer described him as "a personality of alarming force, totally intolerant of the lesser

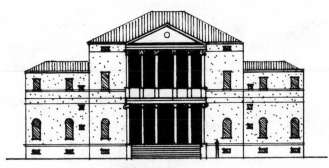

VILLA CORNARO

creatures in his environment."[5] In the painting, Jones is holding a sheet of paper that could be a billet-doux, a list of accounts, a costume sketch, or an architectural drawing, for he was a courtier, an art expert, and a theatrical designer, as well as an architect. He overlapped Palladio—just barely—being born in London in 1573 (Palladio died in 1580). The son of a cloth-worker, he apprenticed as a joiner. Yet at thirty he abandoned this trade. "Being naturally inclined in my younger years to study the Arts of Design," he later recalled, "I passed into for-eign parts to converse with the great masters thereof in Italy."[6] After an extended sojourn in southern Italy, where he appar-ently made high-placed friends, he reemerged in London soci-ety described as a "picture-maker"—that is, a painter. It was in this capacity that he joined the court of James I under the per-sonal patronage of the new queen, Anne of Denmark. Jones's chief occupation was designing the scenery and costumes for masques, or theatrical entertainments, most of them written by Ben Jonson. Jones replaced the Elizabethan arena stage with the Continental proscenium and introduced English audiences to Italian scenery, much of it in the *all'antica* style. For almost thirty years, Jonson and Jones's spectacular combination of drama, dance, and music was the vogue.

When he was forty, Jones accompanied his patrons and friends, the Earl and Countess of Arundel, on a tour of Italy. They visited Naples, Rome, Florence, and Venice, collecting works of art, buying books, and visiting museums, with Jones (who was fluent in Italian) acting as tour guide and artistic con-sultant. They also saw the works of famous Renaissance archi-tects, including Palladio. Jones was familiar with Palladio's treatise, but he was unprepared for the experience of the build-ings. It was love at first sight. The Arundel entourage stopped in Vicenza twice. Jones visited at least three Palladio villas, includ-

ing the Villa Thiene at Quinto, which he was disappointed to
find only partly built. "To this stroke it is finished and nothing
more," he scribbled in the margin of his heavily annotated *Quat-*
tro libri.[7] He interviewed craftsmen who had worked on Palladio's buildings and on Arundel's behalf bought more than two
hundred of Palladio's drawings (Arundel later gave him most of
them). Jones seems to have felt a personal bond with Palladio.
For example, he practiced copying Palladio's signature and
signed his own name in a similar fashion. The two men had
much in common: both were late starters; both came from
humble backgrounds; both were avid readers and self-taught
scholars.

When Jones returned to England he continued to design
masques, but expanded his activities to include architecture. He
was appointed Surveyor of the King's Works, which effectively made him court architect, a role he continued to play
under Charles I. It is no exaggeration to say that Inigo Jones
single-handedly introduced Italian classicism to England.
Although the Renaissance had influenced English scholar-
ship, it had had almost no effect on English architecture.
Jacobean buildings were distinctly old-fashioned, a fusty blend
of decorative Flemish influences and Elizabethan traditions.
Jones's designs were different: spare, rigorous, geometrically
disciplined, and, of course, classical. Although he was working
half a century after Palladio's death, Jones ignored the later generation of Mannerist architects, preferring the simpler styles of
the cinquecento. "All thes composed ornaments, the Which
proceed out of ye aboundance of dessigners and wear brought
in by Michill Angell, and his followers in my oppignion do not
well in sollid Architecture," he complained (in his unique
orthography).[8]

Jones's "solid Architecture" is often called Palladian, but it is really Jonesian, for while he was inspired by his predecessor, he had the self-confidence—and the talent—to go his own way. His buildings, constructed of stone, not plaster, have a precision that is absent from Palladio's domestic work, and despite his theatrical background, Jones—at least on the exterior—was a more severe designer. The house that he built for Queen Anne at Greenwich has an almost austere façade with a rusticated base and a columned loggia in the center, facing a *cortile* flanked by porticoes that recall the Villa Pisani. The Banqueting House at Whitehall Palace, originally designed as a performance hall for masques, is his masterpiece. The restrained pilasters and half-columns of the façade do not prepare one for the spectacular interior with a brilliant ceiling painted by Peter Paul Rubens. "Outwardly every wyse man carrieth a graviti in Publicke places," Jones wrote, "yet inwardly hath his imaginacy set on fire, and sumtimes licentciously flying out, as nature hirself doeth often times stravagantly."[9] Like Palladio, he combined sober exteriors with rich décor, although he disposed of greater budgets than his predecessor, and his splendid interior architecture is not frescoed but the real thing.

Jones followed Palladio's lead in seeking inspiration from antiquity. He modeled St. Paul's Church in Covent Garden on Vitruvius's description of a Tuscan temple, and based the design of his most prominent work, the great portico on the west front of Old St. Paul's Cathedral (which was destroyed some twenty years later in the Fire of London), on Palladio's reconstruction of an ancient Roman temple. Only eight out of forty-six known works survive, but they show Jones to be a true successor of Palladio, applying his principles without copying his designs.

The English Civil War effectively ended Jones's professional life. He served in Charles I's army as a military engineer, was captured, briefly imprisoned, then fined, and died in 1652, three years after his royal patron's execution. Jones's assistant, the talented John Webb, who inherited his master's practice (as well as his collection of Palladio drawings), carried on his brand of austere classicism. However, after Charles II's accession to the throne, tastes changed, and Jones's architecture was out of fashion. Nevertheless, Palladio remained a touchstone for British architects. When John Vanbrugh, a successful dramatist, turned his hand to architecture at the age of forty, having been appointed Comptroller of the Royal Works under Christopher Wren, he ordered a copy of *Quattro libri* from his bookseller. Vanbrugh, who would build such extravagant country houses as Castle Howard and Blenheim Palace, took English architecture in a theatrical and flamboyant direction, yet the springboard for his fertile imagination was Palladio.

Vanbrugh and Wren were not, strictly speaking, Palladians, but Palladianism did eventually return to Britain. It emerged first in Scotland with James Smith, an obscure Edinburgh stonemason turned architect who had spent five years in Italy. Starting in 1685 with his own house, Whitehill, Smith built a number of Palladian country houses in Scotland. His influence spread through Colen Campbell, another Scot, who built what is generally considered the first eighteenth-century Palladian house in England, Wilbury House. In 1715, Campbell published *Vitruvius Britannicus,* a compendium of architectural works in which he championed a stricter classicism based on the "Famous Inigo Jones," and "above all, the great Palladio, who has exceeded all that has gone before him, and surpass'd his Contemporaries."[10] That same year Giacomo Leoni, a Venetian émigré, published the first complete English translation of *Quattro libri.* Leoni's patron was the young Richard Boyle, third Earl of Burlington. Soon after, Burlington engaged Campbell to design a Palladian entrance court and colonnade for Burlington House, the family's London residence.

Campbell encouraged the young earl's interest in architecture. A few years later, Burlington went to Italy to see Palladio's work for himself, retracing Inigo Jones's journey to Venice and Vicenza. He returned to England with an unalloyed devotion to Palladio, and about sixty of the master's drawings (he later acquired most of Webb's Palladian collection, and this entire treasure trove is now at the Royal Institute of British Architects in London, where I saw it). Burlington, who was fabulously wealthy, became a great patron—Horace Walpole called him the "Apollo of Arts." He underwrote a young architect, Isaac Ware, to translate *Quattro libri* (Leoni's version, though also backed by Burlington, was notoriously unreliable), published a collection of Palladio's reconstructions of ancient buildings, and engaged his lifelong friend William Kent, a painter, landscape gardener, and architect, to edit *Designs of Inigo Jones*. The "Architect Earl" was also a practitioner, designing and building a number of notable Palladian houses, some in collaboration with Kent, some on his own.

There are buildings inspired by Palladio in Italy, where a Palladian revival took place in the early eighteenth century, as well as in the Netherlands, Germany, and Poland, and to a lesser extent in France, but nowhere did Palladianism take stronger hold than in the British Isles. Thanks to Lord Burlington's passion for architecture, the talented architects whom he attracted and encouraged, and the revival of interest in Inigo Jones, academic Palladianism flourished well into the nineteenth century. Ware's new translation of *Quattro libri, Vitruvius Britannicus,* and *Designs of Inigo Jones* introduced Palladian ideas to architects who had never been to Italy, or even seen the buildings of Inigo Jones. In the process, Palladianism became fashionable. Between 1715 and 1745, prosperity, changing tastes, and a desire for newness led the landed gentry in England, Scotland, and Ireland to modernize and replace their country houses, producing a building boom not unlike the spurt of villa-building in cinquecento Venice. Palladianism, or rather its British reincarnation, was the preferred style. Sophisticated and elegant, it represented a revival of past glories—not only of ancient Rome but also of Inigo Jones and English royalty. British Palladianism was popularized by an impressive number of architectural manuals, builders' guides, and so-called pattern books, which were intended for "such Gentlemen as might be concerned in building, especially in the remote parts of the Country, where little or no assistance for design can be procured."[11] Between 1724 and 1790, no fewer than 275 new architectural handbooks appeared—as well as 170 new editions of earlier works.[12]

One of the most popular handbook authors was Robert Morris. While he published pattern books for houses and villas, he was also a polemicist. "*Gaiety, Magnificence,* the rude *Gothic,* or the *Chinese unmeaning Stile,* are the Study of our modern Architects," he complained, "while *Grecian* and *Roman Purity* and *Simplicity,* are neglected."[13] In *Select Architecture,* Morris adapted Palladio's designs to the needs of the eighteenth-century English landowner. A "Plain Villa," for example, was a simple rectangular block.[14] A recessed pedimented portico, supported by Ionic columns, marked the entrance. The exterior recalled the plainness of the Villa Poiana, with a molding at the level of the windowsills, a pronounced water table, and modillions under the eaves. The symmetrical plan was recognizably Palladian: in the center was a large entrance hall leading to a public room, and on each side were smaller rooms. Like a Palladio villa, the Morris villa had three levels: a basement con-

All four watch in disbelief as the trinket rolls then settles.

Jillian is as surprised as any of them. She forgot about the tiny thing.

Red gasps and points. "Junkie steal a Chrysler Building! Citizen arrest! Citizen arrest!" Officer Cannell kneels down and lifts up the small building. He looks up at Jillian's open hand dangling directly above the souvenir. "Thief." Red ejects the word from her mouth.

"Damn it." Officer Cannell changes his tune quickly and takes his pad of paper out. "I'm gonna need to see your ID."

Shit. Fuck. Stupid. Shit. Ass. Fuck. Fuck. Jillian's insides cave in and nearly explode outward. She was almost home free. Why did she have to take the meaningless memento?

This is indisputably the stupidest moment of her life.

"It's in my purse." Jillian remembers to go straight for the side pocket—the place where she usually keeps it but never remembers to look. The side pocket is where she keeps her license. But the pocket feels soft, like nothing hard and flat fills it up. A small cluster of receipts, two nickels, and a scrunchy are its only contents. "License, passport . . . ?" the officer adds, as Jillian desperately hunts through the bag.

"It's usually in here. Right here. In this pocket. The zipper pocket. I swear it is." Jillian babbles as she feels around at the bottom of the bag. Her heart is racing, her face flushed. She opens her wallet, pulls out the cards, and counts them aloud: "D'Agostino, Citibank, Visa, old Visa, United Mileage Plus, Air France Frequence Plus, Amex, Corporate Amex, Crunch Fitness, Tiffany's gift card, Gap gift card, new calling card, old calling card, other old calling card, Jivamutki, Saks, expired Brown University Library Pass," but no license.

"Passport . . . ?"

"No . . ." Jillian then remembers Melva and the purple bubblegum and the Ativan and the broken Patina Frost. "Oh my God. You're not going to believe this," Jillian makes sure to sound positive, like she's not lying, which she isn't. "I left my license at McKay's Pharmacy on Twelfth. I did." Officer Cannell scratches his head and looks around. "I did. I swear. Yesterday." The officer is aggravated, even disappointed. She pulls out a thin, laminated card with her picture on it. "I've got Crunch." She feebly turns the gym ID around to the officer. "It's a Gold membership."

Officer Cannell looks at the Crunch Fitness ID. Jillian continues to fuss around in her purse for another pointless minute. She grabs at pens and a lipstick, hoping one might morph into her license. She pulls the price tag off the stolen Fogal stockings and tears it in half. Her heart pumps an excess amount of blood into her neck, causing a prickly rash to emerge.

"Have you ever been arrested, Miss . . . Siegel?"

"No." Jillian's voice starts small but builds. "No! I've never done anything illegal in my life. I mean I pay my bills on time, I vote, I get my teeth cleaned every six months, *everything* . . . on time." She is sure to emphasize the word *everything*. "I bought those socks and I'm an advertising executive and I paid for the socks, I mean . . . look at me . . . do I look like someone who would steal a thing like that?" Jillian goes on and on as if propelled by a motor. Her hands are flying now; she is out of breath and she has to pee. *Shut up, Jill. Jesus.*

"It happens all the time, Miss Siegel." He is not unpleasant like the police on TV. In fact, his pleasantness is frightening; it's what makes it the most real. This is real life, not TV. "And I'm sorry, but without an ID I'm gonna have to take you down to the station. It's procedure. I have no choice here." The officer speaks into his walkie-talkie. "I got a 10–12. I'm coming in."

taining kitchens and servants' quarters, a main floor, and what looked like an attic on the façade but was really a bedroom floor. The plan lacked Palladio's geometrical finesse, for although the entrance hall was square, the proportions of the other rooms were haphazard. On the other hand, utility was well-served: each room had a fireplace; there were two stairs, a large one for the owners and a smaller one for the servants; and to facilitate heating, ceiling heights were kept low, only eleven feet on the main floor, and nine feet on the upper floor. A *serliana* lit the main staircase. Altogether it was a handsome design that supported Morris's claim that "a Building, well proportioned, without Dress, will ever please; as a plain Coat may fit as graceful, and easy, on a well-proportioned Man."[15]

Select Architecture, which was published in 1755 and reprinted only two years later, was particularly popular in the British colonies of the New World: Jamaica, Barbados, the Bahamas, and particularly the thirteen colonies of North America. That period coincides with what one historian has called "the refinement of America," when gentility first appeared, in manners, comportment, dress—and houses.[16] Colonials looked to the mother country for the latest architectural fashion, which has been loosely termed Georgian but was basically Palladian. Since there were few trained architects, gentlemen regularly designed their own homes. When Bishop George Berkeley remodeled his house near Newport, Rhode Island, and produced what is generally considered the first Palladian house in New England, he used Kent's *Designs of Inigo Jones* as a guide. The rusticated, three-arch loggia of Mount Airy, in Virginia, recalls the Villa Caldogno and was copied from James Gibbs's *A Book of Architecture.* Shirley Plantation, another riverside house in Virginia, was based on a plate in *Vitruvius Britannicus.* Armed with Campbell, Gibbs, or Morris, gentlemen built Palladian houses up and down the Atlantic seaboard, from suburban Philadelphia to the Carolinas. Their Palladian features included pedimented porticoes, columned porches, *serlianas* (which Americans called Palladian windows), symmetrically composed façades, and regularly arranged fenestration.

The overmantel of the fireplace in the entrance of Drayton Hall is copied directly from *Designs of Inigo Jones,* so it is likely that the pedimented double portico on the exterior is also based on a published example. In that case, Judge John Drayton, or his builder, must have had a copy of *Quattro libri,* for there are no double porticoes in Campbell, Gibbs, or Morris; indeed, the English Palladians never adopted Palladio's double portico. The Drayton double porticoes—as at Piombino there are two of them, one facing an entrance court, the other the river—are second cousins of the double porticoes of the Villa Cornaro. Subsequently, similar two-story porticoes, often called galleries, appear in many houses, not only on plantations but in suburban villas as well as town houses.

The best-known double portico in the American colonies was that of the capitol in Williamsburg, Virginia. It was built in 1752, more than a decade after Drayton Hall, following the destruction by fire of the original capitol.* The portico was an ungainly affair, judging from a contemporary description.

> The Capitol is a light and airy structure, with a portico in front of two orders, the lower of which being Doric, is tolerably just in proportions and ornaments, save only that the inter-

---

*The double-portico building burned down in 1852; the present-day capitol at Colonial Williamsburg is a replica of the earlier building, which had no double portico.

colonations are too large. The upper is Ionic, much too small for that on which it is mounted, its ornaments not proper to the order, nor proportioned within themselves. It is crowned with a pediment, which is too high for its span.[17]

The severe architectural critic was Thomas Jefferson. Jefferson's interest in architecture was aroused while he was still a student at the College of William and Mary in Williamsburg. With the characteristic obsession that he applied to all intellectual pursuits, he read widely on the subject: Gibbs's treatises, Morris's *Select Architecture, Quattro libri*. He was drawn to Palladianism, partly because it appealed to his rational nature and partly because, as a provincial, he sought the stamp of authority. "Palladio is the Bible," he once advised a friend, "stick close to it."[18] When Jefferson turned twenty-one and achieved economic independence, he started building his own house. He copied the plan from *Select Architecture* but added a double portico. Although the immediate inspiration was probably the Williamsburg capitol, in the handsome drawing (Jefferson learned to draw early—his father was a surveyor), he corrected the proportional inadequacies, probably following the drawings of the Villa Cornaro in *Quattro libri*.*

Jefferson visited northern Italy, including Milan and Genoa, but he did not go to Venice. Few colonial builders ever saw a real Palladio villa, or even a building by Jones or Lord Burlington. So American Palladianism is thirdhand, far removed from its British precedents, and even more distant from its Vicentine roots. American Palladian houses are generally unplastered

---

*Twenty-six years later, after returning from his stay in Paris, Jefferson drastically altered the house, reducing it to one story and eliminating the double portico.

brick, with accents of wood moldings painted white in the characteristic Georgian fashion. The wood trim is delicate compared to Palladio's sturdy stone and plastered brick. American houses rarely have tall basements or attic stories, which gives them a low-slung, close-to-the-ground appearance. Finally, the classical details, which are copied from books rather than from archaeological sites, are stiff and oversimplified. Yet, particularly in the southern colonies, American Palladianism has a curious authenticity. It is not easy to transplant Palladio from the Mediterranean to the rainswept dales of Oxfordshire, or to the Scottish moors. Sir Henry Wotton, who had met Jones during his Italian tour, wrote a handbook on Italian architecture in which he warned that "a good Parler in Ægypt would make perchance a good cellar in England."[19] Alexander Pope ridiculed English architects who "Shall call the Winds thro' long Arcades to roar / Proud to catch cold at a Venetian door; / Conscious they act a true Palladian part."[20] But a Palladian house in Virginia or the Carolinas looks at home. The hot climate makes loggias and porticoes not merely decorative but useful. The strong sun picks out the modeled surfaces, much as it does in the Veneto. Even the presence of porticoes on two sides—one facing inland, another a river, as at Drayton Hall—echoes the situation of many Palladio villas.

American plantation houses, like Vicentine villas, were the administrative centers of vast agricultural estates. They were surrounded by fields, not, as English country houses, by manicured landscapes. Judge Drayton may not have stored his rice crop in his attic, but he lived in the same intimacy with his agricultural surroundings as Giorgio Cornaro. Drayton was not an aristocrat, of course, but like many planters he put on aristocratic airs— neighbors referred to his house as "Mr. Drayton's palace." And the Judge built his grand country house on the banks of the Ashley for much the same reason Cornaro built an imposing villa on the dusty main street of Piombino: to surround himself with the trappings of civilization in a place that was remote, backward, and rustic.

VI

The Brothers Barbaro

fter leaving the Caffè Palladio in Piombino, I head north about fifteen miles to the village of Maser, site of the Villa Barbaro. The villa doesn't open to the public until three o'clock, so I have plenty of time. There is little traffic on this spring Sunday afternoon, and I enjoy the drive. The road passes Altivole, where Caterina Cornaro, the former queen of Cyprus, had her estate, and heads into the heart of the Trevigiana, a region centered on the city of Treviso. There are plowed fields on one side and vineyards on the other. The enormous ragged wall of the Dolomitic Alps looms in the distance. I must be on an old approach road to the villa, for directly ahead, a mile or so away at the base of the mountains, is a vivid splash of yellow. It's fifteen years since I've seen the Villa Barbaro, but the colorful silhouette is unmistakable.

The road veers to one side and the house passes from view. After more twists and turns I bear along the edge of an escarpment. The Villa Barbaro pops up on the left, several hundred feet away at the top of a gently rising slope. I brake hard and pull off the pavement onto a walled semicircular gravel area surrounding a fountain. Atop the dry basin a bearded Neptune holding a trident gazes across the road at the villa, seemingly transfixed by the view.

The yellow hue is not uncommon in Veneto country houses,

but here, freshly painted and juxtaposed against white trim, it makes Palladio's architecture appear delicate, quite different from the severe monumentality of his first houses. The villa is broken into several parts: a central block, which he called the *casa del padrone,* or the master's house, flanked on each side by arcaded wings terminating in ornate pavilions. The wings are extremely long, the entire building stretching out more than two hundred feet from end to end. The pavilions, which resemble huge bookends, have their gables decorated with colossal curved brackets. In *Quattro libri,* Palladio showed a walled courtyard in front of each pavilion, which would have effectively shortened the house and created a formal entrance court in the center. This would also have made the pavilions less prominent, bringing the architectural focus back to the central block. But no matter, the villa is magnificent, and ever so confident, sounding a joyful fanfare across the Trevigian plain.

The central block is two stories high, like the Villa Cornaro, but it does not have a portico; instead, the entire end of the house resembles an ancient temple. The illusion is twofold, for the four giant, white-painted Ionic columns, which from this distance appear to be freestanding, are half-round and attached to the façade. As he did often, Palladio explored a new motif in several houses at once; he built another two-story temple-fronted villa in nearby Bassano for Count Giacomo Angarano,

VILLA BARBARO

a Vicentine friend. To complete the temple effect, he dispensed with the attic and basement in both houses, and placed the service functions—kitchens, wine-making rooms, granaries—in flanking outbuildings. He put the main rooms on the upper floor, to take advantage of views and cooling breezes.

The clients at Maser were also Palladio's friends: Daniele Barbaro, whom he had met years before and who had helped him in Venice, and his brother Marc'antonio. Like Giorgio Cornaro, the Barbaros belonged to the upper reaches of the Venetian aristocracy. Their father, Francesco, who had been governor of Verona as well as a senator, had sent both of his sons to the University of Padua. Marc'antonio went into the diplomatic service and subsequently held various important governmental posts. Daniele, the older brother, had a scholarly bent and stayed in Padua studying philosophy, mathematics, and astronomy. This was during the late 1530s, and as an academic humanist he naturally participated in Alvise Cornaro's intellectual circle, which is where he met Andrea di Pietro, soon to be Palladio.

Daniele remained in Padua for a decade. In 1549, his father died and left his estate at Maser, which had belonged to the family for two hundred years, to his two sons, then both in their thirties. The brothers did not divide their inheritance, and decided to jointly enlarge the medieval house that was on the site. Palladio's earliest sketches for the villa date from this time, although it wasn't until almost a decade later that construction began.[1]

Palladio was a natural choice as architect, since for at least two years previous he had been collaborating with Daniele on a new edition of Vitruvius. Daniele was translating the Latin text into Italian, while Palladio drew the accompanying illustrations. The project was interrupted by Daniele's departure, three months after his father's death, to serve as Venetian ambassador in London. Two years later he was recalled to Venice and appointed patriarch-elect of Aquiléia, an important religious office (he never married but it is unclear if he was ordained). He was not required to live in Aquiléia, at the eastern borders of the Republic, so for the next few years, as the translation of Vitruvius, and the design of the villa, took shape, he and Palladio were often together. Daniele was seven years younger than Palladio, but he seems to have assumed Trissino's role of patron and intellectual mentor. The pair traveled to Venice, where the Barbaros had a house; in 1552, they went to Trento, where Daniele was the official Venetian delegate to the final session of the great religious council. Two years later they visited Rome.

When Barbaro and Palladio went to Rome they studied the antiquities—with an eye to Vitruvius—but they also toured two modern country houses, collecting ideas for the planned villa at Maser. The Villa Giulia, which Pope Julius III was building on the outskirts of Rome, had supplanted the Villa Madama as the most elaborate and beautiful house in the city, designed by no fewer than three architects: Vasari, Giacomo da Vignola, and Bartolomeo Ammanati. Its most striking feature was an elaborate garden whose centerpiece was a nymphaeum, or fanciful semicircular loggia, replete with stucco sculptures and fountains. The second project, also under construction, was equally spectacular. It was a country retreat at Tivoli, about twenty miles east of Rome, belonging to Cardinal Ippolito d'Este, a friend of Daniele Barbaro (who dedicated his translation of Vitruvius to the cardinal). At Tivoli, Barbaro and Palladio were given a tour of the elaborate water gardens by d'Este's architect, Pirro Ligorio.

In 1556, Barbaro's Vitruvius was published in Venice—to

great acclaim. He acknowledged Palladio's contribution in a high-blown tribute:

> For the important illustrations I used the work of Messer Andrea Palladio, architect of Vicenza, who, of all those whom I have known personally or by hearsay, has, according to the judgment of excellent men, best understood the true meaning of architecture and vastly profited from it, having not only grasped its most beautiful and subtle principles but having also put them into practice, both in his beautiful and exquisite drawings of plans, elevations, and sections and in the execution and erection of many and superb buildings, both in his own country [Vicenza] and elsewhere; works which vie with the ancients, which enlighten his contemporaries, and will arouse the admiration of those yet to come.[2]

The construction of the Barbaro villa began soon after the book appeared.[3] The reasons for the long gestation may have been professional demands on the brothers' time, or simply lack of building funds, for they were not independently wealthy. The villa's protracted design was likely also caused by their architectural ambition. Daniele took his avocation seriously. When he commissioned his portrait—now in Amsterdam's Rijksmuseum—he donned his bishop's robes but had himself portrayed surrounded by his architectural books and sitting at the base of a classical column. Marc'antonio, an amateur sculptor, also had a passion for architecture, so much so that he was later nicknamed "The Builder."* The Barbaro brothers were

---

*Late in life, Marc'antonio oversaw the construction of Palmanova, a fortress town with an extraordinary star-shaped plan.

THE VILLA BARBARO IS MASTERFULLY INTEGRATED INTO ITS SITE
AT THE FOOTHILLS OF THE DOLOMITIC ALPS.

connoisseurs and Palladio's friends, but this did not necessarily make them ideal clients. I can well imagine them bombarding him with suggestions, especially Daniele, who had considerable architectural experience. In Padua, he had laid out the university's new botanical garden—one of the first in Europe. In Venice, he had planned the iconographic program for the ceiling of the main council chamber in the Doge's Palace, and personally designed a palazzo on the island of Murano (probably with the help of either Palladio or Sanmicheli).[4] He also knew many architects and it has been suggested that he canvassed their advice about his proposed villa.[5] Such opinionated clients, no matter how well-intentioned, considerably complicate an architect's job. Palladio later wrote that architecture was a "profession everyone is convinced they know something about."[6] He must have been thinking of the Barbaro brothers.

The villa at Maser was, in any case, a challenging project. The site, a hill called Castellano (Lord of the manor), contained a medieval fortified house.[7] Evidence of old fireplaces in the attic of the *casa del padrone* indicates that Palladio reused the exterior walls of the old structure in their entirety. This meant that he had to find a way to accommodate the space needs of not one but two households within the tight dimensions of the relatively small *castello*.

The *castello* was built into the slope, and he took advantage of the situation to open the upper floor of the house to a large rear terrace cut into the hill, a landscape feature no doubt influenced by the stepped gardens of Tivoli. The villa at Maser had water features, too. The terrace was the site of a natural spring that fed a fountain that "forms a little lake that serves as a fishpond," he wrote. "Having left this spot, the water runs to the kitchen and then, having irrigated the gardens to right and left of the road which gently ascends and leads to the building, forms two fishponds with their horse troughs on the public road; from there it goes off to water the orchard, which is very large and full of superb fruit and various wild plants."[8] The troughs are gone, but they must have been located in the semicircle where I am parked.

The formal approach road is still here, but is permanently gated. Leaving my car, I walk down the highway and follow the signs to the side entrance. The large parking lot near the house is starting to fill up with cars and a couple of tour buses, and there is already a crowd of people milling about in front of a locked gate. I usually wander through Palladio's villas alone, but clearly that will not be the case today.

A custodian opens the gate and the crowd swarms into a small courtyard at the eastern end of the house. From this vantage point, it is obvious that the giant curved brackets of the pavilion are nothing more than screens masking a small box-like structure that in a modern building might house an air-conditioning unit. Judging from the rows of small holes, it's a dovecote. Pigeons were a familiar sight on *terraferma* farms since they provided food, fertilizer, and communications— homing pigeons could reach Venice from Maser in less than an hour. The contrast between the grand architectural gesture in front and the utilitarian pigeon coop behind reminds me of false-fronted buildings of the Old West.

A tall arched opening signals the entrance to the arcaded loggia. People are pushing their way in and lining up to buy tickets, so I walk around to the front of the villa until things settle down. The upper part of the pavilion contains a giant zodiac dial, reflecting Daniele's interest in astronomy (the corresponding face of the other pavilion has a sundial). His other interest, Roman antiquity, is expressed by the plaster statues that occupy the niches in the piers. First dour Charon, the god of death, then Flora, the Roman goddess of flowers, next the huntress Diana with her dog, and finally wily Mercury, messenger of the gods and patron of merchants. The antique theme of gods and goddesses is echoed in the *mascheroni,* or masks, that adorn the keystone. It was long thought that the sculptural plasterwork that abounds in this villa was the work of Alessandro Vittoria, an artist who frequently collaborated with Palladio, but many historians now credit Marc'antonio Barbaro.[9] That seems likely—some of the modeling is distinctly amateurish.

The irrepressible Marc'antonio (who was in between postings when the villa was being completed) did not miss a chance to practice his art. Probably under his brother's direction, he crammed the tympanum of the pediment of the *casa del padrone* with symbolic statuary. The composition is dominated by an imperial double eagle adorned with the Barbaro coat of arms and surmounted by a papal tiara. Two smaller crests refer to the families of their mother and of Marc'antonio's wife. The male figures astride dragonlike dolphins must be the brothers, although they are fondling naked buxom maidens, which seems inappropriate for Daniele the churchman. Yet the fraternal allusion is unavoidable. The frieze, which is broken in two by a garlanded cornucopia, bears a shorthand inscription DAN. BARBARUS. PA. AQUIL. (Daniele Barbaro, Patriarch of Aquiléia) under one figure, and ET. MARCUS. ANT. FR. FRANC. F. (and his brother Marc'antonio, sons of Francesco) under the other. Each brother grasps one horn of an ox skull that is the centerpiece of this cheerfully pagan composition.

Ox skulls, or bucrania, were a common classical motif, but one that Palladio rarely used in villas. The striking giant brackets that recall the scrolls on the façade of Alberti's Santa Maria Novella in Florence, which Palladio probably had seen, are like-

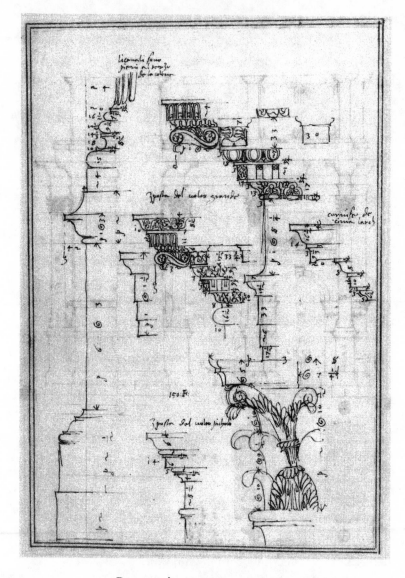

PALLADIO'S SKETCHES OF DETAILS
FROM THE ARCH OF CONSTANTINE, LATE 1560S
(RIBA, XVII/5 *verso*)

wise unusual. So are the tall arched windows that interrupt the entablature. The window frames are more delicately modeled and the façades are more articulated with moldings than other Palladio villas. Such stylistic anomalies have caused some historians to question whether the Villa Barbaro was entirely Palladio's creation.[10] In fact, despite the uniformity of Palladian houses in Britain and America, there is no such thing as a typical Palladio villa. Some of his designs incorporate temple fronts, some do not; some have pedimented windows, some have plain openings; some porticoes are supported by elaborate Corinthian columns, others by unadorned piers. His fertile imagination brimmed with ideas. In a later villa for Count Marc'antonio Sarego of Verona, for example, he struck out in an entirely new direction and dispensed with temple fronts and porticoes entirely, instead planning the two-story house around courtyards. As published in *Quattro libri,* the house consisted of two back-to-back courtyards: one enclosed, for residential functions; the other, U-shaped, for farm use. Only a part of the first courtyard was built, but its colonnade is astonishing. "The columns are Ionic and made of unpolished stone," Palladio wrote, "as seems appropriate here, since farms seem to require things which are rather plain and simple instead of refined."[11] The giant stone columns (Sarego owned a quarry), which Palladio had already used once before in the Antonini house in Udine, are composed of rusticated drums of different thicknesses, piled crudely one on top of the other. They look like stacks of huge stone doughnuts.

The Villa Sarego is Palladio at his most whimsical, but there are underlying consistencies in his work: ingenious planning that neatly combines rooms of predetermined proportions within simple rectangular buildings; inflexible biaxial symmetry of plan and elevation; the taut geometry of the façades; the fusion of everyday building materials and techniques with antique elements; and a sophisticated aesthetic playfulness. If there is one current that underlies Palladio's sense of style, it is what one historian has called his penchant for "telling details."[12] Perhaps because he was trained as a stonemason, Palladio was particularly appreciative of the carved elements that adorned the exteriors—and interiors—of his otherwise rather plain villas. The pages of *Quattro libri,* and many surviving sheets of his drawings, are covered with minutely dimensioned cornices, friezes, moldings, and capitals. While the deployment of these details formed the basis of Palladio's style, the *manner* of deployment varied greatly. Sometimes he re-created entire parts of ancient buildings, such as the Villa Barbaro temple front, sometimes he merely sketched in a molding or two. The quantity and intensity of detail varied from abundant to minimal, depending on the circumstances of the commission—the site, the functional program, the budget, and the client. The last was a particularly important consideration, for Palladio believed that houses should not only be functional, well-built, and beautiful, but that they should also express what he called *convenienza,* or suitability.

> One must describe as suitable a house which will be appropriate to the status of the person who will have to live in it and of which the parts will correspond to the whole and to each other. But above all the architect must observe that ... for great men and especially those in public office, houses with loggias and spacious, ornate halls will be required, so that those waiting to greet the master of the house or to ask him for some help or a favor can spend their time pleasantly in such spaces; similarly, smaller buildings of lesser expense and ornament will be appropriate for men of lower status. . . .[13]

Thus what might appear to be stylistic variety in his villas was really a conscious fitting of houses to their owners. "As far as possible one must (as I have said) pay particular attention to those who want to build," Palladio wrote, "not so much for what they can afford as for the type of building that would suit them."[14] Bonifacio Poiana got a house with a soldierly bearing; the Foscari brothers got a sort of suburban palazzo; and Giorgio Cornaro got a house that would both glorify his ancestors and impress on his visitors that this second son was not taking second place. What would suit the Barbaro brothers? They clearly qualified as "great men in public office," but they were also scholars and dilettantes. Daniele's literary interests are reflected in the Latin maxims that surmount the windows of the front façade: OMNIA TUTI BONIS (All is safe for good people); HOSPES NON HOSPI (A guest not a stranger); NON SOLUM DOMINI (Not only for the master); and NIL TECTI SUB TECTO (Nothing hidden under this roof). The sayings convey a genial hospitality that is the classical equivalent of a "Welcome" doormat.

Convenienza was also affected by the particular nature of the Barbaro estate. At only one hundred acres (largely vineyards), it was considerably smaller than Pisani's fourteen hundred acres at Bagnolo, by cinquecento standards a hobby farm. Maser was not, however, merely a temporary pastoral retreat. The house appears to have been the brothers' permanent year-round home, at least as permanent as their demanding public careers allowed. Consequently, the Villa Barbaro is less countrified than most of Palladio's villas. He incorporated elements from his urban projects: pedimented windows and sculpture niches from the Palazzo Civena; a balustraded balcony from the Palazzo da Porto; *mascheroni* from the Basilica; and bucrania from the Palazzo Chiericati.

Having now seen several Palladio villas, I'm more critical of

SCULPTURES BY MARC'ANTONIO BARBARO ADORN PALLADIO'S
RICH AND MANNERED ENTRANCE TO THE VILLA BARBARO.

the Villa Barbaro than I was on my first visit. It's a beautiful house that responds eloquently to its bucolic setting, but it is occasionally awkward. The scribed pattern of the stonework lacks Palladio's usual flair. The little balustraded balconies are uncharacteristically fussy. The arcaded wings have his usual robust proportions, but the central block is too delicate to hold its own; nor is the abrupt collision of house and arcades fully resolved. Similarly brusque is the relationship between the ornate temple front of the *casa del padrone* and the rather plain sides. Having the brothers looking over his shoulder—and probably contributing their own ideas—has slightly blurred Palladio's normally penetrating eye.

A panorama of vineyards and fields spreads out below the villa. On the left, in the distance, is a large stone barn, on the right, some houses. The Villa Godi has a dramatic outlook, but that stolid house perched on its walled bastion is isolated from its setting; the Villa Barbaro embraces its surroundings: the formal garden, a gravel drive leading down to the fountain near the road, and beyond that a long, poplar-lined allée.

Originally, visitors from Venice arrived by the allée, pausing at the Neptune fountain, which is in the center of a sort of forecourt. Here, while watering their horses, they had their first full view of the villa. On the semicircular wall that defines the back of the court still stand the two statues that were the putative household gods of the Villa Barbaro: on the east side Saturn, the patron of agriculture, and on the west the goddess Fortuna with one foot atop a sphere indicating the uncertainty of fate. Progressing up the drive, visitors passed between additional pairs of Olympian deities, arriving at two lions, symbols of St. Mark and the Republic. Alighting from horseback, the travelers climbed several steps to a paved stone terrace where they were greeted by their welcoming hosts. The terrace is unusual, more than forty feet square, paved in pink and white marble, and bounded on two sides by long stone benches. The Barbaro brothers were enthusiastic patrons of the theater, and it is likely that this was originally a performance space, for which the façade of the house formed a classical backdrop.[15]

The crowd of visitors has thinned out, so I return to the entrance courtyard. An arched opening leads into one end of the arcaded wing. The tall space resembles a long porch and is derived from a traditional Trevigian farm building called a *barchessa*. *Barchesse* were long barns whose south-facing sides consisted of open arcades providing sunny, protected outdoor areas for unloading wagons and doing farmwork. The custom of combining country houses and *barchesse* was established early in the Trevigiana and can be seen in the nearby Villa Tiretta, built by an unknown architect in 1500.[16] About forty years later, when Sanmicheli designed the Villa La Soranza at Treville, he adopted the same model of a residential block flanked by two arcaded *barchesse*. La Soranza (now demolished) was a famous villa, "the most beautiful and the most commodious that had been built in those parts up to that time," according to Vasari.[17] Treville is only ten miles from Maser, and it is impossible that Palladio, who admired Sanmicheli, did not know about it.

The local pedigree of the Maser arcades is a reminder that Palladio, the famous reviver of the *all'antica* style, was also interested in regional traditions.[18] But his *barchesse* were unusual. The Sanmicheli's *barchesse* were barns, places to store animals and farm implements, but at the Villa Barbaro the arcaded wings were an integral part of the house. On the lower floors they contained kitchens, cellars, and service spaces, and on the upper, suites of rooms for the owners. The covered spaces of *barchesse* were traditionally for farm use, but Palladio specifically referred to the Maser arcades as "loggias," and expected them to be used by the owners "for walking in, eating in, and other pastimes."[19] On the other hand, the fancy end pavilions contained mundane uses such as stables and rooms for pressing and storing wine, so the Maser arcades had a utilitarian side, too. Palladio was usually careful to articulate the functional elements of his villas, but such distinctions are somewhat obscured at Maser. It is likely that as he struggled to incorporate the demands of his clients and fit his design to the existing *castello,* he had to compromise.

Palladio's earliest idea for the villa has survived in the form of a proverbial napkin sketch, crudely drawn on the back of a used sheet and obviously intended for his own use, for it includes three impatient scratches made to unclog his pen.[20] The unfinished drawing is the sort of sketch architects make to get the creative juices flowing. Palladio placed a large entrance hall and a monumental staircase inside the old *castello,* adding separate suites of rooms and a *sala* for each brother in the two arms of the *barchesse.* He located a new vaulted loggia in front of the house, which recalls the theatrical loggia in Alvise Cornaro's garden, and sketched in a large terrace. The germ of the Villa Barbaro plan is already here, and it was refined in a second drawing, made at a later date, in which he eliminated the outdoor room and the grand entrance hall, introduced a cruciform *sala,* and moved the monumental stair to the rear.[21] When the house was built, he dispensed with the elaborate stair altogether, substituting two enclosed staircases—a fancy one for family and guests, and a plain one for servants.

The Villa Barbaro would originally have had public reception rooms on the ground floor (which today contains the living room, the dining room, and a study) and the more private family quarters above. Although the current owners still use the front door, paying visitors enter the villa via an open-air service stair that is located within the arcade. At the top of the stairs, on the landing outside the door, is a box of felt slippers. The box is empty, which means that I have to wait until somebody leaves—an effective method of crowd control.

The Villa Barbaro, which accommodated two households, has two *salas* and no fewer than thirteen rooms, yet it feels unexpectedly intimate. I am standing in one arm of a vaulted, cruciform *sala,* similar to the Pisani *sala* but much smaller and with a proportionately lower ceiling. The old *castello* into which the house was fitted was narrow, so the ends of the cruciform room correspond to the exterior walls and have large windows—French doors, really—surmounted by glazed arches, facing south, west, and east. The abundance of light and view gives the *sala* a cheerful domestic feeling.

Behind me is an arched doorway leading to a room that is called the *Salone.* The *Salone* is the "head" of this figural plan whose "body" is the *casa del padrone* and whose "arms" are the *barchesse.* Square with a tall vaulted ceiling, this is, in effect, a second *sala,* providing access to the rear terrace garden and to suites of rooms on each side: Daniele in the east wing, Marc'antonio and his family in the west. The suites are closed to the public, but one can look inside the spacious chambers through a glass door. The inviting room is furnished as a study. The focus of the view from the *Salone* and its adjoining rooms is the nymphaeum, a hemicyclical garden structure with niches containing yet more statues of Olympian gods. In the center is a grotto whence rises the spring that feeds the elaborate water system. Two jets of water spout from the breasts of a nymph that stands above the pediment and splash into a semicircular pool—the "fishpond"— next to a stone terrace enclosed by tall conifers. Despite the

clumsiness of some of Marc'antonio's sculptures, the effect is
magical.

The *Salone* is also called the Sala dell'Olimpico since the
frescoed ceiling contains several images of Olympian gods.
The decoration of this room sets the theme for the rest of the
house. The exact meaning is in dispute, however, for Daniele
Barbaro, who devised the allegorical program, left no explanation, and cinquecento iconography is notoriously difficult to
decipher. For example, art historians have variously identified
the female figure astride a serpent in the center of the ceiling
as representing Divine Love, Divine Wisdom, Providential
Fortune, and Transcendent Grace.[22]

The upper walls of the *Salone* are frescoed with a trompe
l'oeil balcony, rendered in foreshortened perspective. The balcony is peopled with members of Marc'antonio Barbaro's family. On one side are his two elder sons and their pet monkey, and
on the other, his youngest son, his wife, and an old nurse.[23]
Beside them are more pets—a Pekinese and a parrot. Like
most of the frescoed figures, the members of the household are
life-size. Mary McCarthy, for one, found the effect of the family group inexplicably sad. "It is a stage house inside a real
house," she wrote, "an idea that sounds sportive and playful, a
mirror trick, but that is too well executed to be amusing, like a
sort of game, where the children playing it work themselves up
till they begin to cry."[24]

As at the Villa Godi, the frescoes in the house are a mixture
of illusion and reality, of gods and ordinary people, of antique
allegory and visual puns. The walls of some rooms are frescoed
with country landscapes; a ceiling creates the illusion of sky seen
through the arboreal canopy of a vine bower. Classically attired
young women, sometimes identified as muses, stand in niches
holding a variety of musical instruments: a violin, a trombone,

a mandolin, and an unusual boxlike instrument called a Bernaise tambour that looks like a hurdy-gurdy. In addition to Daniele's allegorical scenes, there are occasional comic touches: a brush and a pair of shoes on a windowsill; a small dog half-hidden behind a column. A page boy looks out from behind a half-open door surrounded by an actual stone frame, opposite a corresponding real door.

The frescoes of the Villa Barbaro have been described as "one of the supreme decorative achievements of the Italian Renaissance."[25] They are the work of Paolo Caliari, who was called Veronese, one of several artists from Verona who had been trained by Sanmicheli. Veronese's first villa frescoes were done for Sanmicheli's Villa La Soranza when he was only twenty. He also frescoed parts of Palladio's Palazzo da Porto in Vicenza. Under Daniele Barbaro's direction, Veronese worked on the decoration of the council chamber ceiling in the Doge's Palace, which brought him great fame. Thus when he came to Maser, in the late 1550s, he was not only an experienced painter, he was also familiar with villa decoration, and knew both Palladio and Daniele Barbaro.

There is no evidence that Palladio had a hand in the design of the frescoes. Indeed, the complicated architectural frameworks in some of the rooms alter, rather than simply enhance, the experience of the actual spaces. Perhaps that is why Palladio artfully neglected to credit the painter by name in *Quattro libri* (although a few years later they would work together again in Venice). Thanks to Veronese's masterful frescoes, the Villa Barbaro is probably the most visited of Palladio's villas, which is ironic since it is in many ways the least representative. Palladio's villas are usually surrounded by fields, not gardens. The abundantly decorated exterior lacks the sober, almost ascetic presence of his best work. The somewhat convoluted plan does not demonstrate his usual clarity. Yet whatever awkwardness working with the Barbaro brothers produced, the collaboration seems to have brought out a new side of Palladio. Even if this is not the best resolved of his villas, it is surely the most light-hearted: theatrical, flamboyant, exuberant—and happy.

An Immensely Pleasing Sight

ell, it had to happen. The large gates of the Villa Badoer are chained and padlocked. The forecourt in front of the house is littered with construction debris and crisscrossed by power cables casually slung from temporary posts. An improvised shed made out of sheets of corrugated metal stands forlornly next to a beautiful stone fountain. The pristine lawn that I've admired in photographs is now beaten earth overgrown with clumps of weeds. A large signboard announces Lavori di Restauro e Manutenzione—restoration and maintenance work. The sign says that the *lavori,* which apparently started five years ago, are due to be completed next month, and indeed, despite the disorder of the forecourt, the house itself is freshly plastered and painted. There does not appear to be a last-minute rush, however—it's ten o'clock in the morning on a Friday yet the place is deserted.

The house stands on the banks of the narrow Scortico River in the center of the village of Fratta Polesine, in a region that was the southern extremity of the Venetian Republic. The Villa Badoer is, in many ways, the classic Palladio villa. This house has it all: an impressive portico, a noble pediment supported by six giant Ionic columns, a monumental staircase, and two majestic curved loggias that form quarter circles on each side of the forecourt.

An unpaved lane runs beside the house, across from an open shed belonging to a neighboring farm. A burly man working on a piece of machinery looks up. I explain that I am interested in the villa.

"They've been spending money on the repairs for years," he says gruffly.

I hear the displeasure in his voice. Actually, I'm happy the house is being taken care of, but I don't want to get into an argument, so I nod my head understandingly. Mollified, he unbends.

"Go around there"—he points—"you'll be able to see the back."

At the end of the lane, flat, treeless fields stretch out to the horizon. The dark, cultivated earth comes right up to a tall wall that hides the villa from view. I walk beside the wall down a track as far as an opening, a counterpart to the front gate. This, too, is locked, but I can look in.

The walled area in the rear of the house is about the same size as the forecourt. It is even more of a mess, recently dug up and dotted with piles of earth. There are stacks of construction materials—drainpipes, lumber, concrete blocks—as well as a parked truck and a cement mixer. No workmen in sight. Architecturally, this side of the house is unimpressive—just rows of shuttered windows without frames or pediments. The unrelieved, white stucco façade is as plain and unadorned as an International Style villa of the 1920s. *Quattro libri* shows a portico on the back of the house, which would have made a front-back arrangement of recessed and projecting porticoes comparable to the Villa Cornaro. Without the portico the rear of the villa looks incomplete.

I briefly consider climbing over the gate, but it's too high. Retracing my steps, I meet the farmer again.

"It's closed," I say. "Is there any way that I can get in?"

"Try the front," he says, adding something that I can't understand.

I protest that the front is locked, too, but he waves me on encouragingly and returns to his work. The front gates are very tall, with spiky tops that resemble spears. Nothing to be done here, I think, pulling disconsolately on the padlock. It falls open! I look around—there is no one in the street. Quickly unwrapping the chain, I open the gate and slip in.

Feeling nervous, I hurry across the forecourt. A small door next to the entrance stairs is ajar. The basement is a series of rooms spanned by broad vaults supported on brick walls. The plastered ceilings are painted white and the interior is surprisingly bright, lit by windows cut high into the vaults. The basement housed "the kitchen, cellars, and other places of practical use," according to Palladio.[1] One of the rooms has a large fireplace—this must have been the kitchen—and the rest are bare, except for sawhorses and scattered power tools.

A stair leads to the main floor, which is murky since most of the windows are shuttered. A piece of scaffolding stands in one corner. The room smells of fresh plaster. There are ghostly outlines of white pails and polyethylene sheets where a section of wall is being repaired. The atmosphere is different from my other visits. With the empty rooms and the construction debris the house appears unclothed, as it must have done when it was brand-new, centuries ago.

The shutters in the two far rooms are open, and the frescoes—"of brilliant inventiveness by Giallo Fiorentino," according to Palladio—are plainly visible, although somewhat deteriorated.[2] The architectural framework is simple, almost severe. In one room, the entire lower portion of the wall is painted to resemble marble panels, and the upper is divided into vertical strips by closely spaced faux pilasters supporting a painted entablature; in another room, the vertical panels extend from floor to ceiling. The subjects, rendered with an air of stylized fantasy, are ancient gods and goddesses as well as grotesques. The panels are painted in a flattened manner without trompe l'oeil effects, and are surrounded by decorative borders, which makes them resemble delicate wall hangings or banners. The effect of this ordered, geometrical composition is considerably less scenographic than Veronese's lush frescoes at Maser. It also directly complements the architecture, which could not have displeased Palladio.

It doesn't take me long to see all the rooms. Despite its grand loggias and imposing portico, the Villa Badoer is a small house with only two rooms and two little *camerini* on each side of the narrow *sala,* which reminds me of the center hall of an American Colonial house. The floor plan is not one of Palla-

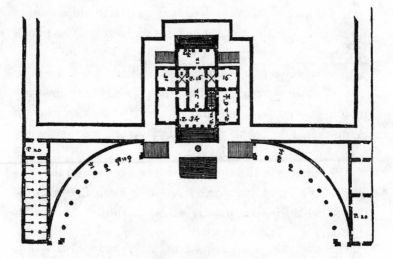

PLAN OF VILLA BADOER, FROM *QUATTRO LIBRI*

dio's best: the large rooms can be reached directly only by
going outside through the portico, and the intimate *camerini* are
little more than passageways. This awkward arrangement is
similar to that of the Villa Poiana, but in the intervening decade
Palladio had developed much more sophisticated plans, such as
La Malcontenta and the Villa Cornaro, and it is unclear why he
went back to this earlier layout.

There are fireplaces only in the two larger rooms. Unlike the
Barbaro fireplaces, for which Marc'antonio created fantastically
carved mantels, these have austere stone surrounds. As far as I
can see, this is the only dressed stone in the interior. With the
exception of two vaulted *camerini,* the eighteen-foot ceilings of
the rooms and the *sala* are flat with closely spaced beams. The
details of this house are distinctly on the plain side compared to
the elaborately decorated Villa Barbaro. Palladio, perhaps breath-
ing a sigh of relief, has returned to simpler ways.

The wide brick staircase—there is only one—continues
from the main floor to the attic. At the landing there is a window looking out onto the entrance portico. Palladio usually
reserved such spacious and well-lit stairs for two-story villas.
Since there were few rooms on the main floor, perhaps guests
were expected to sleep upstairs, although Palladio specifically
referred to the attic as a "granary."[3] Unfortunately the door to
the attic is barred, and the padlock is firmly locked. I descend
the stairs all the way to the basement and go back outside.

I keep expecting someone to show up and chase me away,
but it's as empty as before. The most unusual feature of the *cortile* is the pair of curved loggias that seem to embrace it like two
arms. Unlike the arcaded *barchesse* of the Trevigiana, these are
not barns. Instead, the freestanding structures resemble the porticoes of the Villa Pisani. The design is simplicity itself: a clay-
tiled shed roof spanning between a rear brick wall and a

colonnade. From a distance, the Tuscan columns looked small next to the towering portico, but close-up they are huge–fourteen feet tall, with massive shafts that are at least two feet in diameter. The columns have no bases but stand directly on the ground. The pavement inside the loggia is made of rounded cobblestones like an ancient Roman street in Pompeii. Vasari described the porticoes as "very beautiful and fantastic."[4] The sinuous curved space is a startling contrast to the rigorous rectangular geometry of the house.

The curving back wall is blank, save for a door-size gate. It leads to an open-air courtyard with an odd triangular shape, the walls meeting the bulging curve in tightly squeezed angles. I am reminded of the enigmatic cylindrical forms in the buildings of Louis Kahn, but that is reading too much into it; for Palladio this was merely a leftover space, the result of combining the curved loggia with an outbuilding containing "the rooms of the estate manager, the accountant, the stables, and other offices essential for an estate."[5]

A second gate opens to the rear yard. The sides and back of the villa are unremarkable, almost banal. Palladio wrote that "the cornice runs around the house like a crown," but all that is left of the regal effect are the blocky modillions under the eaves and a single, thin molding, or fascia, a few feet below.[6] In addition, the side wall is marred by two chimney flues that appear to be the same vintage as the house (Palladio usually hid flues inside the thick walls). There is another unusual feature: the house is surrounded on three sides by a raised brick terrace. Palladio illustrated this in *Quattro libri* and called it a "pedestal." In fact, this is not a base but a bulwark. The flat Polesine plain, which was recently dredged marshland, was prone to flooding by the mighty Po River, so Palladio built the basement entirely aboveground and added this massive earthwork to reinforce the basement walls.

Recrossing the triangular courtyard, I return to the curved loggia. An arched opening at the end closest to the house leads directly to a tall flight of steps. An elaborate system of stairs and landings, edged by decorative balustrades, not only provides access to the portico and joins the house to the loggias, but also connects to the brick terrace on the sides and back of the villa. The many landings provide a theatrical setting, and one can imagine the staircase functioning as a viewing platform for musical or dramatic performances.

A final flight of broad stairs leads to the portico, whose pediment is supported by six tall Ionic columns. A giant temple front atop a flight of stairs has become such a familiar sight to us that it's hard to imagine how striking it must have appeared to Palladio's clients. Evidently it appealed to them, for he used this motif over and over again, on city houses as well as villas. There were many permutations: four or six or even eight columns; Doric, Ionic, or Corinthian orders; projecting (like La Malcontenta); flat against the façade (like the Villa Barbaro); or recessed, as it is here. The giant portico in all its forms became a Palladio trademark, and the most imitated of all Palladian motifs, a standard feature of British country houses, large and small. In America, the best-known Palladian portico is undoubtedly that of the White House in Washington, D.C. This building has a convoluted pedigree. James Hoban, an Irish architect and a protégé of George Washington, won the competition to build the President's House in 1792, with a design based on Kildare House in Dublin. (He added the portico when he rebuilt the house after it was burned down by the British during the War of 1812.) Kildare House had been designed by Richard Castle, a German

THE PORTICO AND STAIRS OF THE VILLA BADOER
ARE AMONG PALLADIO'S MOST MONUMENTAL.

expatriate architect (perhaps from Kassel) who is generally credited with introducing Palladianism to Ireland. Castle, in turn, based his work on Campbell, who looked to Inigo Jones. And Jones's first portico was the one that he designed for a brewhouse on the grounds of James I's new residence in New-market, shortly after returning from his Italian journey.[7]

Between 1776 and 1783, the Vicentine architect Ottavio Bertotti-Scamozzi published a four-volume compilation of Palladio's works that included measured drawings of most of the surviving buildings. The elevations of the Villa Badoer show an inscribed masonry pattern, which would have softened the rather sterile effect of plain white stucco. A discerning observer, Bertotti-Scamozzi characterized the villa as having "an air of magnificence which is surprising."[8] *Surprising* is exactly the right word. The house has a small and rather awkward floor plan, a rudimentary *sala*, flat ceilings, unpretentious frescoes, almost no stone details, and undecorated fireplaces. Yet it also boasts a majestic portico, elaborate exterior staircases, and, of course, the curved loggias. Palladio generally pitched his architecture at a consistent intensity: manly simplicity at the Villa Poiana; lordly magnificence at La Malcontenta; and archaeological refinement at the Villa Barbaro. By these standards, the Villa Badoer is strik-ingly *in*consistent.

Given Palladio's concern for *convenienza,* one can only sur-mise that the villa's unexpected blend of modesty and extrava-gance had something to do with his client. We do not know much about "the magnificent Signor Francesco Badoer." Despite Palladio's characteristically high-flown accolade, he has been described by a modern historian as "a modest figure whose public career was devoid of outstanding episodes."[9] Although he served the Republic as a senator and a member of the ruling council, Badoer belonged to an undistinguished branch of a famous Venetian family. The second of three surviving sons, he received a modest inheritance when his father died but married well—his wife, Lucietta Loredan, was wealthy. In 1538, Lucietta's only brother, Zorzi, the head of the family, died at twenty-six. He left no heirs and no will. Following the custom of the time, the bulk of the vast Loredan fortune, which consisted of palazzos and warehouses in Venice and several estates on the *terraferma,* was divided among his brothers-in-law: his widow's two brothers, and his two sisters' husbands. It took ten years to sort out the complicated inheritance, which left Francesco Badoer owner of 460 acres of farmland in the Polesine. The estate was exceptionally valuable since the region had recently undergone massive drainage and reclamation that turned it into the breadbasket of the Republic. Badoer must have been excited by this windfall, but at the same time he was a cautious man, for it was another eight years before he built a house. The site was a seven-acre plot in Fratta, next to the newly dredged Scortico River, which provided easy access to Venice.

The Villa Badoer was designed in 1556, and construction started the following year.[10] This was a busy period for Palladio. In Vicenza, he continued to oversee the building of the Basilica

VILLA BADOER

and two new palazzos, one for Count Giovanni Valmarana and another for his old client Bonifacio Poiana. There were several new Vicentine villa clients—the Counts Odoardo and Theodoro Thiene (relatives of the brothers for whom he had earlier designed a villa at Quinto), the Counts Francesco and Lodovico Trissino (no relations to Giangiorgio Trissino), and Signor Francesco Repeta. Thanks to the patronage of the Barbaro brothers, Palladio's reputation among high-born Venetians continued to grow. In 1559, Sanmicheli died, leaving Palladio as the leading architect of the *terraferma,* and second only to Sansovino in the Republic.

Palladio did not have an office staff in the modern sense, although at this time he was assisted by his sons. The eldest, Leonida, has been identified as the draftsman of several drawings and is usually referred to by historians as an architect; Marc'-antonio, a stone carver (who died in the 1560s), also helped with drawings; and Silla, the youngest, appears to have been a kind of secretary.* In addition, Palladio's nephew Marc'antonio, also a stone carver, occasionally lent a hand. Palladio's personal responsibilities did not end with providing plans and details to the builders and masons. He negotiated with contractors on behalf of the client, kept accounts, ordered materials, and generally oversaw the work. The last was important, since the *all'antica* style was a novelty in the out-of-the-way places where his villas were built, and it needed his close supervision to ensure that the classical details were carried out correctly. In that regard, Palladio also functioned as a teacher. For example, his description of his own simple method of making the gentle tapering, or entasis, of a column sounds like the sort of practical advice he might give to a provincial stonemason.

*Palladio's other son, Orazio, was studying law.

I usually make the profile of this swelling like this. I divide the shaft of the column into three equal parts and leave the third at the bottom plumb vertical; beside the lowest point of the column I place on edge a very thin ruler as long as the column or a little longer, and take that part which extends from the lower third upward and curve it until the end reaches the point of diminution at the top of the column under the neck: in line with that curvature, I mark it, so that I obtain a column which is a little swollen in the middle and tapers very gracefully.[11]

Paolo Gualdo, who knew Palladio in later life, gave a particularly endearing picture of the architect on the building site: "He kept [his workmen] constantly cheerful, treating them with so many pleasant attentions that they all worked with the most exceptional good cheer. He eagerly and lovingly taught them the best principles of the art, in such a way that there was not a mason, stone cutter, or carpenter, who did not understand the measurements, elements, and rules of true architecture."[12]

Fratta is about fifty miles from Vicenza, which is a long ride on horseback, and since the Badoer commission was relatively small, it has been suggested that Palladio may not have closely supervised the construction.[13] If that was so, the local builders must have followed the plans with exceptional care, for the drawings in *Quattro libri* and the finished house are remarkably alike. The curved loggias are slightly shorter—six bays instead of ten—than those shown in the treatise, but this may simply have been the result of fitting the house onto a tight site. It is not known why the rear portico was never finished. Perhaps Badoer changed his mind in midconstruction, for there are attic and basement windows in the spaces that would have been occupied by the portico and its stairs. There are no surviving design drawings or sketches of the Villa Badoer, so it's impossible to be certain about such changes, which may simply reflect a client torn between magnificence and frugality, wishing to "put on a good front"—and saving money in the back. There may be another explanation. Two coats of arms are frescoed over the front door of the villa, the Badoer and the Loredan. Francesco Badoer and Zorzi Loredan had been friends, so it was natural for the grateful villa-builder to commemorate his benefactor. What is odd is that the two crests are of equal size and intertwined. It would have been customary for the Badoer crest to be dominant, unless, of course, it was Lucietta who insisted on equal billing for her brother—and herself. This suggests a strong-willed and perhaps ambitious woman. Is it farfetched to imagine that the striking architectural contrasts in the Villa Badoer reflect the wishes of a second client, one who could claim that the finances to build at all came through her line? It would hardly be the first time that a husband and wife made conflicting demands on their architect.

Was it Lucietta who encouraged Palladio to incorporate the impressive curved loggias into his design? He had invented this device a few years before the Villa Badoer, in 1554, when he was designing a villa for Cavaliere Leonardo Mocenigo, a valued Venetian client.[14] The Villa Mocenigo was a house planned around a courtyard, like the Villa Sarego, and in his preliminary sketch plan Palladio drew a square-doughnut, with the formal entrance, from the Brenta canal, through a rectangular U-shaped *cortile* flanked by straight *barchese*. After finishing the plan Palladio must have had second thoughts, for on top of the *barchessa* he drew a curved loggia. One can sense the excitement of discovery in this hurried scrawl. The magnificent Mocenigo villa on the Brenta canal took about ten years to build. Since the house was demolished in 1835, we cannot be sure of its final design; Palladio's last sketch plan shows curved loggias on the entrance

THE VIEW FROM ONE OF THE CURVED LOGGIAS
OF THE VILLA BADOER DELINEATES THE COMPLEXITY
AND RICHNESS OF PALLADIO'S STAIR DESIGN.

side and rectangular loggias on the rear, but the plan in *Quattro libri* has curved loggias on both sides. Inigo Jones saw the villa in 1613, after the house had been drastically remodeled by Mocenigo's son but when the curved loggias were still intact. "This villa is otherwise ordered for I saww yt and yt is les and as I remember hath these circular loggias," he noted.[15] He was so impressed by the "circular loggias" that he used them in a design for a country house in Northamptonshire.[16]

Palladio wrote that curved loggias "make an immensely pleasing sight," and used them several times.[17] They are a perfect blend of utility and delight. Like a *barchessa,* they provide a sheltered space for various activities, but they are not parts of barns, serving chiefly as covered walkways, linking the house to distant outbuildings. Architecturally, the low loggias create an attractive setting that leads the eye to the higher pedimented temple front, which is the center of the composition. By curving the loggias, Palladio also achieved a startlingly novel effect: parallax—that is, the experience of the ever-shifting views between the staggered columns as one walks around the curve. Palladio was obviously influenced by his recent visit to the Villa Giulia in Rome, whose large hemicycle faces the garden, but his use of low, curved loggias to define a welcoming entrance court as well as to dramatize the main building was entirely original.

Since the Villa Mocenigo has been demolished, and both the Villa Trissino and the Villa Thiene at Cicogna—the other Palladio villas with curved loggias—were never completed, the remote Villa Badoer is the only surviving example of Palladio's curved loggias. However, thanks to Inigo Jones—and to the designs in *Quattro libri*—circular loggias became one of the most popular British Palladian motifs. Robert Adam and James Gibbs both used curved loggias in country houses, and through Gibbs's treatise, the device migrated to America, where it was

adopted by eighteenth-century planters. Mount Airy in Rich-
mond County, one of the largest Virginia plantation houses, has
enclosed curved loggias leading to outbuildings. George Washington built curved loggias when he expanded Mount Vernon.
The delicate open loggias lead to outbuildings containing the
kitchen and servants' quarters.[18] Mount Vernon incorporates
other Palladian elements: a large pediment over the entrance; a
rear portico that serves as a grand garden piazza, or porch; and
a beautiful *serliana* window in the main dining room. The
contemporary American architect Allan Greenberg, who
admires Washington, has built a handsome modern version of
Mount Vernon in Connecticut.[19] The outbuildings contain a
pool house and staff quarters. In another house with a distinctly
Palladian plan, Greenberg enclosed the curved loggias to make
a kitchen and a garden room, and used the outbuildings for a
bedroom suite and the garages.[20] The two wings embrace a
gravel entrance court and still "seem like arms, to gather in those
who approach the house," as Palladio poetically wrote more
than four centuries ago.[21]

Palladio's impact on classical architecture was decisive. He
developed a simple set of architectural elements (vocabulary)
and straightforward rules (grammar) that inspired and were used
by succeeding generations of architects. In that regard, his
influence on the language of building is comparable to the lasting impact that William Shakespeare has had on the English language. Palladio and Shakespeare both belong to the sixteenth
century—Palladio was born in 1508, Shakespeare in 1564—yet,
like the playwright, the architect does not seem a distant figure.
Not because of his buildings, which relatively few people have
seen, but rather because his way of making architecture—with
noble porticoes and welcoming curved loggias—has become
our own.

*   *   *

The front doors to the Villa Badoer are more than twelve feet high, surrounded by a beautiful carved stone frame. Above the doors are the intertwined *stemmi* of the Badoer and the Loredan, and on each side frescoed grotesques of welcoming jesters surmounted by festoons; larger panels are repeated over the two smaller doors that lead to the rectangular rooms on either side. The portico ceiling consists of extremely deep wooden coffers, mimicking the masonry coffers of ancient Roman vaults.

The floor of the portico is raised high above the ground and provides a vantage point overlooking the courtyard. Directly in front of the villa gates is a small bridge, and on the other side of the Scortico River the busy shopping street of Fratta. It's nearing lunchtime, and there are people on the sidewalks. Suddenly I feel vulnerable and exposed, an interloper who has wandered onto the stage.

I slip out of the front gate, replacing the chain, and look for a place to eat. Sure enough, a sign advertises a Ristorante Palladio. The large dining room is full of workers. A noisy group of fifteen or more men with ruddy faces and overalls occupies a long table in the center; the rest of us, alone or in pairs, sit at smaller tables. No menu is offered, and for ten minutes nothing happens. Service in such local eateries—the Italian equivalent of American diners—is usually pretty quick. Suddenly a flurry of waiters appears, wheeling carts loaded with steaming plates. They fan out into the room bringing us the first course. There is a lull while we dispose of the dishes—gnocchi for me—and soon after the empty plates are whisked away, a second convoy of carts appears. This time the choice is between fish, chicken, and a dish that I don't recognize. I've treated myself with the gnocchi, so I virtuously opt for the fish—some sort of small perch or trout—even though I dislike picking bones out of my teeth. A final cart carries desserts, and I choose something that resembles flan.

The noise in the room has diminished considerably, in inverse proportion to the rising general level of contentment. I finish a cup of espresso that dampens the effect of a half-liter of wine and call for the bill. The waiter brings a small, tulip-shaped glass of clear liquid.

"Signore," he says with a flourish.

It is not a question. Not wishing to appear rude, I accept the complimentary drink. The grappa is delicious.

Leaving the restaurant considerably lighter-headed—and heavier-bodied—than I was when I arrived an hour ago, I walk down the street. Passing the villa, which still appears to be empty, I have a sudden urge to go back in and take a second look. But while I was eating someone has secured the padlock. Was my ingression observed? Or was the man in the lane really the caretaker? I mentally tip my hat to him, and make my way back to the car.

Emo

he back of the Villa Emo at Fanzolo looks out over a vast, featureless lawn, ending in a line of trees, that has replaced the "square garden of eighty campi trevigiani, through the middle of which runs a stream that makes the site very pretty and delightful," as it was described by Palladio.[1] Beyond the trees lies the plain of the Trevigiana, flat as a billiard table, a patchwork of plowed fields, hedgerows, and irrigation ditches. It is a hazy day, otherwise I could see the foothills of the Dolomites far to the north. In the same direction, only seven miles away, is the Villa Barbaro.

So close and yet so far. The rear of Barbaro is characterized by a secret garden with an ornate nymphaeum and a tinkling fountain; the back façade of Emo is almost bleak. There is no portico nor, according to *Quattro libri,* was one intended; no pediment, no columns or pilasters, no *serliana,* no thermal window, not even the usual line of modillions beneath the eaves—no classical motifs of any kind. The simplest of fascias, or horizontal bands, marks the division between the tall basement and the main floor. The window openings don't have frames. Someone has painted the shutters green, but the touch of color only serves to emphasize the plainness of the architecture. The house is flanked by two lower wings whose backs are a utilitarian assortment of doors and windows. The roofs are punctuated by more than a dozen stubby chimneys. At the end of each long wing is a dovecote in the form of a squat watchtower.

The building is astonishingly long, stretching about four hundred feet between the two towers. The left wing shows signs of once having been a warm ocher color, but its plaster walls, long without paint, are dark with patches of mold. Yet the weather-beaten condition, while hardly charming, does not undermine the architect's intentions, quite the opposite. This is the most antique of Palladio's villas, but instead of recalling the ancient city of majestic temples and monuments, it makes me think of another Rome: the orderly world of frugal military engineers, hard-traveling centurions, and implacable colonial administrators. This could easily be a barracks outpost in one of the far-flung reaches of the empire. The architectural historian Vincent Scully called Emo "ruthless," which accurately describes its soldierly, unsentimental soul.[2]

A gravel path takes me to a curving double stair—an eighteenth-century addition that replaced the original straight stair—in the precise center of the house. The stair leads to a pair of doors that open into the *sala*. The imposing room is a large cube, about thirty feet high. My eye is drawn to the ceiling, coffered like a deep egg-crate, which is unique among Palladio's villas. The coffers were discovered in the late 1930s hidden behind an ornate nineteenth-century plaster ceiling.[3] They are unpainted wood, carried on intersecting beams. The entablature and giant fluted Corinthian columns, like the rest of the décor of this dazzling room, are frescoed by Palladio's old collaborator Giambattista Zelotti.

The Emo frescoes bear comparison to those of the Villa Barbaro. Zelotti and Veronese, who were almost the same age, had been apprentices together under Sanmicheli and had jointly decorated Palladio's Palazzo da Porto. But by the 1550s they were going their separate ways. There is no doubt that Veronese, whose fame in Venice came to rival that of Titian and Tintoretto, was the more accomplished painter. But in many ways Zelotti was a better decorator—that is, he was more sensitive to the architecture and more interested in the purely ornamental aspects of his art. Palladio worked with him several times, not only at the Villa Godi and La Malcontenta but also at the Villa Caldogno, the Palazzo Chiericati, and again, here, at the Villa Emo, their happiest collaboration.

It's easy to see Palladio's hand in the design of the frescoed architectural elements. The lower part of the wall is a faux marble dado that incorporates the doors leading into the side rooms. Prisoners in Michelangelesque poses recline next to piles of war trophies atop the dado ledge. The upper part of the wall contains frescoed niches with bronze statues of gods and goddesses symbolizing the elements; between the niches are lifelike scenes representing manly Roman virtues. Below, frescoed bronze panels depicting military processions allude to ancestral Emo victories over Lutherans and Turks. The festoons of wild roses that are slung between the columns and trail down to the floor form a gay counterpoint to the martial theme.

Above the door that I have just entered is an elaborate wood carving of the Emo coat of arms—alternating diagonals of crimson and silver—set within gilded scrolls and surmounted by the winged lion of St. Mark. Two mailed fists emerge dramatically from the wall on each side, one holding a sword, the other a general's mace crowned by a helmet. The effect is at once magnificent and slightly lugubrious. On the opposite wall, a frescoed ceremonial archway topped by a broken pediment forms a somewhat precarious perch for two reclining, half-clothed maidens representing Abundance and Prudence. Zelotti painted their garments draped casually over the edge of the pediment, throwing complicated shadows on the moldings below. The archway frames the entrance vestibule, whose double doors are filled with translucent leaded-glass panes. The faux marble dado continues into the vestibule, and includes frescoed niches whose allegorical bronze statues of Conjugal Love and Household Economy (a woman holding a roll of accounts) welcome the visitor. The upper part of the walls and the vaulted ceiling depict a charming grape arbor with wooden trelliswork, twining vines, and a hovering winged cherub.

The plan of the Villa Emo is simplicity itself. Eschewing cruciform *salas* and intricate geometry, Palladio returned to the straightforward layout of his second villa, the Villa Valmarana: back-to-back portico and *sala,* sandwiched between suites of rooms lined up one behind the other. The plan is simple but refined: the largest rooms are accessed directly from the *sala;* the medium-size rooms have their own exterior entrances from the portico; the small rooms sit snugly in between. The medium and small rooms have Palladio's favorite proportions—a square, and a square and a half—while the large rooms are a square and two thirds. With great finesse, he placed the two staircases between the loggia and the *sala,* producing a plan that resembles a tic-tac-toe diagram. The main room dimensions in *Quat-*

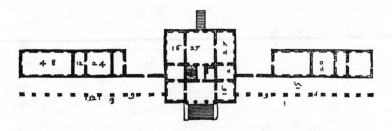

PLAN OF VILLA EMO, FROM *QUATTRO LIBRI*

tro libri are 16 and 27 Vicentine feet, which sounds arbitrary until
I realize that both measures are a multiple of 5⅓ Vicentine feet
(27 feet is five modules rounded-off; the actual dimension in the
house is 26 feet 7 inches, which is almost exactly five modules).⁴
In fact, all the spaces in the Villa Emo are modular: the small
rooms are two by three modules, the medium rooms are three
by three, the large rooms and the portico are three by five, and
the *sala* is five by five. In terms of simple mathematical ratios, this
is the most perfectly resolved of all Palladio's villas, and since it
is very beautiful, it's a compelling argument for simple room
proportions. I'm not sure if the actual size of the module is significant; it was probably merely a convenient way to subdivide
16 feet. Using a module enabled Palladio to achieve dimensional
control. Since workmen did not carry measuring tapes, all
they needed was a stick 5 feet 4 inches long, and a simple set of
instructions: "make the portico three by five sticks, the *sala* five
by five sticks," and so on.*

The large room on the west side of the *sala* is frescoed with
scenes from the life of Hercules. Like all the rooms, it has a flat
ceiling supported by closely spaced beams. Next is a small
room with a proportionately lower ceiling, decorated with
grotesques. This anteroom leads to a square room whose decorative theme is the arts. This room is assumed to have belonged
to the original owner, since his portrait is included in a lunette
over the door. Palladio's client, Leonardo Emo, is also called
Leonardo the Younger, to distinguish him from his illustrious
grandfather. The formidable Leonardo the Elder was a victori-

---

*Frank Lloyd Wright used a house-planning grid—usually two feet
by four feet—that was inscribed in the concrete floor-slab; R. M.
Schindler, who practiced in California in the 1930s, used a four-foot
house module laid out on the building site and keyed to the drawings.

A THRESHING FLOOR LEADS UP TO THE SIMPLE DORIC PORTICO
OF THE VILLA EMO.

ous general in the war, governor of the province of Friuli, *podestà* (mayor) of Verona, and the moving force behind the agricultural development of the Trevigiana. He reclaimed land, dug canals, and built mills. He also introduced the cultivation of *granturco*—corn—recently brought from America, which replaced millet as the Venetian staple and, incidentally, led to the invention of polenta. At the age of sixty-two he retired to his estate at Fanzolo. When he died, he left half of the farm to his namesake and grandson, Leonardo, then seven, who had been living with him since his own father had died. Twenty years later, in 1559, Leonardo commissioned Palladio to design a new country house.

It is always interesting to speculate how a client chooses an architect, whether by a social connection, a recommendation, or a chance encounter. In this case the connection was familial: Leonardo the Younger's mother, Andrianna, was the sister of Francesco Badoer. Since Leonardo was still only twenty-seven—one year beyond his majority—it is possible that his mother not only recommended Palladio but also played a role in the building process. If so, she was a better client than Lucietta Badoer, for Palladio delivered a flawless design. As so often happened, the house was built on the occasion of a marriage—a particularly propitious marriage; Leonardo was betrothed to Cornalia Grimani, a member of a most eminent Venetian family and the direct descendant of a famous doge. Hence the new villa had to proclaim the Emos' own distinguished heritage, not least Leonardo's grandfather's military exploits. This may explain the soldierly appearance of the house, and the martial atmosphere of the *sala* with its war trophies, mailed fists, and manly themes. At the same time, a marriage was a joyful occasion, and Zelotti introduced festive motifs such as the gay floral decorations and the grape arbor in the entrance vestibule. The west rooms were for Leonardo, the east side was for Cornalia, the love story of Venus and Adonis forming a pendant to Hercules, and the myth of Jupiter and Io balancing the Arts. In the first room, a gilded bust of Venus—perhaps also a likeness of Cornalia—looks down from above the door. Distracting loud sounds come from a television monitor in the corner of the cavernous room. It is playing a video recording about the villa, and showing a fireworks display. The flickering little image on the screen is a paltry thing compared to Zelotti's magnificent frescoes.

A small room decorated with grotesques leads to a corner room that serves as the ticket office. An elderly woman sits at a table. I bid her good-bye—this is my second visit in two days—and step outside.

The Emo portico is impressive. It rises the full height of the house, including the attic—about thirty feet. The ceiling, like that of the *sala,* consists of deep wooden coffers. The four—only four—giant columns across the front have puzzled scholars since Bertotti-Scamozzi, for they are Doric but with a plain Tuscan entablature, and their proportions and intercolumniation are neither exactly Doric nor Tuscan. Once more, Palladio is bending the rules. In any event, this is the simplest order of any of his villa porticoes, and it gives the house a moving, austere dignity. The walls of the loggia are richly frescoed with corresponding columns and frescoed door and window frames, draped with festoons of flowers. Zelotti's cheerful depictions of gods and goddesses, including Ceres, the goddess of plenty, soften Palladio's severe architecture.

In place of the usual monumental stair, the Villa Emo has a broad ramp. Although Sansovino used a gently ramped entrance at the Villa Garzoni, ramps were uncommon in Veneto country houses, and the purpose of the Emo ramp has been a matter of conjecture. One historian has suggested that a ramp made it easier to roll casks or drag bundles into the house; another has surmised that the south-facing ramp was used for drying newly threshed grain; yet another guesses that it was an equestrian ramp, allowing riders to dismount at the front door.[5] None of these explanations is convincing; kitchens and cellars were in the basement, not on the main floor, and the flat landing halfway up the ramp would be superfluous for both drying grain and for riding. I think the ramp was intended for entering the house on foot, and was another of Palladio's continuing experiments with ceremonial entrances. After trying ramped stairs in the Villa Cornaro, he built a true ramp at Emo, which both complements the villa's hard, Roman appearance and provides a particularly regal way of ascending to the portico.

At the foot of the ramp is a large paved area that is usually referred to as a threshing floor. Palladio recommended that threshing floors should be close enough to a villa so that the work could be overseen, but he also specified that they "must not be too close to the owner's house because of the dust."[6] The Emo threshing floor seems a little close, on the other hand the paved area also serves as a grand entranceway leading up to, and visually balancing, the wide ramp.

The arcaded wings are much longer than those of the Villa Barbaro and were intended uniquely for farm functions. Built in the form of *barchesse,* they perfectly evoke Palladio's ideal of

VILLA EMO

THE BARCHESSA OF THE VILLA EMO PROVIDED A PROTECTED
OUTDOOR SPACE FOR WORKING, UNLOADING WAGONS,
AND STORING FARM IMPLEMENTS.

farm buildings in close proximity to the gentleman's house. "The covered outbuildings for items belonging to the farm should be built for the produce and animals and connected to the owner's house in such a way that he can go everywhere under cover so that neither the rain nor the blazing summer sun would bother him as he goes to supervise his business; this arrangement will also be of the greatest use for storing wood under cover and the infinite variety of other objects belonging to the farm that would be destroyed by the rain and sun," he wrote, adding almost offhandedly, "besides which these porticoes are extremely attractive."[7] And so they are. The arcades recall a cloister, the monastic effect heightened by the simplicity of the design: no *mascherone,* no keystones over the arches, and simple stone imposts. The flanking *barchesse* serve as foils to the only classical element of the entire house, the elevated portico, whose four columns support a simple entablature and pediment. The tympanum contains figural decoration: two winged victories holding a shield bearing the Emo coat of arms. Otherwise, the front has the same hard simplicity as the rear.

Palladio's description of the Villa Emo in *Quattro libri* is terse, only seven lines. Indeed, he has less to say about this house than about almost any of the others, and although he mentions the back garden—and Zelotti's frescoes—he is more closemouthed than usual about his own intentions. Yet his very brevity and the beautifully spare layout of the page are revealing. Emo is like a quickly drawn sketch, its basic elements distilled from two decades of practice, nothing extraneous allowed to interfere with the essence of the idea. This is the work of a confident master in full possession of his powers. In many ways, the Villa Emo appeals to me most of all the Palladio villas. It is neither a retreat nor a *villa suburbana,* but a true farm. Commodity, firmness, and delight are in perfect balance; truly, nothing can be added,

nothing taken away. The relationship between the arcades and
the house is subtly controlled by the two perfectly proportioned
dovecote towers, which emphasize the predominance of the
central block. There is not even a hint of grandiosity; instead the
sober architecture is sublime, calm, dignified. It is also extremely
simple. Like Beethoven during his so-called third period, Palladio's full command of his art allowed him to achieve his
aims with utterly uncomplicated means. (In the last decade of
his life, he developed a rich and ornate style, but that was after
he stopped building villas.) In the Villa Emo he returned to the
minimalist classicism of his youth, further enhanced by his
profound knowledge of antiquity. Rather than simply mimic
classical forms, however, he did something more subtle, and
more affecting: he evoked an intangible whiff of the Roman
past, the remembered fragrance of a distant time.

Leonardo Emo, who never became a soldier but served the
Republic as an administrator in banking and public finance,
clearly loved this house.[8] He died at only fifty-four in one of the
great plagues that decimated the Veneto at the end of the sixteenth century. In his will he had taken the unusual step of
authorizing his wife to dispose of any of his property if the need
arose, "But I beg that no part of the villa in Fanzolo be sold."*[9]

In 1565, Zelotti completed the frescoes, and Leonardo and Cornalia were married. The 1560s saw Palladio's practice expand,
finally, to Venice. His first Venetian commission was modest
enough. The abbot of the Benedictine religious order, whose
church and monastery were on the island of San Giorgio Mag-

---

*Leonardo Emo's request was honored for more than four hundred
years. In 2001, in what must have been a wrenching decision for the
Emo descendants, the villa was put up for sale.

giore opposite the Piazzetta di San Marco, asked him to complete an unfinished refectory and its vestibule. Palladio added lofty vaults and thermal windows, creating a dramatic setting for a painting by Veronese. The severe, white space impressed Vasari, who met Palladio in Venice in 1566, and thought the refectory "very large and most beautiful."[10] At about the same time the order of Lateran canons commissioned Palladio to enlarge the convent of Santa Maria della Carità (today the Accademia di Belle Arti). For this large project, Palladio designed something unusual: "I endeavored to make this house like those of the ancients."[11] The new convent was based on his reconstruction of a Roman town house, with a Corinthian atrium ringed by colossal Composite columns, connected to a three-story cloister and a refectory. It is not clear exactly how much of this ambitious scheme was realized since only a few fragments, including one side of the cloister and a splendid spiral staircase, survived a 1630 fire. The first two stories of the cloister are open arcades (today glazed), with half columns— Ionic over Doric; the third, which contained the monks' cells, is enclosed and has flat Corinthian pilasters. The beautifully built arcades are unplastered brick with stone trim—these are the brick columns that so impressed Sir Henry Wotton. The effect is at once sensuous and severe. Goethe, who saw the Carità in 1786 during his tour of Italy, revisited the cloister several times and considered it the best of Palladio's buildings. "The funniest thing is the way I expound all this to my hired servant," he wrote in his diary, "because when you're full of a thing, you can't stop talking about it, and you keep looking for some new angle from which to show how wonderful it is."[12]

Palladio's strict interpretation of the *all'antica* style was a novelty in Venice. While Vasari, a sophisticated Florentine, found the convent "marvelous" and "the most notable" of Pal-

ladio's projects in the city, the plain, almost ascetic style did not
appeal to the average Venetian, judging from a piece of popular doggerel that has survived from this period.[13]

> *Non va il Palladio per male a puttane;*
> *Che se tal volta pur gli suol andare*
> *Lo fa, perchè le esorta a fabbricare*
> *Un atrio antico in mezzo Carampane.*[14]

> Palladio does not go to whores for iniquity;
> But even if at times he plays the rake,
> 'Tis but to encourage them to make
> In mid-Carampane, an atrium of antiquity.

What is striking about the verse, which attests to Palladio's
celebrity, is that though it lewdly ridicules his obsession with
ancient architecture—the Carampane was Venice's brothel district—it does so with affection. "A nature so amiable and gentle, that it renders him well-beloved with everyone," observed
Vasari.[15]

Palladio's next major commission came from yet another of
Venice's many religious orders. San Francesco della Vigna was
a Franciscan church in the eastern district that had been built
by Sansovino thirty-five years earlier, but whose front façade
remained unfinished due to disagreements between the various
sponsors of the church. Finally, the responsibility for complet-
ing the work fell on the patriarch of Aquiléia, Giovanni Grimani. Undoubtedly influenced by Daniele Barbaro, his
appointed successor, and perhaps also encouraged by his young
cousin Cornalia Grimani (soon to be Emo), he dismissed
Sansovino and gave the job to Palladio.

The imposing façade of Istrian stone facing the *campo* has

nothing to do with Sansovino's church—it is all Palladio. This was his opportunity to shine, and he made the most of it. He set out to solve a problem that had bedeviled Renaissance architects for a hundred years: how to adapt ancient Roman temple architecture to a Christian church. Architectural propriety required that there be a relationship between the façade and what lay behind it, yet it was unclear how a classical temple front could be successfully combined with a tall nave flanked by lower side aisles. Using his knowledge of antiquity and his extensive experience designing villa porticoes, Palladio resolved the apparent contradiction. He juxtaposed two overlapping temple fronts of different sizes and scales. A pediment supported on four giant Corinthian columns signified the tall nave, and a lower pediment, carried by shorter columns, signified the aisles (which in this case were actually chapels). The columns of San Francesco are engaged—that is, they are three-quarters round and their connection to the wall is concealed behind the inward curve of their shaft, which makes them appear freestanding. The result is a modulated façade of great sculptural richness but one that is also classically correct, with the large and small orders skillfully combined atop a tall base. While architects since Alberti had been adapting ancient Roman architecture to church façades, no one had ever done it with such authority and aplomb.

Construction started immediately, and when Vasari visited Venice the base was already finished. San Francesco was an important project for Palladio, but it was only a façade. His real breakthrough came when the Benedictines, obviously pleased with their refectory and perhaps galvanized by the boldness of his design for San Francesco, asked him to build an entirely new monastic church to replace the old one at San Giorgio Maggiore. A large church, with grand interior spaces—and an immense building budget—was a true test of a Renaissance architect's powers. Vasari saw the model and predicted, correctly, that the new church "will prove a stupendous and most lovely work."[16] The church combined Palladio's interest in antiquity—the nave resembles a Roman basilica—with a richness and magnificence, inside and out, that all Venetians could admire.

San Giorgio catapulted Palladio into the first rank. As his religious work in Venice increased, he accepted fewer and fewer villa commissions; while he designed fourteen country houses in the 1550s, there were only four in the 1560s. The munificent Leonardo Mocenigo commissioned a second villa, and Palladio produced a similar two-story design for Count Annibale Sarego of Verona, Marc'antonio's brother. For some reason, neither house was built. There was a third two-story house, this one with curious *castello* towers, designed for Count Giovanni Valmarana, for whose brother Palladio was building a palazzo in Vicenza.* All three of these villa designs are rather stodgy, with imposing two-story porticoes but unrefined plans. I have the impression that Palladio accepted these commissions more out of a sense of obligation to faithful clients, or their brothers. His attention was elsewhere. I cannot imagine that, approaching sixty, he was unhappy to give up the hard travel associated with building houses in remote rural locations in exchange for a more settled life in the city. Yet during that eventful and busy decade he found time for one final country-house commission—his last villa.

---

*The Villa Valmarana at Lisiera, outside Vicenza, still exists, although in much altered form, having been almost completely rebuilt after suffering damage in the Second World War (yet worth a visit for its evocative setting).

IX

The Last Villa

he unpaved lane—a track, really—skirts the flank of Monte Bèrico, part of the Bèrici hills that dominate the southern outskirts of Vicenza. The slopes are largely without buildings, so it feels like countryside, although my destination is "less than a quarter of a mile away from the city," as Palladio wrote—a short walk from my hotel.[1] I round a corner and the domed silhouette of a building materializes out of the morning haze. The villa sits on high ground, lightly shrouded by bare tree branches, its architectural details blurred.

The lane joins a paved road and the building disappears from view behind a high stone wall. Halfway down the steep hill a large formal gateway signals the entrance. A caretaker lets me in. The gate is at the bottom of a ramped drive that is cut into the hill like a long slot, defined by two retaining walls, one of which is actually the side of a farm building. The gravel carriageway is edged by cobblestoned walks. The villa looms dramatically at the top of the drive. It has the usual Palladio accouterments: a broad staircase leading to a portico; a tall main floor; an abbreviated attic; statues on the parapet. Its exceptional feature is a squat dome that caps the red-clay-tiled roof.

It is only when I reach the top of the drive that the house exerts its full impact. The portico atop a broad staircase has counterparts on the other two sides and, although I can't see it from here, on the back as well. This square house has not one but four temple fronts! Palladio succinctly explained his reasoning:

> The site is one of the most pleasing and delightful that one could find because it is on top of a small hill which is easy to ascend; on one side it is bathed by the Bacchiglione, a navigable river, and on the other is surrounded by other pleasant hills which resemble a vast theater and are completely cultivated and abound with wonderful fruit and excellent vines; so, because it enjoys the most beautiful vistas on every side, some of which are restricted, others more extensive, and yet others which end at the horizon, loggias have been built on all four sides; under the floor of these loggias and the hall are the rooms for the convenience and use of the family.[2]

VILLA ROTONDA

Simple enough, yet the effect is extraordinary. The location is a low knoll that has been transformed into a grassy podium by a surrounding retaining wall. The land drops away on all sides. The vistas, while hardly as bucolic as in Palladio's day, are still impressive. Since the house itself is raised on a tall basement, it looms prominently against the sky, the top of the bulging dome creating the effect of one hill on top of another. Palladio wrote that he provided the house with four loggias to take advantage of the views, but that simple explanation is disingenuous. For one thing, La Rotonda is actually oriented not to the views but to the sun; the house is turned precisely forty-five degrees to the north-south axis, ensuring that even in winter all rooms receive some sun. For another, he could have responded to the views in different ways. He could have made the front more prominent than the other sides, or combined projecting and recessed porticoes, in the manner of the Villa Cornaro, or done a dozen different things. Instead, he made the four sides identical.

Palladio had been thinking of such a house for a long time. Twenty-five years earlier, at the beginning of his career, he had made a drawing of a square villa with a central *sala* rising up into a domed lantern, a roof structure with windows on four sides.[3] Although the façades in the drawing are not identical, the tall lantern is symmetrical, with four pediments above four thermal windows. In a second version, he made the *sala* octagonal, perhaps influenced by a square house with an octagonal *sala* and two loggias that was illustrated in Serlio's treatise.[4]

For years, Palladio had no occasion to build a domed house, but the idea stuck. He returned to it in a project begun in the late 1550s, a villa for the Trissino brothers, which has already been mentioned. The site, which Palladio called "stunning," was a hilltop near the village of Meledo, on the Guà River. "At the top of the hill should be the circular hall, surrounded by

The Villa Rotonda, on a hilltop on the outskirts of Vicenza, is Palladio's most imitated house.

rooms," he wrote, adding that "because each face of the house has wonderful views, there are four Corinthian loggias."[5] The loggias, however, were not identical; two were projecting, and two were recessed. Moreover, the villa had a definite front, facing a huge forecourt defined by curved loggias and *barchesse* that cascaded down the hill. Had it been built, it would have been Palladio's most spectacular villa; the splendid drawing in *Quattro libri* could be a movie set for *Ben-Hur*. But the ambitious project was abandoned in 1563, with only a part of a *barchessa* completed, when one of the brothers died. Yet another precursor of the domed house on Monte Bèrico was Palladio's historical reconstruction of an ancient sanctuary at Praeneste, which he drew in the late 1560s. The hilly site outside Rome was covered in ruins, terraces, the remains of colonnaded structures, and traces of a small temple at the very summit. He imagined a sort of wedding cake of colonnades and loggias, surmounted by a circular domed temple with four identical Ionic porticoes.[6] Palladio was fascinated by circular temples and illustrated several in *Quattro libri,* including Bramante's beautiful chapel, called the Tempietto, overlooking Rome from Montoria, the only modern building in his treatise, apart from his own work. Thus in a variety of projects the images of domed circular buildings on hilltop sites simmered in his imagination.

Climbing the wide stair between massive abutments on which stand heroic statues, I reach the portico. From up here the view of the Bèrici hills is even more spectacular. The front doors open into a wide vaulted passage. There are rooms on each side, but the focus is the arched entrance into the *sala*. And what a *sala!*—a circular space under a breathtaking hemispherical dome. Not large—about thirty-five feet in diameter—the dome rises to a height of fifty feet, higher than any Palladio *sala,* and has a round hole, or *oculus,* at the top. The most famous domed space in the cinquecento was the Pantheon, then known as La Rotonda, which gave the villa its nickname.[7]

The use of a domed circular space, normally associated with ancient temples and Renaissance churches, in a domestic setting has struck some historians as odd. Certainly, Palladio was aware that the ancient Romans did not use circular rooms in their homes, nor was the dome intended to have religious overtones. The domed *sala,* like his temple porches, is a reminder that he was first an architect interested in form, and second an archaeologist. Moreover, as the images of domed pavilions picturesquely perched on hilltops amply demonstrate, he was an architect with a romantic streak.

While undoubtedly aware of the similarity, Palladio did not play up the resemblance to the Pantheon. For example, he did not design the dome with coffers, like the Roman original, and although the plan of the *sala* is often described as round, it is really a cruciform, with four tall vaulted passages like the arms of a Celtic cross. The quadripartite theme abounds: four passages, four porticoes, four entrances, inside the *sala* four doors leading to four staircases, and above them four windows. Encircling the room, well below the springing of the dome, is a balustraded gallery, accessible from the attic.

Although the *sala* is not artificially lit, it is surprisingly bright. Daylight comes from the doors leading to the porticoes and streams in through the *oculus.* The seven-foot-diameter hole was originally open to the sky—Inigo Jones described a "Net to cover the top Hole to keep out the Flies"—and a perforated stone drain in the shape of a faun's face in the center of the floor allowed rainwater to drop into the basement.[8] It is a shame that the *oculus* is now capped by a small cupola. Palladio once described an ancient Corinthian house as having an "unroofed space in the middle," and the original Rotonda *sala* would have recalled such an atrium, especially for the first thirty or forty years of its life when the dome was unfinished.[9]

I regret that the *oculus* is not open, but in any case Palladio's architectural intentions are somewhat obscured by the florid stucco decorations, plaster figures, and frescoes that cover the underside of the dome. These were carried out in the 1580s and represent different tastes and fashions. So do the showy, billboardlike eighteenth-century frescoes on the lower walls and in the passages. How much more beautiful this evocative space would be with white painted walls forming a neutral backdrop to the carved stone door and window frames.

Walking from room to room, I make a quick circuit of the house. The experience of the identical porticoes with their different views is delightful, a bit like being in a revolving restaurant; the view changes while the architecture stays the same. The round *sala* is surrounded by eight rooms, arranged in four suites. All the rooms have shaped ceilings: low flat-vaults in the small rooms (with *amezati*, or mezzanines, above) and high coved ceilings with elaborate stucco decorations in the larger rooms. Except for the domed *sala*, the interior is surprisingly intimate. "Far more space has been lavished on the stairs and porticoes than on the house itself," wrote Goethe after visiting the villa, adding that the "hall and rooms are beautifully proportioned, but, as a summer residence, they would hardly satisfy the needs of a noble family."[10] That is how it appeared to an eighteenth-century German aristocrat; in fact, with eight rooms and a generous *sala*, La Rotonda is larger than most Palladio villas.* It just doesn't feel overwhelming.

---

*The exterior dimensions of La Rotonda are about 80 by 80 modern feet, compared to roughly 75 by 70 feet for the Villa Emo, and 60 by 80 feet for La Malcontenta.

I return to La Rotonda three days later. It is Saturday morning and misty. Since today the interior is closed to the public,
there are no other visitors. I sit outside and sketch. The overall
conception of La Rotonda is straightforward, yet the exterior
details are anything but simple. The cap of the abutments turns
into a fascia that girdles the house at the level of the main
floor. A very complicated molding, about four feet wide, runs
around the house at the level of the architrave frieze. It consists
of a cyma recta (or ogee molding), a flat fascia, a pulvinated (or
cushion-shaped) molding, and three stepped bands of dimin-
ishing size. This molding, like the others, is made of plastered
brick, except at the corners, where, to guarantee the sharpness
of the profile, Palladio has substituted carved stone. Like the
gently swelling tapering of the columns, this optical refinement is a reminder that Palladio's style, however coolly
rational and historical its roots, was ultimately concerned with
perception and experience.

How many visitors have sat here, marveling at this extraor-

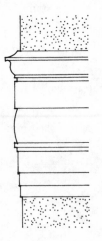

EXTERIOR MOLDING
AT THE VILLA ROTONDA

dinary building? Immediately on his arrival in Vicenza, Goethe hurried up Monte Bèrico to see the house, which he found to be "located just where such a building belongs, the view is unimaginably beautiful." Yet he added a curious comment in his diary: "here the architect was free to do whatever he liked and he almost went a bit too far."[11]

A bit too far; I can see what Goethe meant. At first glance the self-assured Rotonda, with its four identical temple fronts, appears slightly preposterous, a facile tour de force, an architectural parlor trick. "It is not done well," said Samuel Johnson of a dog walking on its hind legs, "but you are surprised to find it done at all." Yet after spending time in and around the villa, under its lofty dome, within its princely porticoes, there is little doubt that, surprising as it may be, the domed house *is* done well. If it's a parlor trick, Palladio the magician is too fast for me. La Rotonda exerts a strange allure, which is why I've come back to look at it again. Goethe, too, was entranced, and returned the following evening; "one more occasion for me to admire his towering genius," he noted.

The most striking characteristic of La Rotonda is, of course, its extreme symmetry, both inside and out. In turning to this form of composition, Palladio, like all Renaissance architects, was influenced by the remains of ancient Roman buildings and by the writings of Vitruvius, who taught that "since nature has designed the human body so that its members are duly proportioned to the frame as a whole, it appears that the ancients had good reason for their rule, that in perfect buildings the different members must be in exact symmetrical relations to the whole general scheme."[12] That is why La Rotonda is so baffling. It is not human at all. It is all fronts, like those spooky two-faced Venetian carnival masks, worn on the face and back of the head. If buildings are supposed to mirror the human body, what sort

of being has four faces? The projecting stair abutments of La
Rotonda stick out like the paws of a great sphinx, the mythical
creature with the head of a woman and the body of a lion. The
analogy strikes me as particularly apt not only because the
porches are Ionic—supposedly the female order—but also
because the four-headed house really is sphinxlike—mysterious,
enigmatic, and a little monstrous.

The very qualities that make La Rotonda a distinctly odd
villa—it is not my favorite—have also made it the most influential Palladio building. This distinction has to do with the idealized geometry of a circle in a square, the domed room, its
iconic pavilionlike quality, and its extraordinary rapport with its
prominent hilltop site. While architects have copied various
Palladian motifs, no single villa of his, indeed, no house anywhere, has had so many distinguished imitators. The first to
have a go was Vincenzo Scamozzi, a young Vicentine who was
Palladio's student at about the time La Rotonda was built.
Scamozzi, something of a prodigy, did not stay a pupil long but
quickly struck out on his own, and though only in his early

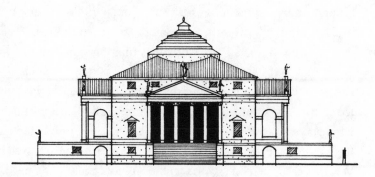

VILLA ROTONDA

twenties was soon receiving commissions for villas and palazzos. In 1576, he was approached by Vettor Pisani, who wanted
a country retreat on the dramatic hilltop site of La Rocca in
the Bèrici hills. This was near Bagnolo, where years earlier Vettor had built a villa with Palladio (who by the 1570s was no
longer accepting villa commissions). Scamozzi's solution was a
Rotonda-like house consisting of a round domed room set in
a square block. Each side has a loggia, but the house is not symmetrical, for there is an Ionic portico on the front and *serliana*
loggias on the back and sides. The handsome villa has the
magisterial presence of its forerunner, and its domed central
room, chaste and without distracting frescoes, is extremely
beautiful. More than thirty years later, Scamozzi designed
another domed villa, the Villa Molin near Padua, which recalls
Palladio's first drawing of a domed house. This time he used a
square central *sala* that rises up into a lantern with four thermal
windows. He again eschewed strict symmetry and provided but
a single portico.

Scamozzi's relationship to Palladio was complicated. As far as
we know, he was the only student to have been taken on by Palladio (other than his own son, Leonida). After Palladio's death,
Scamozzi was generally considered to be the great architect's
successor (Leonida having died some years before), and he was
called upon to complete several unfinished Palladio projects,
including the Teatro Olimpico, an extraordinary theater in
Vicenza, which had been commissioned by the Olympic Academy, of which Palladio was a founding member. Scamozzi also
completed the dome of the Villa Rotonda. During a long and
successful career he designed many buildings: villas for Vicentines and Venetians, the beautiful Palazzo Trissino (now
Vicenza's city hall), and the sweeping Procurazie Nuove on the
south side of the Piazza San Marco in Venice. He also published

AT THE VILLA ROTONDA, PALLADIO DESIGNED FOUR IDENTICAL
PORTICOES OVERLOOKING FOUR DIFFERENT VIEWS.

his own architectural treatise, ambitiously titled *L'idea dell' architettura universale*. The treatise is notable for hardly mentioning Palladio. According to Inigo Jones, who met the sixty-five-year-old Scamozzi in Venice, the architect harbored bitter feelings toward his old master. This may be why he sold Jones and Arundel his entire collection of Palladio drawings, which he must have received from Silla, Palladio's sole surviving son. Scamozzi, who was well-educated, considered himself Palladio's social and intellectual superior, and while his own achievements were considerable, his reputation never equaled that of Palladio, who was always the one visitors like Jones wanted to hear about. In short, Scamozzi was jealous. Though he was an exceptionally gifted architect, like Antonio Salieri he had the misfortune to live in the shadow of a genius.

Jones, too, admired La Rotonda, although he had some reservations about the clay-tile roof, which he thought "does not look well, considering the richness of the Statues, and Beauty of the Building."[13] Characteristically, he did not copy the domed house but used it as a springboard. He made drawings of several villas with domed central halls, though they were not built and likely were studies done for his own amusement. The houses are variations on a theme: one is octagonal with an octagonal central hall; another is round with a round hall; a third has a cruciform plan with an octagonal hall.[14] The resulting triangular and wedge-shaped rooms don't appear very practical. The most interesting design is an octagonal plan with a round hall that, unlike the others, is not domed but open to the sky like a giant atrium.

The Scottish architect James Smith also produced a design for a domed house. Smith, who had been to Italy, introduced the Palladian style to Scotland in the late 1600s in a series of country houses. His domed house was a close copy of La Rotonda, with a circular hall, a similar room arrangement, and four porticoes; the main changes are the addition of more fireplaces and the modification of the porticoes from six columns wide to four. There is no evidence that the house was built, and like Jones, Smith probably made the design as a theoretical exercise.

The four drawings of Inigo Jones's domed houses have survived in William Kent's *Designs of Inigo Jones,* which was published in 1727. By then there were two famous domed houses in England. The first, Mereworth Castle, was designed by the Scottish architect Colen Campbell, who knew James Smith and owned many of his drawings, including the domed house study.[15] The exterior of Mereworth, built in 1725 in Kent, is a close approximation of La Rotonda: the same size, with four identical Ionic porticoes, stucco walls, stone trim, and many of Palladio's details. "I shall not pretend to say, That I have made any Improvements in this Plan from that of *Palladio,*" Campbell wrote somewhat defensively, but he went on to list the advantages of his design, the chief being his ingenious incorporation of twenty-four chimney flues into the double skin of the dome.[16] Although the circular domed room of Mereworth is the formal reception area, the main public space is the so-called Gallery, a long, comfortably furnished room that occupies one entire side of the house; the main floor also includes a dining room and a drawing room. The shape of the dome distinguishes Mereworth from La Rotonda, for it is modeled on the tall dome that Palladio illustrated in *Quattro libri,* not the flatter version that was actually built by Scamozzi.

A second domed house was built a few years later in the outskirts of London by Campbell's aristocratic patron, Lord Burlington, for his own use. Chiswick House was an addition to an existing Jacobean house, and its chief function was to accommodate Burlington's art collection, although the main floor included a bedchamber with a dressing room for Lady Burlington, and the basement housed his private apartment and library (the kitchens were in the main house; there was no attic). Chiswick is an artful blend of Palladio, Jones, and Scamozzi by a talented neophyte (this was Burlington's first architectural work). The plan is a square with an octagonal Jonesian hall. The attractive flattened dome is carried on an octagonal drum like Scamozzi's La Rocca, but instead of an *oculus,* the drum is pierced by four thermal windows like the Villa Molin. The tall Corinthian porch distinctly recalls La Malcontenta, but the sides of the house have *serlianas* like La Rocca, and the rear façade has three *serlianas* that are obviously derived from an unbuilt Palladio project.[17] Burlington was intimately familiar with Palladio's drawings since he owned most of them. He had acquired Jones's entire collection, which he supplemented by additional drawings that he bought on his Italian travels; he is said to have discovered a trove of Palladio drawings in the stables of the Villa Barbaro. Yet Chiswick House, with its delicate ornament, almost dainty scale, and richly encrusted interiors, is not Palladio, it is Burlington; exquisite rather than powerful, elegant rather than sublime.

Two more domed English country houses were built in the 1750s. The first is sometimes attributed to Isaac Ware, who with Burlington's support had published the definitive translation of *Quattro libri.*[18] Foots Cray Place, in Kent, was built for a wealthy London pewterer. It has an octagonal hall capped by a hemispherical dome that roughly resembles the version in Palladio's treatise. The house is built on a hilltop, which distinguishes it from Chiswick and Mereworth, which are on flat sites. The front and back of Foots Cray have Ionic porches; the other two sides have flattened temple fronts. The plan is surprisingly unsymmetrical, given Ware's familiarity with Palladio, convenience taking precedence over geometrical elegance. The second domed house, known as Nuthall Temple, was in Nottinghamshire and was designed by a relatively unknown architect, Thomas Wright. Although the house no longer exists, it is illustrated in the fourth volume of *Vitruvius Britannicus.* This is La Rotonda as seen through the eyes of Scamozzi and Burlington. The octagonal hall is covered by a flat dome resting on an octagonal drum, pierced not by thermal windows but by *serlianas.* The plan is the most Palladio-like of the four British houses, with a strict axial symmetry and small, medium, and large rooms. Mimicking La Rocca, Wright used only one portico, balancing it with the curved bay window of the salon on the opposite side. Like Ware, he paid attention to creature comforts: the domed room was provided with a fireplace, and the two staircases (one for the owners, the other for servants) were more generous, important since the bedrooms were on the upper floor.

The four English villas are attractive enough, but they only serve to underline Palladio's achievement: a domed house is a very simple idea that is anything but simple to pull off. None of the four British architects had Palladio's breadth of experience, and it shows. There are too many compromises, too many fussy details, not enough discipline. Although the pieces are there, they fit together awkwardly; the seams show. And without the magician's sleight of hand, the trick falls flat.

Builders in the sixteenth, seventeenth, and eighteenth centuries adapted Palladio's domed house, but how would it suit a modern family? In 1993, Alvin Holm, a Philadelphia architect, built a domed house inspired by La Rotonda for Richard and Susan Wyatt and their two daughters on the outskirts of Pittsburgh. The first architectural impression is English rather than Italian. The exterior of the house is brick with white-painted wood trim. The interior of the hemispherical dome, slightly smaller than the original, is painted Wedgwood blue, like the hall at Mereworth. An upper gallery overlooks a room that is hexagonal in plan, like Foots Cray and Nuthall. The domed room functions like the large center hall of a traditional American Colonial house: a combination of foyer, reception room, and circulation space. Since it is lit by an *oculus,* it provides a bright focus for the variety of public and private rooms that surround it: four bedrooms on the upper floor (whose basic layout is not much different from its eighteenth-century English predecessors, although more space is devoted to bathrooms and closets) and a variety of public rooms below. Mereworth Castle had a gallery, and Nuthall a saloon, and while the Wyatt house includes living and dining rooms, pride of place is given to that particularly late-twentieth-century contrivance, the family room. Family rooms have largely replaced living rooms in new houses, so the large paneled room with an elaborate patterned ceiling is directly across the hall from the front door. The kitchen is next to the family room, and it includes an informal eating area that looks out over the garden through a handsome *serliana* window. The architectural décor of the Wyatt house is resolutely classical and distinctly formal, but the absence of corridors and the airy central hall give the interior a modern feeling, not an open plan in the Modernist sense but certainly an open atmosphere.

When Holm first saw the Wyatts' hilltop site, he was reminded not only of La Rotonda but also of Thomas Jefferson's hilltop house at Monticello. Monticello has a flat dome on an octagonal drum that resembles Chiswick, although it is compromised since the space under the dome is not a central hall but a menial attic room, invisible and barely accessible from the main floor. Jefferson designed two other houses. One was his unsuccessful entry in the architectural competition for a new President's House, a faithful rendition of La Rotonda, copied from Leoni or Ware's translation of *Quattro libri,* with one novel modification: the ribbed dome consisted of alternating segments of masonry and glass that would have made it an extraordinary presidential beacon at night. The other house was Poplar Forest, Jefferson's country retreat near Lynchburg, Virginia. The octagonal plan, clearly inspired by Inigo Jones, is neatly subdivided into five rooms surrounding a central hall. The rooms ingeniously share chimneys and include a parlor, two bedroom suites, and two smaller rooms; there are two Doric porticoes.[19] The central hall is not round but square, and is used as a dining room.

Poplar Forest does not have a domed room. In an uncharacteristic bid to economize, Jefferson opted for a flat roof, making the dining room a twenty-foot cube into whose ceiling he cut a narrow, sixteen-foot-long skylight. The Wyatt house has a domed room but no external dome. Holm's first sketches featured a flattened Palladian dome on the exterior, but his clients worried that their home might be mistaken for an institutional building, so the dome was concealed behind a large slate roof. In any case, despite its four fronts, the exterior of the Wyatt house does not resemble La Rotonda. There are Palladian motifs such as axial symmetry, pedimented porches, and *serlianas,* but the pragmatic accommodation of form to function is unmistakably American—Jeffersonian rather than Palladian. Each of the four temple fronts is different. The entrance is the familiar double portico of Drayton Hall—Ionic over Doric; an open pedimented porch above a glazed sunroom faces the swimming pool; the main garden façade is a pilastered double portico; and the fourth side has an open pedimented porch above a two-car garage. Of course, this accommodation to

"Watch out for Alfie?"

"Not Alfie! LP. Loss Prevention. The security guys. The Faux Police." Shelly and Jillian stand with their backs to the display surveying the room. "You can't miss them. They have to dress real nice for work, like Dockers and some nerdy shirt. But then they have to wear these fugly shoes, you know, so they can chase you down and stuff. You'll know when you see one. They look like walking potatoes." Shelly wipes the doughnut crumbs from her chest. "C'mon. Put this on." She reaches down into the depths of her jeans pocket, pulls out two fake diamond rings, and squeezes one onto her finger. "All the way from Chula Vista."

"What is it?"

"It's a wedding ring." Shelly puts another ring on Jillian's left hand. "I now pronounce us wife and wife." Shelly laughs into her sleeve.

"Very funny. What's it for?"

"For our *anecdote*." She pronounces the word perfectly, like she'd been practicing. "You need an anecdote for Beauty Cash." Shelly points to a stack of huge Henckel Knife Block boxes nearby. "Scoop one a them up, quick."

"Wait. We can't forget the mantra." Jillian looks out to the left and touches pinkies with Shelly. *"It is mine. It is mine. It is mine."* The girls hum out the words quickly without moving their lips.

"Okay. Go on."

Jillian walks over to the big box. "This?" Jillian whispers loudly. "We can't *cut* this thing, Shelly." The box nearly weighs Jillian down. "Plus everything in this store has sensors on it. We'll never get out with a thing like this."

"I told you—we're not going to *cut* it. We're just going up to the counter." Shelly starts gnawing on her cuticles. The two girls walk up to the counter, and Jillian heaves up the heavy box onto the surface.

"Stop that. You look guilty already." Jillian pushes Shelly's hand away from her mouth. "Now what, mastermind?"

"Now you just look around and try not to look like a klepto. Try and look married."

"To you?"

"No, lesbo. *To a guy.*" Shelly wiggles her ring finger in front of her and hums to herself. Feeling silly but game, Jillian follows suit. Jillian is fully aware of how crazy they must look, but enjoys the ridiculous moment. The two girls continue to look around the store until a salesgirl comes up to the counter.

"Can I help you?"

"I'm not sure if we're in the right department." Shelly's voice is an octave higher than normal and vaguely but unidentifiably accented. She looks and sounds convincingly confused. The saleswoman lifts up the knife block box and turns it around.

"*It is mine,*" Shelly says aloud. "I just have returned back from my honeymoon in three European cities and one Chinese one"— Shelly puts her left hand on the counter and wiggles her finger— "and my best friend, who also just got hitched"—Jillian smiles, raises her eyebrows, and places her left hand on the counter too—"and just got back from her honeymoon in the Grand Bahamas, is helping me with my gift crap."

"Congratulations." The saleswoman looks as if she's trying to follow Shelly's *anecdote*.

"She got another knife block from someone else." Jillian smiles at the saleswoman. This must be the stupidest thing Jillian has ever done, but the very dumbness of it makes it entertaining.

"So you want to make a return?"

"Yes," the two say simultaneously with a smile.

"But I looked everywhere and I couldn't find my gift receipt." Shelly thrusts her hands into her pockets and swirls them around for a bit.

"Billy and Brandon gave it to her." Jillian nods sincerely. "Our gay friends." Jillian smiles to the woman.

The saleswoman looks on the bottom and on the top of the box. Jillian's heart picks up the pace—maybe there is some indicator on the box that shows that it wasn't actually bought, that it utilitarian requirements undermines the purity of the original concept, yet Palladio's ingenious idea of a hilltop house looking in four directions, with a domed space at its center, persists, even in this altered form.

The man who commissioned La Rotonda had relatively simple requirements. He was a fifty-two-year-old retired cleric, Monsignor Paolo Almerico. As a young canon of Vicenza's cathedral, the well-born Vicentine had been accused of murder and imprisoned, and although ultimately exonerated, he had left the Republic with a cloud over his head. Nevertheless, able and ambitious, he persevered in his career and served two successive popes in the influential post of referendary (the person who screened papal petitions). He eventually returned to Vicenza, where, "to enjoy himself he retired to his place on a hill outside the town," according to Palladio.[20] Almerico owned agricultural land in the vicinity, but his new house was not a *casa di villa;* it had neither outbuildings nor *barchesse,* and there was no *granaro,* which is why Palladio referred to the attic merely as a "place in which to walk around the hall."[21] La Rotonda has sometimes been described as a "pleasure house" or a "belvedere," which gives the impression that it was not a permanent residence.[22] In fact, in 1567, a year after commissioning the house, Almerico sold the family residence in Vicenza, and three years later he was described as living in his new home.[23] Almerico was a bachelor, and that may explain the unconventional layout of La Rotonda: four distinct suites of two rooms were useful for entertaining guests.* The plan, however formal, functioned extremely well,

---

*The cleric was a worldly man who had at least one illegitimate son. The son inherited La Rotonda on Almerico's death in 1591, and immediately sold it.

and one can imagine large numbers of the monsignor's Roman friends living comfortably in the house without tripping over each other. Each room has direct access to the outside—and to an airy portico—and the *sala* is located out of the traffic flow so that social events can continue undisturbed by comings and goings.

Palladio had met Almerico thirty years earlier, when the canon commissioned the Pedemuro workshop to build a cathedral portal—the design and execution of which are generally credited to the stonemason Andrea di Pietro. The old relationship, as well as the idyllic hilltop site, and the willingness of Almerico to build a domed house, surely persuaded Palladio to undertake the commission. Construction progressed extremely quickly by the standards of the time, and by 1570 the final decorative touch was in place—the eight statues on the stair abutments. However, for unexplained reasons, the construction of the dome lagged and the central room remained unroofed. It has been suggested that Almerico may have run low on funds, but perhaps, like the Wyatts, he was having second thoughts about the propriety of a house with a dome.

Palladio's great treatise, *I quattro libri dell'architettura,* was published in 1570. It was more than 340 octavo pages, profusely illustrated with simple, uncluttered woodcuts, organized in four books. Palladio described the basics of construction and the five orders in the first book, his own palazzos and villas in the second, bridges and sundry structures (including the Basilica) in the third, followed by a book on Roman temples. He planned as many as six additional volumes, on ancient baths, theaters, amphitheaters, harbors, and fortifications. To reach a wider readership, *Quattro libri* appeared in three editions, one consisting only of Books I and II, another of Books III and IV, as well as an omnibus volume.

Palladio dedicated the first two books to his friend and client Count Giacomo Angarano, a Vicentine nobleman who had commissioned a palazzo in Vicenza and a villa on the Brenta, and the second two to Emanuele Filiberto, Duke of Savoy, a great patron of the arts whom he had met in Turin. He also singled out the mentors of his youth, Giangiorgio Trissino ("one of the most illustrious men of our time") and Alvise Cornaro ("a gentleman of exceptionally fine judgment"), and praised Marc'antonio Barbaro ("a Venetian gentleman of great intellect"). Yet his supporter and patron Daniele Barbaro received no thanks or accolades—he was mentioned in connection with the translation of Vitruvius, but was coolly referred to merely as the "Most Reverend Barbaro."[24] There appears to have been a falling-out between the two, caused perhaps by something that occurred during the design of the villa at Maser, either concerning the instructions given to Veronese, or something else. In any case, when Daniele published the second edition of his Vitruvius in 1567, he rewrote his praise of Palladio, making it less effusive.[25] Barbaro died without warning the year *Quattro libri* was published, and though he mentioned Palladio affectionately in his will, he pointedly listed the architect among his household servants, not bequeathing him a personal memento—his main gifts to his brother were his books and his astronomical instruments—but rather the modest sum of fifteen ducats (he left his principal servants forty ducats each, and his valet two hundred).[26]

That same year, Palladio moved his household to Venice, perhaps emboldened by the death of Jacopo Sansovino, his only architectural rival. Ironically, his next major commissions were back in Vicenza: the Palazzo Barbaran, and an important public building, the Loggia del Capitaniato. The Loggia, which stands on the Piazza dei Signori opposite the Basilica, was the

official residence of the *capitanio,* or Venetian governor of
Vicenza. It is a splendid building, representative of the direction
that Palladio's secular architecture was taking in the final decade
of his life. Four giant engaged Corinthian columns rise the full
height of the façade. The columns are unplastered brick, like
those of the Carità, but there is nothing subdued or severe about
this design—every square inch of the walls is covered with a riot
of high-spirited stone and plaster decoration. The side wall in
particular is rich in pictorial embellishment, as it commemorates
the Venetian naval victory over the Turks at Lepanto. Compared
to the severity of La Rotonda of only a few years earlier, the
Loggia represents a new and unexpected facet of Palladio's fertile imagination.

The architectural exuberance of the Loggia belies the great
sadness that had descended on the Palladio family. In 1572, two
of his sons died: Leonida, the eldest, who was helping with the
architectural work, and Orazio, who had graduated a doctor of
civil law from the University of Padua. One can imagine the
pride that Palladio felt in their achievements. We do not know
the cause of their deaths, which occurred within a few months
of each other, but they most likely resulted from one of the
epidemics that regularly swept through the city.

A few years later, an extremely severe plague decimated the
Venetian Republic, killing more than half a million people and
reducing the population by as much as a third. The calamity
brought Palladio an unexpected commission. During the
plague the Venetian Senate declared that it would erect a
church to Christ the Redeemer—*Il Redentore*—as an offering.
A site on the island of Giudecca was chosen, Palladio was
appointed architect, and construction began in 1577. The
façade continues the illusion of two overlapping temple fronts
that he had begun in San Francesco and continued in San

Giorgio Maggiore, but the design is tauter and is achieved with simpler means. Palladio's virtuoso composition of Corinthian columns and pilasters is an extraordinary fusion, as Ackerman wrote, of "the intellectual and the sensuous."[27] The monochrome interior, which shimmers in the pale Venetian light, is surely one of the most beautiful church interiors anywhere.

With both San Giorgio Maggiore and Il Redentore under construction, there was no doubt that Palladio was now the premier architect in the city. This had been confirmed a few years earlier when he was invited to design a temporary triumphal arch and loggia for Henri de Valois's state visit to the city. One of those responsible for that commission, as well as for Il Redentore, was Marc'antonio Barbaro, who as the procurator of St. Mark's was an important personage in Venetian politics and one of Palladio's most vocal supporters. Palladio originally proposed a centralized domed church for Il Redentore. Though the idea was rejected in favor of a more conventional solution, it appealed to Marc'antonio, who invited Palladio to build a miniature version as a private family chapel in the village of Maser adjacent to the villa. Legend has it that it was here, on August 19, 1580, while he was working on the chapel, that Palladio died. He was seventy-one.

There are two commemorative statues of Andrea Palladio: one was placed outside Chiswick House by Lord Burlington in the 1720s, the second was erected in 1859 beside the Basilica by Vicenza's belatedly grateful citizens. The Palladio of Chiswick is a beardless young man, with rounded features and a romantic air, while the Palladio of Vicenza resembles a stern, bearded philosopher. For many years, Palladio's physical appearance, like that of Shakespeare, was a matter of conjecture since no reliable likeness had survived. It was not until 1980 that a contemporary portrait turned up. It was painted by his friend Giambattista

Maganza in 1576, when Palladio was sixty-eight. Palladio is bald, with regular, attractive features and a neatly trimmed full beard flecked with white. He looks fit and is dressed in a dark tunic and a linen shirt with an embroidered collar, proper but not ostentatious; he could be a functionary or a small-town magistrate. He is holding a paper scroll that identifies him as "Architeto Vicentino," attesting to the fact that he has been made a citizen, a singular honor and a major social advance for his whole family. Somewhat awkwardly he also grasps a pair of metal dividers. The common drafting instrument, used to transfer dimensions from one part of a drawing to another, is a reminder of the importance of geometry in his work. Architects were commonly portrayed with the tools of their trade—Titian painted his friend Giulio Romano holding an architectural plan. Titian's Giulio—a tortured *artiste*—casts a melancholy look at the viewer as he points to his drawing. Maganza's Palladio, by contrast, appears composed, his forthright avuncular gaze remarkably gentle. He looks into the distance with a mixture of unperturbed calm and cool intelligence. It is the countenance of a man who sees the world exactly as it is.

X

Palladio's Secret

he Villa Saraceno at Finale di Agugliaro is one of Palladio's early villas and not particularly renowned, which may be why I left it until last. I was driving to Finale, which is about fifteen miles south of Vicenza, when I was rear-ended by a delivery van. The rest of the drizzly afternoon was spent chatting to a friendly policewoman, waiting for a tow truck, and having my fender straightened and a sheet of plastic taped over the shattered rear window. By the time I got back on the road, I was in no mood to look at a villa. Taking the accident as an omen, I dropped the car off at the rental agency and spent the final days of my trip on foot. It was a chance to wander around Vicenza, where, as Vasari pointed out, there are so many Palladio buildings that "even if there were no others there, they would suffice to make a very handsome city with most beautiful surroundings."[1] I never did get to Finale on that trip.

After returning to Philadelphia, I came across a reference to the Villa Saraceno.[2] The magazine article described how the house had recently been restored by a British trust that rescues old buildings and rents them to holidayers. I could live, for however short a time, in a Palladio villa! This was too good an opportunity to pass up, and together with two friends, my wife, Shirley, and I booked the villa for the following March.

"You have to see these buildings with your own eyes to real-

LIKE MANY OF PALLADIO'S COUNTRY HOUSES,
THE VILLA SARACENO WAS THE HEART OF A WORKING FARM.

ize how good they are," Goethe had written. True enough, but experiencing a building is not the same thing as looking at a painting in a museum. Paintings are meant to be looked at; architecture should be lived in. Buildings reveal themselves slowly; they must be seen at different times of day and under different conditions, in sunlight and darkness, in fog and rain. Houses particularly should be appreciated in small doses. For days on end you may be unaware of your surroundings, then one day you stop what you are doing, look around, and indescribably but unmistakably you feel that everything, including yourself, is in the right place. That is the experience of architecture. That's what I wanted—to wake up under Palladio's roof, eat a meal in front of his fireplace, and watch the sunset from his loggia. If only for a short period I wanted to call a Palladio villa home.

I also wanted—although I didn't admit this to anyone, hardly even to myself—to discover Palladio's secret. What made his houses so attractive, so imitated, so perfect? I'd traveled from villa to villa, studied *Quattro libri,* pored over photographs and plans, and read scholarly papers, but I still wasn't sure that I knew the entire answer. Now I had eight days to find out.

I'm alone in the villa, the others have gone to the food market in Padua. The house is silent, except for the occasional crackling of burning logs in the fireplace. Pale mid-morning light slips in through tall windows and across the worn refectory table that is spread with my books and papers. It's an ordinary enough room, with white, roughly plastered walls, a reddish terrazzo floor, and an extremely high, dark wooden ceiling.

The Villa Saraceno dates from the first decade of Palladio's career, roughly the same time that he was designing the Villa Poiana, which is only a few miles away. As happened so often,

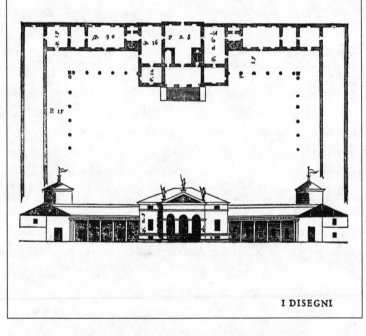

DE I DISEGNI DELLE CASE DI VILLA DI ALCVNI
Gentil'huomini di Terra Ferma.   Cap. XV.

D VN luogo del Vicentino detto il FINALE, è la seguente fabrica del Signor Biagio Sarraceno: il piano delle stanze s'alza da terra cinque piedi: le stanze maggiori sono lunghe vn quadro, e cinque ottaui, & alte quanto larghe, e sono in solaro. Continua questa altezza ancho nella Sala: i camerini appresso la loggia sono in uolto: la altezza de' uolti al pari di quella delle stanze: di sotto vi sono le Cantine, e di sopra il Granaro: il quale occupa tutto il corpo della casa. Le cucine sono fuori di quella: ma però congiunte in modo che riescono commode. Dall'vna, e l'altra parte ui sono i luoghi all'vso di Villa necessarij.

I DISEGNI

A PAGE FROM *QUATTRO LIBRI*, VILLA SARACENO

his client was the younger of two brothers, Giacomo and Biagio Saraceno. They belonged to a Roman ecclesiastical family that generations before had moved to Vicenza and established itself in the professions.[3] Their grandfather had bought the Finale estate, which they inherited on their father's death in the late 1530s. Giacomo, the elder, got the customary lion's share and forthwith built a large country house known locally as the Palazzo delle Trombe, perhaps because of its trumpetlike rain spouts. The spouts are gone but the house still stands, surrounded by a working farmyard. It is sometimes claimed that Giacomo's villa was designed by Sanmicheli, but it is more likely that the sturdy, rather conventional design was the work of a local builder.* A decade later, around 1548, the younger brother commissioned a villa of his own. He turned to Palladio, who by then was making a reputation for himself with the Basilica, a project with which Biagio, as a member of the city council, was intimately familiar. The site for the villa was an existing medieval farmyard, just down the road from Giacomo's house.

The Villa Saraceno has a checkered history. Biagio died in 1562 and left the house to Leonardo, the younger of his two sons. When Leonardo died without an heir, the property passed to his brother Pietro, clearly his father's second choice. Something of a ne'er-do-well, Pietro fathered several illegitimate sons, but since Biagio's will specified that only lawful offspring could own the villa, the house was inherited by Pietro's daughter Euriemma. Thus the villa passed to her husband's family, the Caldognos (whose ancestor had also built a Palladio villa). A later Caldogno widow, Lucietta, who ran the estate for thirty years

---

*Perhaps Giacomo engaged the Pedemuro workshop, where Andrea di Pietro was still working as a stonemason, for the window arrangement of the Palazzo delle Trombe anticipates the Villa Godi.

(1650–80), altered the east wing to provide rooms for her two sons. Lucietta's descendants rented the house and fields to tenant farmers, and finally sold the property at auction in 1838. After changing hands several more times, the estate became a dairy farm, ceasing operation at the end of the Second World War. Housing was in short supply in postwar Italy, and the villa and its adjoining farm buildings were crudely subdivided and turned into a tenement, housing as many as thirty people. Thirty-five years later, abused and run into the ground, the villa was finally abandoned, and for fifteen years stood empty, at the mercy of the elements. The Landmark Trust bought the property and spent five years restoring the building. Since 1994, the Villa Saraceno has been occupied by scores of delighted visitors, judging from the comments in the guest book.

I read this potted history in a scrapbook I found in the living room. The villa has a small library that includes several guidebooks, the inevitable Penguin edition of *Death in Venice,* and a beat-up paperback facsimile edition of Isaac Ware's translation of *Quattro libri.* I set Thomas Mann aside for evening reading, and turn to the familiar pages of the famous treatise. It feels strange to be looking at a floor plan of the Villa Saraceno—as I sit inside the villa. Palladio listed Saraceno first among the villas belonging to "some gentlemen of the *terraferma,*" perhaps because it was the smallest and simplest of his published designs. The house is about seventy-five feet long and fifty feet wide, half the size of the Villa Pisani, which Palladio had completed a few years earlier. The straightforward plan is simple but practical: a south-facing loggia leading to a *sala* with two rooms on each side, a small one in the front and a larger one in the rear. The two larger rooms—today the living room and dining room— are accessible directly from the *sala,* and lead to the smaller rooms. The smaller rooms are at the front of the house, but unlike the Villa Emo, they do not have doors leading to the loggia, which makes them both more private and warmer in the winter. The woodcut in *Quattro libri* shows the house facing a *cortile* formed by two impressive L-shaped *barchesse* with round dovecote towers at the corners, gay pennants at their peaks. "On each side there are all the necessary places for the use of a villa," Palladio wrote. But that was wishful thinking—the noble *cortile* was never built. In the nineteenth century, influenced by a neoclassical revival, an owner added a *barchessa* approximating Palladio's design, but since it was built only on the east side, it has left the house with an endearingly lopsided appearance. The *barchessa* connects the villa to several smaller outbuildings of medieval vintage that were part of the original farmyard.

The room in which I'm working, on the east side of the *sala,* is the dining room. The first time we ate here was magical. It was the evening that we arrived, and we'd asked the custodian, Lorella Graham, to arrange to have dinner ready after we got in from the airport. We were still unpacking when a young couple showed up carrying boxes of groceries and started working in the kitchen. The food was simple, and delicious: a radicchio risotto, sautéed turkey breasts in a lemony sauce, a salad, and cooked pears. We ate at the long table by the flickering light of candles and the glow of the fire. Outside, the winter wind drove the rain against the closed window shutters. We felt like magnificent *signori.*

This room is not exactly as Palladio designed it. Lucietta Caldogno made changes in the mid-seventeenth century, and a hundred years later the ceiling was lowered slightly and a stone stair added to reach a new upstairs bedroom. Since there was no trace of the original rooms, the modern restoration preserved these alterations. The large raised fireplace is thought to be original, however, signaling the longtime use of this room as a kitchen (the modern kitchen is next door in the *barchessa*). The kitchen was inside the house because, despite Palladio's claim that "the cellars are underneath," the Villa Saraceno never had a usable basement. As he did in most of his early villas, Palladio buried the basement about four feet below ground level, but when the first portion (under the room in which I'm sitting) was built, it flooded—he had underestimated the height of the groundwater. Reluctant to raise the basement, which would have increased the cost and altered the external appearance, he continued with the construction but filled the remaining spaces inside the foundation walls with rubble. Thus most of the main floor rests on solid earth. I examined the small section of the basement that was finished, accessible only by an external door. It has long stone cribs, perhaps used for growing mushrooms. Although today the vaulted space is dry, before electric sump pumps it must have been damp for much of the year.

It is not yet noon but I'm hungry—I've still not adjusted to the transatlantic time change. The kitchen is next door, a room about twenty feet square, with large windows overlooking the covered arcade of the *barchessa*. This was probably the original location of the kitchen, before it was moved into the house proper. Of course, in 1550 it would have had merely a large fireplace and worktables. Today, a long U-shaped counter lines the walls on one side of the room, opposite a wooden table with cane-seated chairs. The kitchen is fully equipped with a hooded gas range, ovens, and two dishwashers (although the villa itself sleeps five, the renovated outbuildings can accommodate a dozen people). No attempt has been made to hide the modern appliances, or to historicize the cabinetwork; the countertops and a backsplash are plain white ceramic tile. Dishes and glassware are stored in a sideboard instead of in overhead cupboards. The walls, as elsewhere in the house, are white-painted plaster;

the ceilings, wooden beams; the floor is rough brick. The over-all effect is rustic and informal, sympathetic to Palladio without actually being Palladian.

I take my sandwich and a glass of beer back to the refectory table, throw another log on the fire, and return to *Quattro libri.* The short text describing the Villa Saraceno is Palladio's usual no-nonsense boilerplate:

> At a place in the Vicentine, called Finale, is the following building belonging to Signor BIAGIO SARRACENO [sic]. The floor of the rooms is raised five foot above the ground; the larger rooms are one square and five eighths in length, and in height equal to their breadth, and with flat ceilings. This height also continues to the hall. The small rooms, near the loggia, are vaulted; the height of the vaults is equal to that of the rooms. The cellars are underneath, and the granaries above, which take up the whole body of the house. The kitchens are without the house, but so joined that they are convenient. On each side there are all the necessary places for the use of a villa.[4]

The illustrations in Isaac Ware's translation were copied from the original woodcuts and include the dimensions of the main rooms. Here is an opportunity to confirm if the actual sizes correspond to the numbers in *Quattro libri.* I fetch my tape measure and start in the small room next to the dining room, which is our bedroom. The commodious room, dominated by a tall hooded fireplace, easily accommodates a bedstead, an immense wardrobe, a chest of drawers, and a couple of arm-chairs. According to *Quattro libri,* the dimensions should be 12 Vicentine feet wide and 16 feet long (one of Palladio's favorite proportions, a square and a third). Measuring and converting into Vicentine feet, I confirm that these are almost exactly the

dimensions of the room as built. The text of *Quattro libri* specifically describes the "larger rooms"—the dining room and living room—as "one square and five eighths," that is, 16 by 26
Vicentine feet, but the dimensions on the plan are 16 by 26½.
It appears that Palladio, or his son Silla, who wrote many of the
captions in *Quattro libri,* either made a mistake in the text, or
gave erroneous information to the printer who cut the wood
blocks.* Probably the latter, since my measurement shows the
rooms to be precisely 16 by 26 Vicentine feet.

This leaves one puzzle. The square and five-eighths proportion that Palladio specified—and built—is *not* one of Vitruvius's
five recommended room shapes. This piques my interest, and I
methodically go through the twenty-three villas in *Quattro
libri.* Of the ten villas with 16-foot-wide rectangular rooms, half
follow Vitruvius—that is, they are either 24 Vicentine feet
long (a square and a half) or 26½ feet long (a square and two-
thirds, rounded off). The rest are 26, 27, or 28 Vicentine feet
long. Since it is difficult for the human eye—even Palladio's
expert eye—to appreciate such small differences, and since all
these rooms are presumably equally beautiful, the inescapable
conclusion is that while their general proportions are important,
their precise dimensions don't really matter.

Heresy? Not really. Much has been written about the mathematics of Palladio's room proportions. But it's one thing to
analyze a room using a floor plan from *Quattro libri,* and quite
another to be in the room itself. When I woke up this morn-

---

*Considering that the treatise was compiled over a span of fifteen
years, such discrepancies are exceedingly rare—I found only two other
dimensional errors among the villas: the larger rooms of the Villa
Cornaro are described as a square and three-quarters but the dimensions are 16 by 26½ feet; the *sala* of the unbuilt Villa Mocenigo at Dolo
is described as two and a half squares but is shown as 30 by 76 feet.

ing, my bedroom was darkened by the closed shutters that allow only cracks of daylight to enter. The blurry outline of the walls and ceiling were barely discernible. Not wishing to wake Shirley, I tiptoed out. Empty wineglasses littered the refectory table, and the smell of burnt wood hung in the air. The *battuto* was cold on my bare feet. The dining room, so cozy and convivial the evening before, seemed abandoned and inhospitable. I opened the tall window shutters, which helped to breathe a little life into the place.

The experience of a room depends on so many things; materials, for example. The floor of the Saraceno living room is

VILLA SARACENO LIVING ROOM

brick-red tile, the walls are rough white plaster (surprisingly, some of it original), the wooden ceiling is dark brown, almost black. If the floor were linoleum, the walls plywood, and the ceiling acoustic tile, obviously this would be a different, and considerably less agreeable, room, notwithstanding its identical proportions. It would also be different without the prominent, six-foot-wide frescoed frieze that covers the upper parts of the walls. The frescoes were commissioned by either Pietro Saraceno or his daughter Euriemma in the 1590s; the artist has not been identified. The band of mythological figures significantly affects the room, enlivening the space and altering the perceived proportions of the walls.

A broad wooden molding, similar to a picture rail, defines the bottom edge of the frescoed band. The interiors of Palladio's villas are typically Spartan with simple, almost rustic details; there are no baseboards at Saraceno, for example, and doors and windows are straightforward and unaffected in design. This makes details, such as the fresco molding, the carved stone surround of the fireplace, and the attractive little stone seats under the living room windows, arresting. That is, they catch the eye, and in the process they change the way the room is perceived. More, or different, details would likewise change the Saraceno living room.

The east and west rooms of a villa were commonly referred to as *a mattina* (in the morning) and *a sera* (in the afternoon), recognizing the movement of the sun. The same room bathed in bright sunlight or illuminated with flickering candlelight assumes a different character. At the Villa Saraceno, for example, the living room is bright and sunny *a sera,* and in the evening it is almost cavelike. The dining room, which has north-facing windows, only comes into its own in the evening.

Although I am skeptical that Palladio's secret lies in mathematically precise dimensions, there is no doubt that the rooms in the villa are exceptionally pleasing. We all agree on this—this house feels good. It's hard to pin down exactly why. The peasantlike roughness of the materials contrasting with the elegantly carved stone details has something to do with it; so does the commodiousness of the rooms and their pleasing overall proportions. There must be more to it than that, however. I finally come to the conclusion that what also contributes to the sense of well-being of these rooms is their height: they are extremely tall—nineteen feet according to my measurement. This makes the interior spacious and airy, almost like being outside. At night, with a few candles and the glow of a fire, the ceiling disappears entirely; even during the daytime it is usually outside my cone of vision. The sense of spaciousness is not only, and perhaps not mainly, visual, it is also aural, for tall ceilings affect sound. Under a high ceiling, voices, footsteps, a chair scraping, seem more distant than they really are.[5] When I'm talking to Shirley across the table, she's only five feet away, but I "hear" a larger distance. No wonder that the relatively small Villa Saraceno feels palatial.

Palladio devoted an entire chapter of *Quattro libri* to the height of rooms. He listed more than one way of calculating room height, "to ensure that most of the rooms of different sizes have vaults of an equal height."[6] According to his different formulas, the ceiling of the Saraceno living room, for example, could be 19, 23, 23¾, or 24½ modern feet, and still "turn out beautiful to the eye."[7] Another example of Palladio's pragmatism. Whatever formula was used, the ceiling would be high. Evidently, this was an aesthetic issue. Most ordinary buildings have low ceilings—all one really needs is sufficient headroom, after all. I'm 6 feet 1 inch and I've been in plenty of farmhouses and cottages where I've had to stoop. Tall ceilings produce a wonderful sense of luxury, not only for a 6-footer; everyone likes tall ceilings, as modern real estate agents and homebuilders know. I'm used to ceilings of 9 or 10 feet, but within a day or two, the ceilings of the villa felt normal; a week later, when we checked into a hotel in Venice, I was almost crushed by the low ceiling of our attic room.

Generally, there is a variety of ceiling heights in Palladio's villas. In order to simplify construction, and increase the space in the attic, he made all the ceilings in the Villa Saraceno the same height. To counter the monotonous effect, he added vaults to the two smaller rooms. One of these vaults has been restored, giving a beautiful touch of refinement to the otherwise simple interior. It is likely that Palladio planned the frescoed frieze in the large rooms for the same reason—to effectively lower the perceived ceiling height, thus increasing the contrast with the *sala*.

The *sala* is always the architectural climax of a Palladio villa, and I immediately headed for it the evening we arrived at the house. The room was not only not exceptionally tall for a *sala,* it was not very large and had a flat, uninteresting ceiling. As in the living room, the upper third of the walls was frescoed, though the effect was less successful than in the living room.*
The *sala* was an odd T-shape, the result of two little rooms cut out of each corner, one containing a stair, the other a *camerino,* or small room. There were monumental doors on each side, one leading into the loggia, the other opening to the back of the house, but since it was a blustery night and raining, the doors and the window shutters remained closed. The room had a curiously makeshift quality; on the whole, I was disappointed.

*I surmise that Palladio's original idea was to have a frieze only in the large rooms, and that it was Pietro or Euriemma who added it to the *sala.*

The next day the weather cleared. Early in the morning I went to the *sala,* swung open both pairs of twelve-foot-high doors and unlatched the window shutters. It was like raising the lights on a darkened stage. Through the wide-open doors I could see far into the landscape. Much is made of modern architecture's discovery of the continuity between inside and outside—thanks especially to the invention of plate glass—but the effect was obviously known to cinquecento architects; the two tall doors brought the outside right into the house. Standing in the center of the clay-tiled floor, out one door I could see the loggia and the forecourt, and out the other the open fields behind the house.

Every time I looked through the doorway, across the loggia, and down the garden path, or if I walked from the dining room to the living room, I was looking down—or moving along—an imaginary line, or axis. The two main axes of the Villa Saraceno intersect, appropriately, in the center of the *sala.* That explains the T shape: the upright of the T is the north-south axis of the loggia and the entrance doors, the crossbar is the east-west axis of the large rooms and the *barchessa.* The locations of interior doors and windows reinforce these axes. Standing in the kitchen, for example, I could look through the entire house— a distance of almost a hundred feet—and through three sets of doors see the far window of the living room. Although a Palladio villa is cut up into discrete rooms, such long vistas reinforce an agreeable sense of openness.

Leaving my work in the dining room, I cross the *sala* and go out the back door. The cleared area immediately around the villa, originally the site of the *bruolo,* or orchard, is still bounded by irrigation ditches. Beyond I can see flat cultivated fields interrupted by hedgerows of poplars, and in the far distance the gray outlines of other farms. Two far-off promontories bracket the view: Monte Bèrico on the left and the Euganian Hills on the right.

The ground is spongy and wet—no wonder Palladio had flooding problems. The rear of the villa has no portico, and according to *Quattro libri* none was intended. A pediment over a very slightly projecting center portion and the row of chunky modillions under the eaves are the sole classical motifs; otherwise the façade is relieved only by several flat moldings, one marking the main floor, one at the level of the windowsills, and the third defining the attic. The big doors and the windows have attractive sandstone frames. The wall is roughly plastered where earlier makeshift windows have been blocked up and patched. This side of the villa shows its years, but its bulk and its massive proportions are still impressive.

Quattro libri sometimes gives the false impression that Palladio was only interested in idealized geometry and classical vocabulary. In fact, much of the impact of the villas has to do with their sympathetic relationship to their surroundings. The hilltop sites of Godi and La Rotonda, the canalside setting of La Malcontenta, the foothills backdrop of the Villa Barbaro, are an integral part of their designs. In that regard, Saraceno recalls Emo, for it, too, sits in a flat agricultural plain. Although more than fifteen years separate the two houses, they share the flinty self-sufficiency of a Roman outpost. When we drive back to the villa after shopping in the nearby town, its comforting bulk is visible a long way off, rising behind a surrounding wall. Like the lines of poplars and the long straight canals that crisscross the Vicentine plain, it marks the civilizing hand of man.

The backs of the *barchessa* and the old farm buildings extend to the left. On the right is the brick wall of the compound. After walking around the meadow, to get a view of the house from a distance, I return to the wall, which has a small gate leading into a courtyard about two hundred feet square. The enclosing brick wall is believed to have been built by Palladio, although the ornamental gates on two sides are seventeenth-century additions. The gravel drive that leads from one of the gates to the villa is formally laid out, but this was always a working farmyard, not a ceremonial *cortile*. On the north side stand the villa, the adjoining *barchessa,* and the medieval farm buildings; on the east, another older house, where Lorella and her husband, David, live, additional outbuildings, a large brick barn (parts of which date from the fifteenth century), and an old dovecote tower. Here, even more than in the majestic Villa Emo, one has the sense of the *casa di villa* as an integral part of a farm.

The nineteenth-century *barchessa* gives a general sense of Palladio's intentions. The six massive Tuscan columns and pilasters have an exaggerated taper, and are spaced a little too far apart, but they imbue this rather ordinary space with great dignity. It's too cool to eat at the rough-hewn wooden table that stands in the arcade, but it makes a nice place to sit in the late afternoon, when the setting sun casts long shadows across the flagstones. The covered arcade is deep enough to roll in a wagon—or park a car, which we sometimes do when it rains.

I walk over to the barn and, balancing my notebook on top of an old wellhead, sketch the house. With its plain, three-arched loggia, it belongs to an early villa type that Palladio repeated several times even after he discovered the columned portico. Like the nearby Villa Poiana, the Villa Saraceno has a stripped architectural style of great severity and force. The three arches have prominent keystones and imposts, and are topped by a large pediment. Smaller pediments are repeated over the windows. The row of modillions under the cornice casts a serrated shadow on the plastered wall.

I reflect on the anomaly of the *all'antica* style—that is, the anomaly of Renaissance humanists such as Palladio reviving the architecture of an ancient civilization that was, in addition to its artistic accomplishments, slave-owning, imperialist, and obsessed with power. That power is evident even in this modest house. The three arches of the muscular loggia resemble a stylized triumphal arch. The arches are elongated, for like all of Palladio's villas, this house surges proudly upward, placed high on a basement podium, the tall main floor made even taller by the attic. No doubt such monumental qualities explain the attraction of Palladianism to landed aristocrats in Kent as well as to plantation owners in South Carolina. Yet there is more to Saraceno than its echo of ancient imperial glories. This noble

VILLA SARACENO

but almost rustic building does not have the full-blown classical details of Chiswick or Mereworth. It wears its *all'antica* style lightly, and merely hints at the Roman past. Because of this reserve, Palladio villas are sometimes described as exalted farmhouses, an appellation that captures neither their commanding authority nor their imposing presence. Yet the description has merit, for the unabashedly simple materials and uncomplicated details serve to amplify Palladio's achievement. "There is something divine about his talent," Goethe wrote, "something comparable to the power of a great poet who, out of the world of truth and falsehood, creates a third whose borrowed existence enchants us."[8] That's exactly how I feel about the Villa Saraceno. With its massive walls and clay-tile roof, it is a real farmhouse, but one that incorporates a Roman triumphal arch. Its monumental presence is almost, but not quite, belied by its ordinary plastered brick construction. It is as if Palladio were turning straw into gold. *Enchanting* is exactly the right word for this little architectural masterpiece.

Finishing my sketch, I walk over to the broad steps that ascend to the loggia. The abutment walls date from the seventeenth century (although their design is based on *Quattro libri*). If, as seems likely, they reproduce the original, then this may be the first application of the simple, full-width stair that Palladio would use so often. In some ways, the loggia is the most dramatic space in the villa, taller even than the *sala,* with a high, barrel-vaulted ceiling and three arched openings that recall the Villa Godi. The ceilings and walls are likewise frescoed, although clumsily painted compared to Zelotti, and much worn. Still, the patches of vivid color give a festive air. Two 8-foot-long garden benches fit comfortably on each side of the loggia with room to spare. Perhaps it's because I'm used to modern houses, where everything is "just large enough," that Palladio's amplitude is so striking. Just as the height of the rooms alters my perception of the space, the largeness has unexpected effects. The windows, for example, which are all the same, are 4½ feet wide and no less than 8½ feet tall. When I open the shutters in the morning, it's not like raising a blind at home. Through the tall windows I can see more sky than land, which both brings the exterior into the house and heightens the sense of protective shelter when I close the shutters at night. There are lessons here for anyone building a house today: instead of concentrating on increasingly refined details and exotic materials, focus instead on spaciousness. Make things longer, wider, taller, slightly more generous than they have to be. You will be repaid in full.

The English architect Raymond Erith attributed the generosity of Renaissance architecture to its different units of measure. According to him, the Venetian foot, which like the Vicentine foot is about fourteen modern inches long, "was a better unit for classical architecture because, for instance, if they made a door 3 Venetian feet by 6 Venetian feet, it was big enough to walk through, i.e., it was 3 feet 6 inches by 7 feet by our measurements."[9] (This is exactly the size of the interior doors of the Villa Saraceno.) Of course, measurements are abstractions, and the doors could easily have been made any size, but architects have always had a tendency to round off dimensions to whole numbers. When sketching the plan of a house, for example, and trying to fit the various bits and pieces together, it is easier to remember that clothes closets and kitchen counters are two feet deep, that stairways and exterior doors are three feet wide, that patio doors are six, eight, or ten feet wide, and so on. Using Venetian feet makes everything slightly larger, slightly more generous.

As I write this, I have before me photographs of that eight-day idyll spread out on my writing desk. There are several views of the front of the villa, taken one late afternoon when the winter sun was low on the horizon. It had been a gray, drizzly day, and the four of us were in the loggia watching the sunset. In the photographs, the bare branches against the southwest horizon are burnished with golden halos. We look tiny next to the massive piers and the vast arches; the architecture appears overwhelmingly huge, the people minute. The photographs are startling because when we were in the villa I did not feel overwhelmed at all. Quite the opposite. Palladio's architecture *was* large and powerful, but it was also welcoming and comfortable, not cozy but definitely accommodating.

This accommodation is a matter of scale, not of size. Although size and scale are often used interchangeably in popular speech, their meanings in architecture are distinct. To say that a door is "big" describes its size; to say that a door has "big scale" says nothing about its actual dimensions, but rather characterizes its impact on us—it *looks* big. Scale has to do with relative size: how large or small is the door frame compared to the surrounding wall, how heavy or light is the door handle compared to the door. It is easy to ignore scale, particularly today when so many building components are standardized. But adjusting the size of a baseboard, say, to the size of a room, or the proportion of a window to the proportion of a wall, is one of the simplest way to achieve architectural distinction.

Palladio had this to say about scale: "Beauty will derive from a graceful shape and the relationship of the whole to the parts, and of the parts among themselves and to the whole, because buildings must appear to be like complete and well-defined bodies, of which one member matches another and all the members are necessary for what is required."[10] That is why his drawings of ancient buildings were full of dimensions. It was not only the actual size of things that concerned him, but also the correct relationship between the different parts. Once this relationship was established, any element of classical architecture could be proportionately enlarged or reduced. Corinthian columns could rise the full height of the nave at the church of Il Redentore, support lower arches over side chapels, and also carry miniature pediments in the altarpiece.

The harmonious combination of different scales sets classical architecture apart from the preceding Gothic style, which used the pointed arch motif at a single scale.[11] The rediscovery of scale was one of the great accomplishments of the Renaissance, and Palladio, like his contemporaries, manipulated scale to produce different effects. Classical elements such as columns could be made larger or smaller, more or less delicate, more or less monumental, to alter the atmosphere of a building or a room. For example, the Saraceno loggia is wider than the loggia of the Villa Godi, and has correspondingly larger piers, imposts, and base moldings. But whereas the Godi loggia recedes (literally, by being recessed into the house), the Saraceno loggia asserts itself by jutting forward about six inches from the façade. Palladio further emphasized this effect by creating an incised masonry pattern—now almost worn away—on the

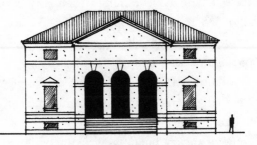

VILLA SARACENO

front of the loggia, but leaving the walls of the house plain to create a contrast.[12] On the other hand, assertive as the loggia is, its scale is commensurate with the scale of the façade, which is why we don't feel overwhelmed; it's big, but it doesn't feel big.

The presence of small and large scales, and the rapport between the parts, accounts, I think, for the sense of well-being that the villa conveys. As Palladio beautifully put it, he aimed to build "in such a way and with such proportions that together all the parts convey to the eyes of onlookers a sweet harmony."[13] This is not exciting architecture; indeed, it is the opposite of exciting—it is composed, serene, ordered. The Renaissance produced many great architects—Brunelleschi was the most daring, Bramante the most inventive, Giulio the most expressive, Michelangelo the most iconoclastic—but in his calm, considered way, Palladio has been more influential than any of them. Generation after generation of architects, professionals and amateurs, aristocrats and commoners, have come to the Veneto, seen his architecture, and fallen under his spell.

Palladio is an architect whose personal style became a Style. The eighteenth-century Scottish architect Robert Adam is another rare example; so is the nineteenth-century American master H. H. Richardson. Palladio was so widely imitated not because he was easy to copy but because the principles that underlie his style were easy to understand, and because his classically inspired vocabulary of architectural elements was rich enough to provide his followers with the means to express their own ideas, whether they were Inigo Jones, James Gibbs, or Thomas Jefferson. Thanks to this suppleness, Palladio's style returned not once but several times, and will likely do so again in the future.

Palladio's architecture is a combination of mathematics, especially geometry, scale, and proportion. At the same time, a

THE VILLA SARACENO, ONE OF PALLADIO'S
SMALLEST AND SIMPLEST HOUSES, PERFECTLY COMBINES BEAUTY
WITH FUNCTIONALITY AND SOUND CONSTRUCTION.

Palladio villa is not a theorem, or a poem, or a painting—it's a building. It is beautiful, but it is practical, too. It is not an abstract creation; it is made of specific materials: smooth reddish *battuto* on the floor, scribed *intonaco* on the exterior, carved stone frames around the doors and windows. Palladio loved to build. I imagine him in the attic, inspecting the huge timber trusses, or walking into the *sala,* fondly running his hands over the stone door frames. His buildings are so palpable, so real. Wotton was wrong about that; we *do* need stuff as well as art "to satisfy our greatest fancy." Perhaps that is Palladio's real secret: his equilibrium, his sweet sense of harmony. He pleases the mind as well as the eye. His sturdy houses, rooted in their sites, radiate order and balance, which makes them both of this world and otherworldly. Although they take us out of ourselves, they never let us forget who and what we are. They really are perfect.

The afternoon is drawing to a close. I lock the *sala* doors—a complicated system of bolts and latches—and go back into the dining room. Embers are smoldering among the ashes of the burnt-out fire. The light has changed in the course of the day and the room has a listless quality. As I gather my notes I hear the sound of a car outside, the slamming of a door, then voices. The others are back. I go outside to welcome them home.

AFTERWORD

About a year after I finished this book, it came to my attention that an old retaining wall in our garden had started to bulge and sag and was in need of repair. Made of stones laid atop each other without mortar, it had to be dismantled and rebuilt. I was not up to the job—the wall is 150 feet long—so I hired a professional to do the work. Over the next four weeks, watching Brian Corrigan and his assistant labor in my garden, I realized that I had not paid enough attention to Andrea Palladio's original calling. Of course, I had understood that the nearly two decades of his youth and early manhood spent working as a stonemason had provided him with useful knowledge of the building crafts. But I had not considered how the actual occupation may have affected him.

I had always imagined Palladio as he appears in the statue beside the Basilica in Vicenza—a pensive scholar, albeit a self-educated one. But, as was obvious from watching Brian at work, handling heavy stones is an intensely physical activity. (So is wielding a stone-carver's mallet and chisel.) However refined and courtly Palladio may have become under Trissino's tutelage, and however gentlemanly he appears in Maganza's portrait, he could not have been a delicate sort—he must have had a rugged and powerful physique. His active and extremely productive life should be seen in that light.

The work of a stonemason involves strenuous activity, but

the pace is stop-and-go, very different from the steady toil of a plasterer or a painter. Brian spent a lot of time considering the piece of wall he was working on, examining the different stones that were laid out on the grass like the pieces of a jigsaw puzzle. It was only after careful scrutiny that he would bend down to heft a stone into place. He did everything calmly and carefully, reinforcing my impression of Palladio as a deliberate sort of person who approached problems in an unhurried, almost ponderous manner. Thus he bided his time during the Basilica competition, waiting until the right moment before submitting the ideas over which he had evidently labored a long time.

When Brian and I discussed how the wall should be rebuilt, he said that the original wall had been placed directly on the ground, and that before rebuilding it he wanted to add a foundation of crushed stone. Wouldn't that add to the cost, I asked. Yes, he said, but if he didn't do it, in another fifty years the wall would start moving again. His evident conviction made me realize that the subject wasn't open to discussion—this was how it had to be done. Palladio may have given "the most intense pleasure to the Gentleman and Lords with whom he dealt," but I wonder if stubbornness wasn't also a part of his character. Not the willfulness of the self-involved architect—"it must be done the way I want"—but rather the considered but obstinate attitude of the experienced craftsman—"this is the right way to do it."

A stonemason contends against gravity and time, which are unrelenting. A badly plastered wall can be patched up, peeling paint can be scraped and re-covered, but a poorly built stone wall eventually will collapse. The stonemason is an innate conservative—or, perhaps, stonemasonry is a craft that attracts men of conservative temperament. The architect Palladio was innovative, sometimes unusually so, but his innovation was always in the context of the tried and true, for when Palladio found something that worked, he stuck to it. His invention was never gratuitous or capricious. And the evidence of superior building is in the villas themselves, standing strong after almost five hundred years.

Like so many who have visited Palladio's villas, I was attracted by their somber beauty and chaste geometry. But since writing this book, I have discovered a more individual and personal connection. I was researching some family background and came across a surprising coincidence, something I had vaguely known but entirely forgotten: both of my parents grew up in houses built in the Palladian style. My mother's family lived in the center of Warsaw in a villa built in 1860 by the Italian architect, Francesco Maria Lanci. On the hundred-foot-long street façade is a tall main floor punctuated by a row of windows with pediments supported by Composite pilasters. A lightly rusticated base indicates the ground floor.

The country house where my father spent much of his childhood is in a village called Lusławice, in southern Poland on the Dunajec River. It did not belong to my grandfather; he was merely a houseguest—for more than twenty years. The house was a *dwór,* or manor house, built in the early nineteenth century. It is a long low structure, without a basement or attic, but with an elegant central pedimented portico supported by four Doric columns. The portico is distinctly Palladian, of course, but even more Palladian is the combination of a rustic structure with an elegant classical appendage.

I felt at home in the Villa Saraceno, for Palladio's architecture was not only a familiar part of my culture and education, it was also in my family history. The universal appeal of Palladio's villas suggests that for many others, too they are not simply beautiful old houses, but in an immediate way their considered proportions and serene spaces provide a palpable connection to the past, bringing history to us, and us into history.

December 2002

THE VILLAS

A chronological listing of Palladio villas requires a caveat. Palladio described twenty-three villas in *Quattro libri,* but he did not include dates, and he did not arrange the designs in chronological order. Rather he "placed them in the text to suit myself." To complicate matters further, he referred to certain villas as completed when they were still under construction, and sometimes when construction had not even begun. Roughly half a dozen additional villas have been attributed to Palladio on the basis of surviving drawings, likewise undated. Completion took years, in some cases, decades. Hence the precise times of design and construction are difficult to establish. Certain villas can be dated on the basis of contracts, wills, and contemporaneous accounts, or on stylistic grounds. The dates of others—Valmarana, Sarego at Santa Sofia—are only roughly known. Some dates are in dispute. The Villa Zen, for example, is dated as early as 1548 and as late as 1566. The captivating little Villa Forni is likewise variously dated, from 1541 to the 1560s. Moreover, its attribution, like that of the Villa Caldogno, is contested; some say it might have been designed by Alessandro Vittoria, a sculptor who often worked with Palladio. The fate of the Villa Ragona can only be guessed at despite its inclusion in *Quattro libri,* for it has vanished without a trace—possibly it was never built. Thus the list below includes conjecture, and the sequence of projects is necessarily imprecise.

Location of Palladio's Villas

1. Villa Godi, Lonedo di Lugo
2. Villa Pisani, Bagnolo
3. Villa Poiana, Poiana Maggiore
4. Villa Foscari, Malcontenta
5. Villa Cornaro, Piombino Dese
6. Villa Barbaro, Maser
7. Villa Badoer, Fratta Polesine
8. Villa Emo, Fanzolo
9. Villa Almerico (La Rotonda), Vicenza
10. Villa Saraceno, Finale di Agugliaro

The First Decade: 1540–50

Villa Godi, Lonedo di Lugo Vicentino (Vicenza)
Included in *Quattro libri*. Survives.

Villa Piovene, Lonedo di Lugo Vicentino (Vicenza)
Not included in *Quattro libri*. Survives. Fragments may be by
Palladio. Attribution is contested.

Villa Valmarana, Vigardolo di Monticello Conte Otto (Vicenza)
Not included in *Quattro libri*. Survives.

Villa Gazoto, Bertesina (Vicenza)
Not included in *Quattro libri*. Survives, though in poor condition.

Villa Pisani, Bagnolo di Lonigo (Vicenza)
Included in *Quattro libri*. Survives. Porticoes destroyed.

Villa Saraceno, Finale di Agugliaro (Vicenza)
Included in *Quattro libri*. Survives.

Villa Thiene, Quinto Vicentino (Vicenza)
Included in *Quattro libri*. Unfinished. Fragments survive.

Villa Muzani, Malo (Vicenza)
Not included in *Quattro libri*. Destroyed in 1919.

Villa Poiana, Poiana Maggiore (Vicenza)
Included in *Quattro libri*. Survives.

Villa Chiericati, Vancimuglio di Grumolo delle Abbadesse
(Vicenza)
Not included in *Quattro libri*. Survives.

Villa Caldogno, Caldogno (Vicenza)
Not included in *Quattro libri*. Survives. Attribution is contested.

Villa Angarano, Angarano di Bassano del Grappa (Vicenza)
Included in *Quattro libri*. House was vastly altered in eighteenth century, only *barchesse* survive.

The Second Decade: 1550–60

Villa Foscari (La Malcontenta), Gambarare di Mira (Venezia)
Included in *Quattro libri*. Survives.

Villa Forni, Montecchio Precalcino (Vicenza)
Not included in *Quattro libri*. Survives in poor condition. Attribution is contested.

Villa Schio, Montecchio Precalcino (Vicenza)
Not included in *Quattro libri*. Destroyed.

Villa Cornaro, Piombino Dese (Padova)
Included in *Quattro libri*. Survives.

Villa Pisani, Montagnana (Padova)
Included in *Quattro libri*. Survives.

Villa Ragona, Ghizzole di Montegaldella (Vicenza)
Included in *Quattro libri*. No trace.

Villa Thiene, Cicogna di Villafranca (Padova)
Included in *Quattro libri*. Only an outbuilding was built. Survives.

Villa Barbaro, Maser (Treviso)
Included in *Quattro libri*. Survives.

Villa Mocenigo, Dolo (Venezia)
Included in *Quattro libri*. Built, remodeled. Demolished in 1835.

Villa Sarego, Santa Sofia (Verona)
Included in *Quattro libri*. Partially built. Survives.

Villa Trissino, Meledo di Sarego (Vicenza)
Included in *Quattro libri*. Only a fragment was built. Survives.

Villa Repeta, Campiglia dei Berici (Vicenza)
Included in *Quattro libri*. Burned in seventeenth century.

Villa Zen, Donegal di Cessalto (Treviso)
Included in *Quattro libri*. Survives in poor condition.

Villa Emo, Fanzolo (Treviso)
Included in *Quattro libri*. Survives.

The Third Decade: 1560–70

Villa Mocenigo, Marocco (Treviso)
Included in *Quattro libri*. Not built.

Villa Sarego, Miega di Cologna Veneta (Verona)
Included in *Quattro libri*. Partially built. Destroyed.

Villa Valmarana, Lisiera di Bolzano (Vicenza)
Included in *Quattro libri*. Not built according to original
design; rebuilt in 1969. Survives.

Villa Almerico (La Rotonda), Vicenza
Included in *Quattro libri*. Survives.

Readers interested in visiting the surviving villas may consult
Caroline Constant's *The Palladio Guide* (Princeton Architectural Press, 1985, revised 1993).

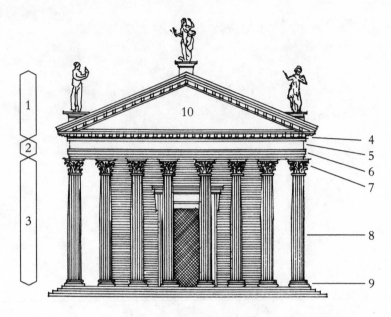

The Parts of Classical Architecture
After Andrea Palladio's drawing of the Temple of Jupiter Stator, Rome

1. Pediment
2. Entablature
3. Column
4. Cornice
5. Frieze
6. Architrave
7. Capital (Corinthian)
8. Shaft (fluted)
9. Base
10. Tympanum

GLOSSARY

Acanthus: Prickly Mediterranean plant whose stylized leaf is represented in classical decorations such as the capitals, or headpieces, of Corinthian and Composite columns.

Apse: Semicircular or polygonal recess, usually with a half-domed ceiling. Palladio used apses in the entrance loggia of the Villa Pisani.

Barchessa: Traditional barn of the Trevigiana region in the Veneto; the roof is extended to form a sheltered arcade on the south side. Palladio incorporated *barchesse* in the designs of the Villa Barbaro and the Villa Emo.

Bucrania: Decorations in a Doric frieze representing ox skulls and recalling the sacrificial function of Roman temples. Palladio used bucrania in town houses such as the Palazzo Chiericati and in suburban villas such as the Villa Pisani in Montagnana, but rarely in country houses.

Capital: Headpiece or carved block at the top of a column. While the columns in Palladio villas are made of brick—plastered or unplastered—capitals and bases are generally carved stone.

Column: Basic element of classical architecture. Columns consist of three parts: bases, shafts, and capitals, or headpieces. They may be entirely freestanding or engaged—that is, part of the wall. A flat representation of a column that is part of the wall is called a pilaster. Ancient Roman columns were made of stone, but Palladio's columns are usually plastered brick.

Composite order: An order is the entire assembly of columns and entablature. The composite order is Roman in origin and its capital combines Ionic volutes with Corinthian acanthus leaves. Palladio rarely used this ornate order in country houses, the early Villa Gazoto being a rare exception.

Corinthian order: Athenian order whose capital consists of stylized acanthus leaves. Palladio designed beautiful Corinthian columns for the upper porticoes of the Villa Cornaro.

Dado: Lower section of a wall that is decorated differently from the upper section—for example, a plaster wall might have a dado of inlaid stone. Palladio often had faux marble dados frescoed on the walls of his villas.

Doric order: Greek order distinguished by an extremely simple saucer-shaped capital consisting of several moldings, and by its complicated frieze consisting of alternating panels called triglyphs and metopes. Doric, because it is the simplest order, usually represents the manly virtues, which may be why Palladio chose it for the Villa Emo, one of his most robust designs.

Entablature: Horizontal beamlike element that is supported by columns. The entablature is divided into three parts: the architrave at the bottom, the frieze in the middle, and the cornice at the top under the eaves. Palladio derived the exact profiles of his entablatures from studies of Roman ruins. The entablature could be a real beam, as in the Villa Emo, or a flattened representation of a beam, as at the Villa Pisani.

Entasis: Classical columns are always narrower at the top, and the subtle curved taper is referred to as entasis. This effect not only gives columns a gracious shape but it also creates the optical illusion that the columns are perfectly straight, since a column without entasis will appear to be bulging at the top.

Fascia: Plain, flat horizontal molding projecting slightly from the surface of a wall. Palladio often used fascias to demarcate floor levels on the exterior of his villas.

Fluting: Vertical grooves of concave profile carved into the shafts of columns. Although ancient Roman columns are almost always fluted, Palladio rarely used fluted columns since his plastered brick columns could not be carved. The stone columns in the interior of San Giorgio Maggiore are fluted.

Giant column: Any column more than one story high. Also called colossal column. Palladio introduced giant columns to domestic architecture when he used them first in the portico of the Villa Chiericati.

Groin: Line formed by the intersection of two vaults. Commonly found in the cruciform *salas* of Palladio villas.

Hemicycle: Semicircular columned structure. A freestanding hemicycle is the focus of the rear garden of the Villa Barbaro.

Impost: Block-shaped headpiece at the top of a pier from which an arch springs. Usually stone, but in Palladio villas often plastered brick.

Intercolumniation: The distance, measured in column diameters, between two columns. Columns can be spaced closer or farther apart. Vitruvius described five different intercolumniations: pynostyle (1½ diameters); systyle (2 diameters); eustyle (2¼ diameters); diastyle (3 diameters); and araeostyle (4 diameters). Palladio favored eustyle for villa porticoes, but used wider spacing such as araeostyle for flanking loggias and arcades.

Ionic order: Said to have originated in Ionia, today western Turkey. The chief distinguishing feature of the Ionic capital is a pair of decorative spirals, or volutes, that resemble ram's horns. Ionic was Palladio's favorite order and he used it in most of his villas, including the four porticoes of the Villa Rotonda.

Mascherone: Grotesque mask, used to adorn the keystone of arches—a common Renaissance motif. It appears in Palladio's Basilica and also in the arcades of the Villa Barbaro.

Modillions: Decorative rows of small, closely spaced brackets just below the eaves that are part of the cornice. The ancient Romans generally used modillions in conjunction with the Ionic and Corinthian orders. Palladio incorporated stylized block modillions in almost all his villas, regardless of the order, because it was a simple and inexpensive way to incorporate a classical reference.

Oculus: A circular window (literally, eye). Also a round opening in the top of a dome, such as that of the Villa Rotonda.

Order: The entire assembly of columns and beams that forms the basis of classical Roman architecture. The five orders recognized by Palladio are Tuscan, Doric, Ionic, Corinthian, and Composite. They are distinguished by the capitals, the slenderness of the column, and the precise design of the beamlike entablature. The orders can be used individually or in combination. In the three-story cloister of the Carità convent, for example, Palladio used Doric on the lowest level, Ionic above, and Corinthian on the top floor.

Pediment: Triangular gable end of a temple, adapted by Palladio, who used it at a smaller scale over porches, porticoes, doors, and windows.

Portico: Originally a columned and pedimented projection in front of a temple. Adapted by Palladio to the porches and loggias of villas, it was probably the most copied of his architectural inventions.

Pulvinated molding: Decorative horizontal molding that is not flat but softly rounded (from the Latin *pulvinus,* or cushion).

Quoins: Stone blocks, sometimes rusticated, used to emphasize the corners of a building. Not commonly used by Palladio, but quoins do appear in the basement of the Villa Pisani, and on the ground floor of the Palazzo Antonini.

Rustication: Artificially roughened masonry laid with exaggerated joints to create a dramatic texture. In Palladio villas, it may be stone or plastered brick. Palladio commonly used rustication in palazzos, and sometimes in villas. The loggia of the Villa Pisani and the columns of the Villa Serego are heavily rusticated.

Serliana: A tall central arch flanked by two lower rectangular openings. First used by Bramante but later popularized by Serlio in his treatise. Sometimes called a Venetian window, it is widely known as a Palladian window, since Palladio used it so often, especially in the Basilica.

Thermal window: Semicircular window divided vertically into three equal parts. First found in Roman baths, or *therma,* it was widely used by Palladio, not only in villas but also in the naves of San Giorgio Maggiore and Il Redentore.

Torus: Convex molding, usually at the base of a column.

Tuscan order: Simplest of the five orders, said to be derived from ancient Etruscan temples. Tuscan columns are massive and widely spaced, and are sometimes difficult to distinguish from Roman Doric. Palladio reserved the Tuscan order for colonnades and farm buildings.

Tympanum: The flat triangular surface of a pediment. Often the place where Palladio displayed the armorial crest of the villa owner.

Vault: Curved ceiling or roof; a barrel vault is semicircular in cross section. Palladio used vaulted ceilings of different shapes to enliven the interiors of his villas.

Voussoir: Wedge-shaped stone or brick that forms part of an arch or a vault. Palladio often made stylized voussoirs of plastered brick.

Water table: A horizontal molding on the lower part of a building wall, designed to throw rainwater away from the foundations.

ACKNOWLEDGMENTS

I should like to acknowledge the generous advice and personal insights of Douglas Lewis, a distinguished Palladio scholar and curator of sculpture and decorative arts at the National Gallery of Art, Washington, D.C., and the friendly assistance of Deborah Howard of Cambridge University, and Pierre de la Ruffinière du Prey of Queen's University. I relied on the published research of many Palladio scholars (mentioned in the notes), but I would like to single out the published work of James S. Ackerman, Bruce Boucher, Howard Burns, Douglas Lewis, and Lionello Puppi. I used the marvelous new translation of *Quattro libri* by Robert Tavernor and Richard Schofield. Charles W. Hind, head of special collections and curator, and Philippa Martin, of the Royal Institute of British Architects Drawings Collection in London, an invaluable repository of several hundred Palladio drawings, offered efficient and helpful assistance. John Blatteau shared his extensive knowledge of classical architecture. Allen Freeman contributed a CD-ROM version of *Quattro libri*. Richard and Susan Wyatt offered me the hospitality of their Pennsylvania Rotonda, and Alvin Holm provided architectural information about the house. Eva Loeb and David Burns shared the Villa Saraceno—and much more. The Landmark Trust deserves great credit for rescuing the Villa Saraceno, and for accomplishing a sterling restoration. Colleagues and friends at the University of Pennsylvania contributed advice and conversation: Joseph Farrell, Gino Segre, Liliane Weissberg, David De Long, and Julia Moore Converse, director of the Architectural Archives. The staff of the Fisher Fine Arts Library, the Van Pelt Library, and Interlibrary Loans were helpful as always. Throughout much of the writing of this book, Acalya Kiyak served as a diligent research assistant. Jane Herman did a sterling job of copy editing, and Erich Hobbing produced a masterful book design. My longtime editor, Nan Graham, provided encouragement, criticism, and wise advice; Susan Moldow, publisher of Scribner, was equally supportive, as usual. Thanks to Andrew Wylie, my agent. Thanks, also, to the University of Pennsylvania, which granted me the sabbatical that gave me a chance to see the buildings with my own eyes.

March 2000–December 2001

Hotel Palladio, Vicenza

Villa Saraceno, Finale di Agugliaro

The Icehouse, Chestnut Hill, Philadelphia

NOTES

FOREWORD

1. Johann Wolfgang von Goethe, *Italian Journey,* trans. W. H. Auden and Elizabeth Mayer (San Francisco: North Point Press, 1982), 47.
2. Reprinted in Witold Rybczynski, *Looking Around: A Journey Through Architecture* (New York: Viking, 1992), 209–19.
3. James S. Ackerman, *Palladio* (New York: Penguin Books, 1966), 185.
4. Andrea Palladio, *The Four Books on Architecture,* trans. Robert Tavernor and Richard Schofield (Cambridge, Mass.: MIT Press, 1997), 7.
5. Ibid., 66.
6. Paolo Gualdo, "Life of Palladio" (1616) in Douglas Lewis, *The Drawings of Andrea Palladio* (New Orleans: Martin & St. Martin, 2000), 12.

CHAPTER 1: GODI

1. Andrea Palladio, *The Four Books on Architecture,* trans. Robert Tavernor and Richard Schofield (Cambridge, Mass.: MIT Press, 1997), 143.
2. Ibid.
3. Kurt W. Forster, "Back to the Farm: Vernacular Architecture and the Development of the Renaissance Villa," *Architectura* 1 (1974): 6–8.
4. Lionello Puppi, *Andrea Palladio,* trans. Pearl Sanders (Boston: New York Graphic Society, 1975), 239.
5. "Andrea Palladio," *Encyclopaedia Britannica,* vol. 17 (Chicago: Encyclopaedia Britannica, 1949), 149.
6. Palladio, *Four Books,* 57.
7. Quoted in Kurt W. Forster, "Travelers in Search of Palladio," *Palla-*

dio and Northern Europe: Books, Travelers, Architects, eds. Guido Beltramini et al. (Milan: Skira Editore, 1999), 224.

8. Banister F. Fletcher, *Andrea Palladio: His Life and Works* (London: George Bell and Sons, 1902), 75.

9. Rudolf Wittkower, *Architectural Principles in the Age of Humanism* (London: Academy Editions, 1998), 67.

10. See Michelangelo Muraro, *Venetian Villas: The History and Culture,* trans. Peter Lauritzen et al. (New York: Rizzoli, 1986), 146–47; Rudolf Wittkower, "The Influence of Palladio's Villas," *Country Life,* February 25, 1954, 516; Forster, "Back to the Farm," 6–8.

11. Giorgio Vasari, *Lives of the Most Eminent Painters, Sculptors and Architects,* trans. Gaston Du C. de Vere, vol. 3 (New York: Harry N. Abrams, 1979), 2016.

12. Puppi, *Andrea Palladio,* 5–6.

13. Robert Tavernor, *Palladio and Palladianism* (London: Thames and Hudson, 1991), 5.

14. Palladio, *Four Books,* 5.

15. Howard Burns, *Andrea Palladio, 1508–1580: The portico and the farmyard* (London: The Arts Council of Great Britain, 1975), 69.

16. Paolo Gualdo, "Life of Palladio" (1616) in Douglas Lewis, *The Drawings of Andrea Palladio* (New Orleans: Martin & St. Martin, 2000), 11.

17. Ibid.

18. Quoted by Puppi, *Andrea Palladio,* 12.

19. Ibid.

20. Quoted by T. S. R. Boase, *Giorgio Vasari: The Man and the Book* (Princeton, N.J.: Princeton University Press, 1979), 13.

21. Douglas Lewis, "Palladio, Andrea," *Macmillan Encyclopedia of Architects,* ed. Adolf K. Placzek (London: Collier Macmillan Publishers, 1982), 351–52.

22. Vasari, *Lives,* 1574.

23. See Ross King, *Brunelleschi's Dome: The Story of the Great Cathedral in Florence* (London: Pimlico, 2001), 33–34.

24. Douglas Lewis, *The Drawings of Andrea Palladio* (New Orleans: Martin & St. Martin, 2000), 12.

25. Ibid., 115.

26. Fletcher, *Andrea Palladio,* 18.

27. See Bruce Boucher, *Andrea Palladio: The Architect in His Time* (New York: Abbeville Press, 1998), 69; Paul Holberton, *Palladio's Villas: Life in the Renaissance Countryside* (London: John Murray, 1990), 205.

28. Lewis, *Drawings,* 199–201.
29. Ibid.
30. Ibid., 199.
31. Palladio, *Four Books,* 143.

CHAPTER 2: CHE BELLA CASA

1. Andrea Palladio, *The Four Books on Architecture,* trans. Robert Tavernor and Richard Schofield (Cambridge, Mass.: MIT Press, 1997), 121.
2. Howard Burns, *Andrea Palladio, 1508–1580: The portico and the farmyard* (London: The Arts Council of Great Britain, 1975), 187.
3. Palladio, *Four Books,* 124.
4. Douglas Lewis, *The Drawings of Andrea Palladio* (New Orleans: Martin & St. Martin, 2000), 115.
5. S. J. Woolf, "Venice and the Terraferma: Problems of the Change from Commercial to Landed Activities," in *Crisis and Change in the Venetian Economy in the Sixteenth and Seventeenth Centuries,* ed. Brian Pullan (London: Methuen & Co., 1968), 175–203.
6. Palladio, *Four Books,* 5.
7. Ibid., 163.
8. Rudolf Wittkower, *Architectural Principles in the Age of Humanism* (London: Academy Editions, 1998), 63.
9. James S. Ackerman, *Palladio* (New York: Penguin Books, 1966), 177.
10. Palladio, *Four Books,* 273.
11. Giorgio Vasari, *Lives of the Most Eminent Painters, Sculptors and Architects,* trans. Gaston Du C. de Vere, vol. 3 (New York: Harry N. Abrams, 1979), 2016.
12. See Lewis, *Drawings,* 112.
13. Henry Petroski, *The Pencil: A History of Design and Circumstance* (New York: Alfred A. Knopf, 1992), 36–40.
14. *The Palladio Drawings: Palladio. Smythson. Adam* (London: Royal Institute of British Architects, undated), 1.
15. RIBA Palladio XI/22, *verso.* See Lewis, *Drawings,* 226–27.
16. RIBA Palladio XVII/2, *verso.* See Lewis, *Drawings,* 108–9.
17. Palladio, *Four Books,* 57.
18. Leon Battista Alberti, *On the Art of Building in Ten Books,* trans. Joseph Rykwert, Neil Leach, and Robert Tavernor (Cambridge, Mass.: MIT Press, 1988), 310.
19. Palladio, *Four Books,* 77.

20. RIBA Palladio XVII/18, *verso.* See Lewis, *Drawings,* 108–9.

21. Vincenzo Scamozzi quoted in Lionello Puppi, *Palladio Drawings,* trans. Jeremy Scott (New York: Rizzoli, 1989), 22.

22. RIBA Palladio XVI/7. See Lewis, *Drawings,* 109–12.

23. RIBA XVII/17. See Lewis, *Drawings,* 113–15.

24. Lionello Puppi, *Andrea Palladio,* trans. Pearl Sanders (Boston: New York Graphic Society, 1975), 255.

25. Paul Holberton, *Palladio's Villas: Life in the Renaissance Countryside* (London: John Murray, 1990), 215–19.

26. Andrea Palladio, *I quattro libri dell'architettura* (reprint, Milan: Ulrico Hoepli Editore Libraio, 1980), Book IV, 37.

27. Palladio, *Four Books,* 147.

28. Ibid.

29. Alberti, *On the Art of Building,* 301.

30. Palladio, *Four Books,* 78.

31. Deborah Howard, *Jacopo Sansovino: Architecture and Patronage in Renaissance Venice* (New Haven, Conn.: Yale University Press, 1975), 125.

32. Ibid., 124.

CHAPTER 3: THE ARCHED DEVICE

1. Vitruvius, *The Ten Books on Architecture,* trans. Morris Hicky Morgan (New York: Dover Publications, 1960), 80.

2. Andrea Palladio, *The Four Books on Architecture,* trans. Robert Tavernor and Richard Schofield (Cambridge, Mass.: MIT Press, 1997), 233.

3. Caroline Constant, *The Palladio Guide* (Princeton, N.J.: Princeton Architectural Press, 1993), 58.

4. RIBA Palladio XVI/3. See Douglas Lewis, *The Drawings of Andrea Palladio* (New Orleans: Martin & St. Martin, 2000), 132.

5. See Lewis, *Drawings,* 133.

6. RIBA Palladio XVI/4.

7. RIBA Palladio, XVI/4 *verso.*

8. See Lewis, *Drawings.*

9. Palladio, *Four Books,* 136.

10. For background on the Palazzo della Ragione, see Franco Barbieri, *The Basilica of Andrea Palladio,* Corpus Palladianum, vol. 2 (University Park: Pennsylvania State University Press, 1970).

11. For currency conversion, see James S. Ackerman, *Distance Points: Essays in Theory and Renaissance Art and Architecture* (Cambridge, Mass.: MIT Press, 1991), 381, fn. 25.

12. Palladio, *Four Books,* 17.

13. Giorgio Vasari, *Lives of the Most Eminent Painters, Sculptors and Architects,* trans. Gaston Du C. de Vere, vol. 3 (New York: Harry N. Abrams, 1979), 2015.

14. Palladio, *Four Books,* 203.

15. Johann Wolfgang von Goethe, *Italian Journey,* trans. W. H. Auden and Elizabeth Mayer (San Francisco: North Point Press, 1982), 47.

16. Lionello Puppi, *Andrea Palladio,* trans. Pearl Sanders (Boston: New York Graphic Society, 1975), 269.

17. Paolo Gualdo, "Life of Palladio" (1616), in Lewis, *Drawings,* 3.

18. Georgina Masson, "Palladian Villas as Rural Centres," *Architectural Review,* July 1955, 20.

19. Palladio, *Four Books,* 114.

20. Ibid., 136.

21. Denis Cosgrove, *The Palladian Landscape: Geographical Change and Its Cultural Representations in Sixteenth-Century Italy* (Leicester: Leicester University Press, 1993), 149.

22. Palladio, *Four Books,* 6.

23. George Hersey and Richard Freedman, *Possible Palladian Villas (Plus a Few Instructively Impossible Ones)* (Cambridge, Mass.: MIT Press, 1992).

24. Palladio, *Four Books,* 56.

CHAPTER 4: ON THE BRENTA

1. Quoted by Lionello Puppi, *Andrea Palladio,* trans. Pearl Sanders (Boston: New York Graphic Society, 1975), 281.

2. Johann Wolfgang von Goethe, *Italian Journey,* trans. W. H. Auden and Elizabeth Mayer (San Francisco: North Point Press, 1982), 47.

3. See Douglas Lewis, *The Drawings of Andrea Palladio* (New Orleans: Martin & St. Martin, 2000), 196–99.

4. A. C. Landsberg, "An Historic Italian Villa; Malcontenta, Part I," *Country Life* 82 (October 16, 1937): 400.

5. John Ruskin, *The Stones of Venice,* vol. 1 (New York & London: Garland Publishing, 1979), 344.

6. Quoted by Erik Forssman, *Visible Harmony: Palladio's Villa Foscari at*

Malcontenta, trans. Gordon Irons (Stockholm: Sveriges Arkitektur-museum and Konsthögskolans Arkitekturskla, 1973), 12.

7. Leon Battista Alberti, *On the Art of Building in Ten Books,* trans. Joseph Rykwert, Neil Leach, and Robert Tavernor (Cambridge, Mass.: MIT Press, 1988), 151.

8. Ibid., 295.

9. Michelangelo Muraro, *Venetian Villas: The History and Culture,* trans. Peter Lauritzen et al. (New York: Rizzoli, 1986), 120.

10. Alberti, *On the Art of Building.*

11. Vitruvius, *The Ten Books on Architecture,* trans. Morris Hicky Morgan (New York: Dover Publications, 1960), 51.

12. Ibid., 112.

13. Paul Johnson, *The Renaissance: A Short History* (New York: The Modern Library, 2000), 79.

14. Lewis, *Drawings,* 198.

15. Forssman, *Visible Harmony.*

16. Andrea Palladio, *The Four Books on Architecture,* trans. Robert Tavernor and Richard Schofield (Cambridge, Mass.: MIT Press, 1997), 128.

17. See Douglas Lewis, "Patterns of Preference: Patronage of Sixteenth-Century Architects by the Venetian Patriciate," in *Patronage in the Renaissance,* eds. Guy Fitch Lytle and Stephen Orgel (Princeton, N.J.: Princeton University Press, 1981), 374.

18. Palladio, *Four Books,* 57.

19. Rudolf Wittkower, *Architectural Principles in the Age of Humanism* (London: Academy Editions, 1998), 119–29.

20. Ibid., 111.

21. Ibid., 122.

22. Deborah Howard and Malcolm Longair, "Harmonic Proportion and Palladio's *Quattro Libri,*" *Journal of the Society of Architectural Historians* 41, no. 2 (May 1982): 116–42.

23. Ibid., 116.

24. Ibid., 137.

25. Vitruvius, *Ten Books,* 180.

26. Palladio, *Four Books,* 59.

27. Ibid., 128.

28. Quoted in Harold Donaldson Eberlein and Robert B. C. M. Carrère, "Villas of the Veneto: I. The Villa Emo at Fanzolo," *The Architectural Forum* 34, no. 1 (January 1921): 6.

29. Palladio, *Four Books,* 77.

30. Howard Burns, *Andrea Palladio, 1508–1580: The portico and the farm-yard* (London: The Arts Council of Great Britain, 1975), 69.

31. James S. Ackerman, *Distance Points: Essays in Theory and Renaissance Art and Architecture* (Cambridge, Mass.: MIT Press, 1991), 365.

32. Michael Baxandall, *Painting and Experience in Fifteenth-Century Italy* (New York: Oxford University Press, 1972), 6–7.

33. Quoted by Howard Burns, "Building and Construction in Palladio's Vicenza," in *Les chantiers de la Renaissance,* ed. J. Guillaume (Paris: Picard, 1991), 212.

34. Ibid., 75.

35. Burns, *Andrea Palladio,* 69.

36. Manfredo Tafuri, *Venice and the Renaissance,* trans. Jessica Levine (Cambridge, Mass.: MIT Press, 1989), 130.

CHAPTER 5: PORTICOES

1. See Douglas Lewis, "Patterns of Preference: Patronage of Sixteenth-Century Architects by the Venetian Patriciate," in *Patronage in the Renaissance,* eds. Guy Fitch Lytle and Stephen Orgel (Princeton, N.J.: Princeton University Press, 1981), 372–74.

2. Andrea Palladio, *The Four Books on Architecture,* trans. Robert Tavernor and Richard Schofield (Cambridge, Mass.: MIT Press, 1997), 112.

3. My thanks to Douglas Lewis, who is writing a monograph on the Villa Cornaro, for suggesting how the upper *sala* was used.

4. Palladio, *Four Books,* 79.

5. John Summerson, *Inigo Jones* (New Haven, Conn.: Yale University Press, 2000), 107.

6. Ibid., 4.

7. A. A. Tait, "Inigo Jones—Architectural Historian," *Burlington Magazine* 112 (1970): 234–35.

8. Quoted by Nikolaus Pevsner, *An Outline of European Architecture* (Harmondsworth, U.K.: Penguin, 1958), 219–20.

9. Ibid.

10. Colen Campbell, *Vitruvius Britannicus, or the British Architect,* vol. 1 (London, 1715), 1–2.

11. James Gibbs, *A book of Architecture, containing designs of buildings and ornaments* (London: 1739).

12. Richard L. Bushman, *The Refinement of America: Persons, Houses, Cities* (New York: Alfred A. Knopf, 1991), 102.

13. Robert Morris, *Select Architecture* (London, 1757), unpaginated.
14. Ibid., Plate 36.
15. Ibid., unpaginated.
16. Bushman, *Refinement of America,* xii–xiii.
17. Thomas Jefferson, *Notes on the State of Virginia,* ed. William Peden (Chapel Hill: University of North Carolina Press, 1955), 152.
18. Quoted by Jack McLaughlin, *Jefferson and Monticello: The Biography of a Builder* (New York: Henry Holt, 1998), 54.
19. Henry Wotton, *The Elements of Architecture* (London: 1624), 10.
20. Alexander Pope, *Epistle to Lord Burlington* (London, 1731).

CHAPTER 6: THE BROTHERS BARBARO

1. Douglas Lewis, *The Drawings of Andrea Palladio* (New Orleans: Martin & St. Martin, 2000), 204.
2. Quoted by Lionello Puppi, *The Villa Badoer at Fratta Polesine,* Corpus Palladium, vol. 7, trans. Catherine Enggass (University Park: Pennsylvania State University Press, 1975), 36.
3. Lionello Puppi, *Andrea Palladio,* trans. Pearl Sanders (Boston: New York Graphic Society, 1975), 315.
4. Inge Jackson Reist, "Renaissance Harmony: The Villa Barbaro at Maser" (Ph.D. diss., Columbia University, 1985), 130–66.
5. Howard Burns, *Andrea Palladio, 1508–1580: The portico and the farmyard* (London: The Arts Council of Great Britain, 1975), 197.
6. Andrea Palladio, *The Four Books on Architecture,* trans. Robert Tavernor and Richard Schofield (Cambridge, Mass.: MIT Press, 1997), 78.
7. Reist, "Renaissance Harmony," 10.
8. Ibid., 129.
9. Carolyn Kolb, "The Sculptures on the Nymphaeum Hemicycle of the Villa Barbaro at Maser," *Artibus et Historiae* 18, no. 35 (1977): 30.
10. Burns, *Andrea Palladio,* 196.
11. Palladio, *Four Books,* 144.
12. Bruce Boucher, "Nature and the Antique in the Work of Andrea Palladio," *Journal of the Society of Architectural Historians* 59, no. 3 (September 2000):296.
13. Palladio, *Four Books,* 77.
14. Ibid.
15. This theatrical use of the terrace was suggested by Douglas Lewis.

16. See Michelangelo Muraro, *Venetian Villas: The History and Culture,* trans. Peter Lauritzen et al. (New York: Rizzoli, 1986), 146–47.

17. Giorgio Vasari, *Lives of the Most Eminent Painters, Sculptors and Architects,* trans. Gaston Du C. de Vere, vol. 3 (New York: Harry N. Abrams, 1979), 1580.

18. Kurt W. Forster, "Back to the Farm: Vernacular Architecture and the Development of the Renaissance Villa," *Architectura* 1 (1974): 12.

19. Palladio, *Four Books,* 56.

20. RIBA Palladio XVI/5 *verso.* See Lewis, *Drawings,* 203–4.

21. The original has been lost; a copy by John Webb is in the Worcester College Library, I/65. Thanks to Douglas Lewis for providing his own sketch.

22. For different interpretations see Richard Cocke, "Veronese and Daniele Barbaro: The Decoration of Villa Maser," *Journal of the Warburg and Courtauld Institutes* 35 (1972): 231–32; Inge Jackson Reist, "*Divine Love* and Veronese's Frescoes at the Villa Barbaro," *Art Bulletin* 67, no. 4 (December 1985): 622–23; Charles Hope, "Veronese and the Venetian Tradition of Allegory," *British Academy Proceedings* 61 (1985): 416; Douglas Lewis, "The Iconography of Veronese's Frescoes in the Villa Barbaro at Maser," in *Nuovi Studi su Paolo Veronese* (Venice: Arsenale, 1990), 319–20.

23. Mary Rogers, "An ideal wife at the Villa Maser: Veronese, the Barbaros and Renaissance theorists of marriage," *Renaissance Studies* 7 (December 1993): 379–84.

24. Mary McCarthy, *The Stones of Florence and Venice Observed* (Harmondsworth, U.K.: Penguin Books, 1985), 264–65.

25. Cocke, "Veronese and Daniele Barbaro," 226.

CHAPTER 7: AN IMMENSELY PLEASING SIGHT

1. Andrea Palladio, *The Four Books on Architecture,* trans. Robert Tavernor and Richard Schofield (Cambridge, Mass.: MIT Press, 1997), 126.

2. Ibid.

3. Ibid.

4. Giorgio Vasari, *Lives of the Most Eminent Painters, Sculptors and Architects,* trans. Gaston Du C. de Vere, vol. 3 (New York: Harry N. Abrams, 1979), 2018.

5. Palladio, *Four Books.*
6. Ibid.
7. John Summerson, *Inigo Jones* (New Haven, Conn.: Yale University Press, 2000), 80.
8. Quoted by Georgina Masson, "Palladian Villas as Rural Centres," *Architectural Review,* July 1955, 20.
9. Lionello Puppi, *The Villa Badoer at Fratta Polesine,* Corpus Palladium, vol. 7, trans. Catherine Enggass (University Park: Pennsylvania State University Press, 1975), 13.
10. Ibid., 35.
11. Palladio, *Four Books,* 18.
12. Paolo Gualdo, "Life of Palladio" (1616), in Douglas Lewis, *The Drawings of Andrea Palladio* (New Orleans: Martin & St. Martin, 2000), 12.
13. Puppi, *Villa Badoer,* 46–47.
14. RIBA Palladio X/1, *verso.* See Lewis, *The Drawings of Andrea Palladio,* 164.
15. Facsimile of Inigo Jones's copy of Andrea Palladio, *I quattro libri dell'architettura,* vol. 2 (Venice, 1570), 66.
16. Summerson, *Inigo Jones,* 116.
17. Palladio, *Four Books,* 138.
18. Allan Greenberg, *George Washington Architect* (London: Andreas Papadakis Publisher, 1999), 20.
19. *Allan Greenberg: Selected Works,* Architectural Monograph No. 39 (London: Academy Editions, 1995), 86–101.
20. Ibid., 75–79.
21. Palladio, *Four Books,* 156.

CHAPTER 8: EMO

1. Andrea Palladio, *The Four Books on Architecture,* trans. Robert Tavernor and Richard Schofield (Cambridge, Mass.: MIT Press, 1997), 133.
2. Vincent Scully, *The Villas of Palladio,* photographs by Philip Trager (Boston: Little, Brown & Co., 1986), 132.
3. Giampaolo Bordignon Favero, *The Villa Emo at Fanzolo,* Corpus Palladium, vol. 5, trans. Douglas Lewis (University Park: Pennsylvania State University Press, 1972), 31.
4. Harold Donaldson Eberlein and Robert B. C. M. Carrère, "Villas of

the Veneto: I. The Villa Emo at Fanzolo," *Architectural Forum* 34, no. 1 (January 1921): 3.

5. Favero, *Villa Emo*, 25; Martin Kubelik, "Palladio's Villas in the Tradition of the Veneto Farm," *Assemblage,* October 1986, 99–100; Paul Holberton, *Palladio's Villas: Life in the Renaissance Countryside* (London: John Murray, 1990), 187–88.

6. Palladio, *Four Books*, 123. See also Kubelik, "Palladio's Villas," 99–100.

7. Palladio, *Four Books.*

8. Gabriele Poggendorf, *Palladio's Emo in Fanzolo* (Berlin: Marcetus Verlag, 1995), 36.

9. Giampaolo Bordignon Favero, *Villa Emo,* trans. Shirley Guiton (Padua: Romano Bertoncello Brotto Editore, 1983), unpaginated.

10. Giorgio Vasari, *Lives of the Most Eminent Painters, Sculptors and Architects,* trans. Gaston Du C. de Vere, vol. 3 (New York: Harry N. Abrams, 1979), 2017.

11. Palladio, *Four Books*, 105.

12. Johann Wolfgang von Goethe, *The Flight to Italy: Diary and Selected Letters,* trans. T. J. Reed (Oxford: Oxford University Press, 1999), 89.

13. Vasari, *Lives*, 2016.

14. Tomasso Temanza, *Vite dei più celebri architetti e scultori Veneziani* (Milan: Edizioni Labor, 1966), 395. Translation by author.

15. Vasari, *Lives*, 2019.

16. Ibid., 2017.

CHAPTER 9: THE LAST VILLA

1. Andrea Palladio, *The Four Books on Architecture,* trans. Robert Tavernor and Richard Schofield (Cambridge, Mass.: MIT Press, 1997), 94.

2. Ibid.

3. RIBA Palladio XVII/1. See Douglas Lewis, *The Drawings of Andrea Palladio* (New Orleans: Martin & St. Martin, 2000), 103.

4. RIBA Palladio XVI/19B. See Lewis, *Drawings,* 103.

5. Palladio, *Four Books*, 138.

6. RIBA Palladio IX/8 and IX/7. See Lewis, *Drawings,* 187–88.

7. Camillo Semenzato, *The Rotonda of Andrea Palladio,* Corpus Palladium, vol. 1, trans. Ann Percy (University Park: Pennsylvania State University Press, 1968), 12–13, fn.1.

8. Ibid., 21, fn. 11.

9. Martin Kubelik, "Palladio's Villas in the Tradition of the Veneto Farm," *Assemblage,* October 1986, 107.

10. Johann Wolfgang von Goethe, *Italian Journey,* trans. W. H. Auden and Elizabeth Mayer (San Francisco: North Point Press, 1982), 50.

11. Johann Wolfgang von Goethe, *The Flight to Italy: Diary and Selected Letters,* trans. T. J. Reed (Oxford: Oxford University Press, 1999), 46.

12. Vitruvius, *The Ten Books on Architecture,* trans. Morris Hicky Morgan (New York: Dover Publications, 1960), 73.

13. Semenzato, *Rotonda,* 21, fn. 12.

14. William Kent, *Designs of Inigo Jones,* vol. 2 (Farnborough, U.K.: Gregg Press, 1967), plates 14, 16, 17, 18.

15. John Harris, *The Palladians* (London: Trefoil Books, 1981), 59.

16. Colen Campbell, *Vitruvius Brittanicus: or The British Architect,* vol. 1 (New York: Benjamin Blom, 1967), 8.

17. RIBA Palladio XVII/15. See Lewis, *Drawings,* 99.

18. Howard Colvin and John Harris, "The Architect of Foots Cray Place," *Georgian Group Journal* 7 (1997): 1–8.

19. Lucille McWane Watson, "Thomas Jefferson's Other Home," *Antiques,* April 1957, 343.

20. Palladio, *Four Books,* 94.

21. Ibid.

22. See James S. Ackerman, *Palladio* (New York: Penguin Books, 1966), 70; Robert Tavernor, *Palladio and Palladianism* (London: Thames and Hudson, 1991), 78.

23. Semenzato, *Rotonda,* 12–13, fn. 1.

24. Ibid., 5, 67.

25. Lionello Puppi, *Andrea Palladio,* trans. Pearl Sanders (Boston: New York Graphic Society, 1975), 315–16.

26. Bruce Boucher, "The Last Will of Daniele Barbaro," *Journal of the Warburg and Courtauld Institutes* 42 (1979): 280.

27. Ackerman, *Palladio,* 184.

CHAPTER 10: PALLADIO'S SECRET

1. Giorgio Vasari, *Lives of the Most Eminent Painters, Sculptors and Architects,* trans. Gaston Du C. de Vere, vol. 3 (New York: Harry N. Abrams, 1979), 2016.

2. Dan Cruikshank, "Jewel in the Crown," *Perspectives,* May 1994, 34–38.

3. Richard Haslam, "Villa Saraceno, Veneto, Italy," *Country Life*, October 6, 1994, 45.

4. Andrea Palladio, *The Four Books of Architecture*, trans. Isaac Ware (New York: Dover Publications, 1965), 50–51.

5. Christopher Alexander et al., *A Pattern Language: Towns, Buildings, Construction* (New York: Oxford University Press, 1977), 877–79.

6. Andrea Palladio, *Four Books on Architecture*, trans. Robert Tavernor and Richard Schofield (Cambridge, Mass.: MIT Press, 1997), 59.

7. Ibid.

8. Johann Wolfgang von Goethe, *Italian Journey*, trans. W. H. Auden and Elizabeth Mayer (San Francisco: North Point Press, 1982), 47.

9. Lucy Archer, *Raymond Erith: Architect* (Burford, Oxfordshire: Cygnet Press, 1985), 75.

10. Palladio, *Four Books*, 7.

11. John Summerson, *Heavenly Mansions: and Other Essays on Architecture* (New York: W. W. Norton & Co., 1963), 14.

12. Ottavio Bertotti Scamozzi, *Le Fabbriche e I Desegni de Andrea Palladio*, vol. 2, (Vicenza: Giovanni Rossi, 1786), Plate 24.

13. Palladio, *Four Books* (trans. Isaac Ware), 213.

INDEX

Page numbers in *italics* refer to illustrations.